POLISH COMMUNISM IN CRISIS

Polish Communism in Crisis

GEORGE SANFORD

CROOM HELM
London & Canberra
ST. MARTIN'S PRESS
New York

© 1983 George Sanford
Croom Helm Ltd, Provident House, Burrell Row,
Beckenham, Kent BR3 1AT

British Library Cataloguing in Publication Data

Sanford, George
    Polish communism in crisis.
    1. Poland——Politics and government——1945-
    I. Title
    320.9438   JN6766
    ISBN 0—7099—2358—9

0060252

ISBN 0—312—62046—2'

Printed and bound in Great Britain

TABLE OF CONTENTS

ABBREVIATIONS AND GLOSSARY OF POLISH TERMS

In order to maintain uniformity throughout this study I
retain the original initials for Polish terms.

AK	ARMIA KRAJOWA (Home Army)
AKTYW	Literally central core of active members of a party or organisation
Bl	BIULETYN INFORMACYJNY (Information Bulletin)
BPS	BIULETYN PRASOWY SEJMU (Sejm press bulletin of Committee meetings)
CC	Central Committee
CKKP	CENTRALNA KOMISJA KONTROLI PARTYJNEJ (Central Party Control Commission)
CPv	Communist Party
CPSU	Communist Party of the Soviet Union
CRZZ	CENTRALNA RADA ZWIĄZKÓW ZAWODOWYCH (Central Council of Trade Unions)
ChSS	CHRZEŚCIJAŃSKIE STOWARZYSZENIE SPOŁECZNE (Christian Social Association)
DiP	DOŚWIADCZENIE i PRZYSZŁOŚĆ (Experience and Future)
DzU	DZIENNIK USTAW (Bulletin of Laws of the Polish People's Republic)
FJN	FRONT JEDNOŚCI NARODU (Front of National Unity)
FPN	FRONT POROZUMIENIA NARODOWEGO (Front of National Understanding)
FYP	Five Year Plan
GDR	German Democratic Republic
GUKPPiW	GŁÓWNY URZĄD KONTROLI PRASY PUBLIKACJI i WIDOWISK (Main Office for the Control of the Press, Publications and Public Performances)
GUS	GŁÓWNY URZĄD STATYSTYCZNY (Main Statistical Office)
ICPA	Information Centre for Polish Affairs; published News Bulletin and Agencja Solidarność (AS) during 1980-1981
IPPM-L	INSTYTUT PODSTAWOWE PROBLEMY MARKSIZMU-LENINIZMU (Institute of the Fundamental Problems of Marxism-Leninism)
IW	INSTYTUT WYDAWNICZY (Publishing Institute)
KIK	KLUB INTELIGENCJI KATOLICKIEJ (Catholic Intelligentsia Club)
KiW	KZIĄŻKA i WIEDZA (Book and Knowledge Publishing House)
KKP	KRAJOWA KOMISJA POROZUMIEWAWCZA (Solidarity National Co-ordination Committee)
KOR	KOMITET OBRONY ROBOTNIKÓW (Workers' Defence Committee). Later KSS-KOR, KOMITET SAMOOBRONY SPOŁECZNEJ (Social Self-Defence Committee)
KPN	KONFEDERACJA POLSKI NIEPODLEGŁEJ (Confederation of Independent Poland)
KPP	KOMUNISTYCZNA PARTIA POLSKI (Communist Party of Poland)

Abbreviations and Glossary

KSR   KOMISJA SAMORZĄDU ROBOTNICZEGO (Conference of
          Workers' Self-Management)
KW   KOMITET WOJEWÓDZKI (PZPR Provincial Committee)
KZ   KOMITET ZAKŁADOWY (PZPR Factory Committee)
LOK   LIGA OBRONY KRAJU (League for the Defence of the
          Country)
MILLIARD One thousand million
MKS   MIĘDZYZAKŁADOWY KOMITET STRAJKOWY (Inter-Factory
          Strike Committee)
MO   MILICJA OBYWATELSKA (Citizens' Militia)
MON   MINISTERSTWO OBRONY NARODOWEJ (Ministry of National
          Defence)
MP   MONITOR POLSKI (Official Journal of the Polish
          People's Republic)
MSW   MINISTERSTWO SPRAW WEWNĘTRZNYCH (Ministry of Internal
          Affairs)
MSZ   MINISTERSTWO SPRAW ZAGRANICZNYCH (Ministry of Foreign
          Affairs)
ND   NOWE DROGI (New Roads)
NIK   NAJWYŻSZA IZBA KONTROLI (Supreme Control Chamber)
NOT   NACZELNA ORGANIZACJA TECHNICZNA (Supreme Technical
          Organisation)
NPS-G   NARODOWY PLAN SPOŁECZNO-GOSPODARCZY (National
          Social-Economic Plan)
NSZZ   NIEZALEŻNE i SAMORZĄDNE ZWIĄZKI ZAWODOWE (Free and
          Self-Governing Trade Unions)
PAN   POLSKA AKADEMIA NAUK (Polish Academy of Sciences)
PAP   POLSKA AGENCJA PRASOWA (Polish Press Agency)
PGR   PAŃSTWOWE GOSPODARSTWA ROLNE (State Farms)
POP   PODSTAWOWA ORGANIZACJA PARTYJNA (Basic Party Cell)
PPR   POLSKA PARTIA ROBOTNICZA (Polish Workers' Party)
PREMIER   Colloquial usage for Chairman of the Council of
          Ministers
PRL   POLSKA RZECZPOSPOLITA LUDOWA   (Polish People's
          Republic)
PWN   PAŃSTWOWE WYDAWNICTWO NAUKOWE (State Academic Pub-
          lishing House)
PZKS   POLSKI ZWIĄZEK KATOLIKÓW SPOŁECZNYCH (League of
          Polish Social Catholics)
PZPR   POLSKA ZJEDNOCZONA PARTIA ROBOTNICZA (Polish United
          Workers' Party)
REGIME   Although the phrase carries connotations of political
          illegitimacy in contemporary Western and emigré usage
          the term Communist régime in this study is used in a
          value-free and strictly precise manner.   It denotes
          something more restricted than the Communist system
          itself but also wider than Communist leadership in
          general.   In other words, it is the method and style
          of government associated with a particular established
          leadership, such as the Gomułka or Gierek régime.
RM   RADA MINISTRÓW (Council of Ministers; colloquially -
          Government)

Abbreviations and Glossary

RN   RADA NARODOWA (People's Council)
ROPCiO   RUCH OBRONY PRAW CZŁOWIEKA i OBYWATELA (Movement for the Defence of Human and Civil Rights)
RP   RADA PAŃSTWA (Council of State)
SD   STRONNICTWO DEMOKRATYCZNE (Democratic Party)
SDKPiL   SOCJAL-DEMOKRACJA KRÓLESTWA POLSKI i LITWY (Social Democracy of the Kingdom of Poland and Lithuania)
SGPiS   SZKOŁA GŁÓWNA PLANOWANIA i STATYSTYKI (Main School of Planning and Statistics)
SKS   STUDENCKI KOMITET SOLIDARNOŚCI (Students' Solidarity Committee)
SDP   STOWARZYSZENIE DZIENNIKARZY POLSKICH (Leage of Polish Journalists)
SSS   SPRAWOZDANIE STENOGRAFICZNE SEJMU (Stenographic Report of Sejm Proceedings - Sejm Hansard)
SZSP   SOCJALISTYCZNE ZRZESZENIE STUDENTÓW POLSKICH (Union of Polish Socialist Students)
TL   TRYBUNA LUDU (Tribune of the People)
TKN   TOWARZYSTWO KURSÓW NAUKOWYCH (Association for Academic Courses)
TRÓJMIASTO The 'Three-Cities' conurbation of Gdańsk, Gdynia and Sopot
TU   Trade Union
       UCHWAŁA (Resolution)
UJ   UNIWERSYTET JAGIELLOŃSKI, KRAKÓW
       USTAWA (Law)
UW   UNIWERSYTET WARSZAWSKI (Warsaw University)
WKP   WOJEWÓDZKA KOMISJA PRZEDZJAZDOWA (Pre-Congress Provincial Committee)
       WNIOSEK (Motion)
WRN   WOJEWÓDZKA RADA NARODOWA (Provincial People's Council)
WRON   WOJSKOWA RADA OCALENIA NARODOWEGO (Military Council of National Salvation)
WZZ   WOLNE ZWIĄZKI ZAWODOWE (Free Trade Unions)
ZBoWiD   ZWIĄZEK BOJOWNIKÓW O WOLNOŚĆ i DEMOKRACJĘ (League of Fighters for Freedom and Democracy)
ZLP   ZWIĄZEK LITERATÓW POLSKICH (League of Polish Writers)
ZMS   ZWIĄZEK MŁODZIEŻY SOCJALISTYCZNEJ (League of Socialist Youth)
ZOMO   ZMOTORYZOWANE ODWODY MILICJI OBYWATELSKIEJ (Mobile Units of the Citizens' Militia)
ZSL   ZJEDNOCZONE STRONNICTWO LUDOWE (United Peasant Party)
ZSMP   ZWIĄZEK SOCJALISTYZNEJ MŁODZIEŻY POLSKIEJ (League of Polish Socialist Youth)

There is nothing more difficult to arrange, more doubtful of
success, and more dangerous to carry through than initiating
changes in a state's constitution. The innovator makes
enemies of all those who prospered under the old order and
only lukewarm support is forthcoming from those who would
prosper under the new. Their support is lukewarm partly from
fear of their adversaries, who have the existing laws on their
side, and partly because men are generally incredulous, never
really trusting new things until they have tested them by
experience. In consequence whenever those who oppose the
changes can do so, they attack vigorously, and the defence
made by the others is only lukewarm. So both the innovator
and his friends are endangered together. But to discuss this
subject thoroughly we must distinguish between innovators who
stand alone and those who depend upon others, that is between those who achieve their purposes can force the issue and
those who must use persuasion. In the second case they always
come to grief, having achieved nothing; when however they
depend upon their own resources and can force the issue, then
they are seldom endangered. That is why all armed prophets
have conquered, and unarmed prophets have come to grief.
Besides what I have said already, the populace is by nature
fickle; it is easy to persuade them of something, but
difficult to confirm them in that persuasion. Therefore one
should rightly arrange matters so that when they no longer
believe they can be made to believe by force.

Machiavelli, <u>The Prince</u>

Patiently endured so long as it seemed beyond redress, a
grievance comes to appear intolerable once the possibility of
removing it crosses men's minds. For the mere fact that
certain abuses have been remedied draws attention to the
others and they appear more galling; people may suffer less
but their sensibility is exacerbated.

de Tocqueville, <u>The Old Regime and the French Revolution</u>

Hereby it is manifest, that during the time men live without
a Common Power to keep them all in awe, they are in that condition which is called Warre; and such a warre, is as of
every man, against every man. For Warre consisteth, not in
Batell onely, or the act of fighting...but in the known dis-
position thereto, during all the time there is no assurance to
the contrary.... To this Warre of every man against every man,
this is also consequent; that nothing can be Unjust. The
notions of Right and Wrong, Justice and Injustice have there
no place. Where there is no Common Power there is no Law.

Hobbes, <u>Leviathan</u>

FOR MY WIFE

POLISH COMMUNISM IN CRISIS

Chapter One

THE DILEMMA OF COMMUNIST REFORM IN THE SOVIET SPHERE

The problem of the reform of Communist states within the Soviet sphere is a highly complex one but it can be stated simply. There has always been a school of thought in the West that Communist states suffer from too much ideological and institutional inertia and are hampered by too many vested interests to reform themselves. To the contrary, it is often argued that the dynamics of Communist politics normally veer them towards a strengthening rather than a dilution of totalitarianism [1]. Many critics of 'actually existing socialism', such as Rudolf Bahro, have also questioned the capacities for self-reform of Soviet-type systems [2]. The presumption is that, normally, Communist leaderships have little interest in implementing substantive reform from above as this would undermine the bases of their rule which depends on a centralised system of political and economic directives. Pressures for reform from below, from within the party, are usually contained by traditional methods of recruiting, purging, manipulating and controlling party cadres and members spiced with a certain amount of police methods, as in Czechoslovakia in the 1970s. On the other hand, if reform from above and from within the CP is unlikely, the general Western view has been that the development of countervailing social and political forces external to the CP could only produce successful reform or nationalist movements outside the Soviet sphere of Red Army control. But the paradox is that nationalist pressures, at least, are bound to be much weaker in such National Communist states as Yugoslavia, Cuba or Vietnam, where the CP took power in its own right. In the Soviet controlled sphere of Eastern Europe (Poland, Czechoslovakia, Hungary, Bulgaria and the GDR) challenges of the latter national and societal type have induced outright invasion when they have gone beyond the bounds of Soviet tolerance, as in Hungary in 1956 and Czechoslovakia in 1968. Alternatively, they have been tamed and emasculated because of the self-interest and collaboration of the local Communist élites, as in the case of Gomułka's Poland after 1956. The Morton's Fork of Communist Reform within the Soviet sphere in Eastern Europe is therefore that substantive Communist reform is unlikely to emerge from within the top ruling levels of the CP and if it does, as in Czechoslovakia in 1968, the Soviet reaction is particularly strong and rapid. On the other hand, broader societal challenges of the Polish 1980 type, which force the CP to carry out such reforms, must sooner or later prove unacceptable to the Kremlin and their domestic hardline allies and are suppressed through the use of a variety of political and police and military methods at different times.

The repetition of the above scenario in Hungary in 1956, in Czechoslovakia in 1968 and in Poland, in a camouflaged way, in 1981, might seem to support the thesis that such outcomes are inevitable and that Soviet type states are unreformable. However, such an argument suffers from obvious shortcomings. Firstly, the pressures for reform within both the party and society in Eastern Europe have incontestably been very major and recurring ones. The Soviet power holders have had to deal with them in increasingly sophisticated ways. The cases of Yugoslavia, Poland and Hungary provide much evidence that socio-economically modernising socialist states at a certain point produce reform-minded and contestatory second and third generation university educated Communist sub-élites. Recent years have also shown the developing strength and self-awareness of the working class. The successful examples of hardline containment in the GDR and Czechoslovakia and of the successful harnessing of nationalism, as in Albania and Romania, may also prove not to be the norm in the long run. Secondly, it is quite untrue in point of fact to claim that reforms have never been introduced in the USSR and its inner sphere since the death of Stalin in 1953. Major structural reforms of the economy, of the state and local organs and of internal security methods have been introduced at various times. Quite long periods of cumulative reform have also occurred, most notably under Khrushchev in the late 1950s and under Kadar in Hungary for most of the 1960s, not to mention Poland itself in 1955-1957 and 1971-1974.

The problem is partly a semantic one, of defining

and agreeing on the terms to be used, as one of the
great difficulties in both the study and the practice
of Communist politics is that the same words just do
not mean the same thing to different individuals.
What is a Communist reform and when is it really a
reform?   At one end of the spectrum it is quite
clear that a bewildering array of individual reforms
from above in limited organisational spheres and in
administrative methods is carried out by the Communist states on a regular basis.   Even the most
ideologically hardline states have also carried out
very significant economic reforms, as in the GDR in
1965 or in Bulgaria's innovative readjustment of her
agricultural system.   The implication in the West,
especially in its mass media which shapes public
opinion, though, is that a Communist reform is not
really a reform unless it brings about a qualitative
change in the system.   Public opinion in Western
democracies is very heavily, although unconsciously,
ideologically motivated in this respect.   What it
awaits, and certainly hopes for, is the transformation of the totalitarian Communist state into something approximating to the Yugoslav model,with decentralised state and economic systems and some
'self-management' at lower levels.   Nothing else
qualifies as a 'real' reform.   Now this 'reform',
in Western terms, may appear as a 'counter-revolution' to Soviet Communists and their orthodox hardline allies in Eastern Europe.   The matter has been
complicated with the emergence of a significant
Marxist opposition in Eastern Europe during the last
decade which has produced pioneering ideas for the
democratisation of public life within the Marxist-
Leninist frame of reference, although outside the
Soviet one.   Putting the matter very schematically,
one can now proceed to the following definitions.
Firstly, Soviet type CPs deal with the problem of
decentralisation within the party, state and economic
management levels on an everyday technical basis.
Secondly, the question of democratisation can be considered under both liberal-bourgeois and socialist
headings.   The former envisages the 'free play' of
political and social forces, the existence of opposition parties and all sorts of mechanisms which are
irrelevant to the Marxist-Leninist state, except in
mixed, transitional periods,such as when the East
European CPs were taking over power between 1944 and
1948.   The latter involves both a diminution of the
CP's leading role and its readjustment either to make
it concentrate on essential policy making or in even
more advanced versions to transform it from direct

political rule to being more of a moral-inspirational force.

One should also note the argument produced during the Polish crisis that the cyclical recurrence of crises is part of the growing process of a young socialist system and not proof of its unreformability. The novel Communist argument was that it is the strength not the weakness of socialism that allows it to have a house-cleaning every so often in order to overcome its deformations. More questionable is the ideological tenet that the dialectics of socialist development tend naturally towards participation, democratisation and self-management and that the CP's leading role facilitates and does not constrain such trends [3].

The reader needs to be aware of the foregoing considerations as with a few honourable exceptions much of the public presentation and discussion of the Polish crisis of 1980-1981 in the West was almost in terms of a political morality play. Most of the early publications on the subject were inevitably superficial rapportage, far below the standard of such works on Poland in the 1956 crisis as Konrad Syrop's Spring in October [4]. The one notable exception was Neal Ascherson's The Polish August which, although, as is normal on books on Poland, overslanted towards the historical background in order to gain a mass audience and too slight on the events of the crises of 1980-1981 themselves, nevertheless remains the outstanding early study of the subject. The earliest academic analysis related the failures and shortcomings of the Gierek era to the course of events in the reform period from Summer 1980 to the PZPR Ninth Congress in July 1981 and took a somewhat over-optimistic view of the outcome [5].

My main axiom in this study is that the Polish Reform Movement of 1980-1981 can only be understood in terms of the values, presumptions, aims and discourse of the Polish Communist reformers themselves. These, hardly surprisingly, are very different from Western ones and a real intellectual and imaginative jump from Western to Polish realities is required in order to comprehend them. Much of the material which is central to Polish political life, especially the CP literature, may seem dry, turgid and convoluted in style to outsiders and nobody would claim otherwise. I make no apology nevertheless for including large chunks of such nitty-gritty detail, particularly of Polish CP (PZPR) plena, as this is the only sure corrective to the simplifying snap judgements and stereotypes about Poland which, through constant

repetition, have been embedded in the Western mass
consciousness. Neal Ascherson in a review of what
is perhaps the best academic History of Poland since
1863, edited by R.F. Leslie, complained that the
authors had managed the rare feat of making 'the most
dramatic of all European national experiences ...
rather dull' [6]. The author can merely plead that
the tendency to over-dramatise and exaggerate the
special character of Poland's history and current
problems is a much greater sin than the effort to
convey the hard, unglamorous and often prosaic realities of the situation [7].

The brunt of my argument in this study is twofold: firstly, that the key political problem in
1980-1981 was whether the PZPR would be able to
produce Communist reformist leadership and policies
which would be acceptable to both Polish society and
the Soviet leadership, as in October 1956. Cata-
clysmic theoretical alternatives, such as the collapse
of Communist power in the USSR or the outbreak of the
Third World War, interest me, not all in the context
of the realities of 1980-1981. Secondly, my thesis
is that the course of events in the Polish crisis
from Summer 1980 to December 1981 was crucial and
the outcome by no means pre-ordained in terms of Communist politics. It was not inevitable that political alternatives would be narrowed down either to
socio-economic anarchy and political counter-revolution or the imposition of military rule to save
Communism (and the state as well), as was claimed
by General Wojciech Jaruzelski in imposing the
State of War in December 1981. For a while, certainly until after the Ninth PZPR Congress in July
1981, it appeared possible, even quite likely, that
the reformist and centrist elements within the PZPR
would, as in 1956, find common ground with the moderate elements in Solidarity; in this way they would
face the Kremlin, as in 1956, with an insuperable,
although not wholly unacceptable, Polish domestic
fait accompli. This study, starting from the premise
that only reform from within the Communist system,
led by the PZPR and designed to make democratic centralism really work, could have had any chance of
success, given Soviet military power and its politico-
strategic preconceptions, therefore concentrates on
the Polish crisis from the vantage point of developments within the PZPR. It describes the alternatives which were possible within the PZPR framework
and explains the bitter, although not too tragic (in
lives at least) failure of the reform Communist enterprise in this period. I have aimed to produce an

uncommitted academic account based largely on Polish
sources of the realities of Communist reform politics.
My main concern is to see whether a peaceful outcome
avoiding the use of force was possible, and if not
to explain the reasons for this failure.   If my approach seems dominated by political realism it is not
because of any lack of sympathy with the libertarian,
democratic and self-management aims of the national
upsurge of 1980;   a hard-headed appraisal of the
realities of political life in Eastern Europe inevitably produces an acute awareness of the narrowness
of the range of what is politically possible.   As
Adam Bromke has shown, the debate between political
realism and political idealism is one of the most
basic and long running themes in Polish politics [8].
It certainly recurred with a particular sharpness
and was one of the staples of political debate during
1980-1981.
        In the Summer of 1980 a number of separate, but
equally grave, crises with long drawn out historical
antecedents came to a head in Poland.   There are
numerous ways of viewing the causes of the Summer
1980 outburst, but the one point on which there may
be agreement is that no simple monocausal explanation
will do.   It was an economic crisis, a political
struggle within the PZPR, the death throes of the
1956-1980 political system, a working class revolt,
a societal protest of a contestatory type against
authoritarian and corporatist structures, an outburst
of traditional Polish nationalism and the culmina-
tion of a demographic trend which produced an extremely
young, demanding and consumption orientated society.
The downfall of the Gomułka-Gierek system of 1956-
1980 and the course of events in 1980-1981 can also
be usefully explained in terms of the concept of the
'overloaded state' which succumbs to revolution because it cannot satisfy an overwhelming deluge of
pressures, demands and expectations [9].   This in my
view is at least as satisfactory as concentrating on
the epiphenomena of the political demands for democratisation and renewal.   With outstanding exceptions
in the quality press, like Bernard Guetta in Le Monde
and Christopher Bobiński in the Financial Times,
these slogans were invariably swallowed at face value
by the Western mass media because of their ideological values, the realities of the East-West conflict
and the meaningfulness of such stereotypes to public
opinion, especially in Britain, which unlike many of
its continental counterparts is normally woefully
badly informed about East European developments [10].
All in all a sharp dichotomy existed, and still

exists, between the mass media/public and academic debate on the subject.

Sparked off by economic shortages which had worsened during the late 1970s and meat price increases in July 1980, discontent by industrial workers produced two months of country-wide strikes which culminated in mass factory occupations in the Baltic sea coast area, most notably in the Lenin Shipyard in Gdańsk. This not only caused a crise de régime which overthrew the Communist leader, Edward Gierek, but the Workers' Upsurge challenged the foundations of the Communist state by gaining the concession of the right to strike and to organise 'free TUs', thus provoking a crise d'état.

Once the Polish Communist authorities had been humiliated, however, and the illusion of Communist power at factory and local level shattered, the lid was taken off the seething cauldron which constituted Polish society. Consequently a whole series of associated political, economic, social and demographic tensions broke out. These kept the country in a ferment, paralysed such leadership capacity as there was for initiating reforms, overloaded the political system and reduced society almost to the Hobbesian state of the war of all against all (in the struggle for consumption at least) until the imposition of the State of War on 13 December 1981. The general crisis did not end there and then, but a complete sea change was brought about my military rule which, for good or ill, closed the preceding chapter in Poland's history and which is the justification for concluding this study at that point.

In this study I trace out the dynamics and the course of the 'Never Ending' Polish crisis of Summer 1980 to December 1981. There is no inevitability and,on the contrary, many surprises in history; most political analysts agree, however, that the Kremlin and the Red Army would not willingly permit the downfall of the Communist régime in Poland or the readjustment of the postwar Yalta realities. They refused to accept the collapse of Communism in Hungary, a much more peripheral interest, or the democratisation of the Czechoslovak political system in 1968, so it is difficult to lend credence to Polish opposition arguments that Poland could become such a political and economic liability that the Soviets would be willing to concede it a 'Finnish' status. This would preserve the USSR's hold over the country's foreign relations while allowing a non-Soviet Leninist type of domestic political system. The argument of KOR dissidents, like Jacek Kuroń,

that Poland's geopolitical position and Soviet interests necessitated the maintenance of the essential framework of Polish Communist rule but that
this could be transformed from within in order to
allow the existence of countervailing social checks,
such as the Roman Catholic Church and eventually
Solidarity, and that some form of pluralist power
sharing could be arranged, even under conditions of
Communist hegemony as had occurred in 1944-1947,
now with military rule, also appears very dubious
[11].

The key questions to be borne in mind in reading this study are the following, although the limitations of reliable information and space often allow for only very tentative answers. If the overthrow of the Communist system in Poland would inevitably entail a Soviet invasion, to what extent was
it possible to force reform on the PZPR by means of
social, especially workers', pressure from outside,
without producing the same result? [12]. In spite
of the disappointments of 1956 and 1971, what were
the possibilities during the crisis period for Communist reformism? To what extent could the PZPR
produce new leaders and policies which might stabilise the crisis by carrying out the necessary reforms,
by changing its directing personnel at all levels
and by establishing some form of social contract or
agreement with Polish society? To what extent was
it reasonable to envisage the assimilation of the
more TU and less politically minded Wałęsa wing of
Solidarity within such a revised system? How high
a price would the USSR be willing to pay in order to
achieve a peaceful and evolutionary outcome, as in
1956? What were the forces within Poland which
would either support or oppose such changes? Were
significant political mistakes made by the reformists,
within both the PZPR and Solidarity, which led to
the State of War? Finally, given the economic collapse and the overloading of the Polish political
system during 1981 by a wide range of political,
economic, social and local demands, were there any
alternatives apart from political paralysis, economic
chaos and social anarchy to military rule?

I make no secret of the fact that I consider the
events of August-September 1980 to be the greatest
Polish lunacy since the 1863 Uprising. I also view
the sixteen months from the signing of the Gdańsk
Agreement to the imposition of the State of War as
being dominated by a whole series of face-saving
'historical alibis', which were thought up on all
sides in order to conceal the realities of the

situation and to allow the Communist authorities and
Polish society to stagger on towards their showdown
in December 1981. Firstly, a revolution did take
place in August-September 1980. The PZPR lost its
capacity to rule for a while but its international
situation, the relative solidity of its police,
judicial and military forces and the self-interest
of its élite,which controlled all the key positions
in Poland, meant that it was not swept away. The
revolution was, therefore, a strictly limited one,
not 'self-limiting', to the extent that nobody else
took power. Even after Solidarity organised itself
and confronted the Communist system head-on in October-
November 1980 and again in March 1981, it only had a
veto capacity rather than a share in a system of
'dual power'. To conceal these facts and to gain
time, in order to avoid the immediate resort to
physical coercion, the PZPR had to claim that Polish
Communism and its Soviet ally was not universally
hated by the Poles, that the Summer events were
directed not against socialism itself but against
its distortions, that the working class had only in-
dulged in a justified protest and that it would now
become the main agent of socialist renewal. The
PZPR on that basis produced a strategy from the
October Sixth Plenum onwards designed to eliminate
these deformations and to produce a purer and renewed form of socialism. As a militant said at the
Toruń Party Consultative Forum, 'a party which led
the country into such a crisis should normally lose
power but as this is obviously impossible the need
is to change it' [13]. The ambiguity of the situation was that even the most pro-Soviet PZPR hardliners covered their tracks by supporting the renewal verbally and tactically. On the other hand,
Polish society, which had rebelled for largely bread
and butter reasons and a national refusal to accept
economic reality which had aggravated the country's
economic problems for over a decade, was now presented, both in Poland and in the West, as a heroic force
struggling for democracy, uncorrupted socialism,
self-management, the national rights of the Polish
Nation and Society, as well as a whole farrago of
similar fine sounding ideals. This allowed Solidarity
a few months of euphoric national unity when the
Poles, especially the under 35s, believed that everything was possible. The ultimate historical alibi
of course, which dominated Polish politics until the
Ninth Congress in July 1981, was that, as a miner-
delegate said at the Ninth Congress, 'individuals
failed not socialism'. If Polish society and the

genuine sections of the PZPR were guiltless, then
the blame could very conveniently be attached to the
old political élite. Its mistakes, personal corruption and responsibility were often real enough,but
certainly not as all-encompassing as was claimed
after Gdańsk.

Since Zygmunt Bauman launched the idea over a
decade ago it has been accepted that much about
Communist politics can be explained in a schematic
way by examining the relationships and conflicts
between three basic forces [14]. These can be defined as follows: firstly, the Central Political
Elite (CPE) can either be defined in a restricted
way as being composed of the few hundred top political leaders and functionaries or it can be regarded
in a much wider way as being made up of the 180 to
300,000 or so (and some would claim more) office
holders in all walks of life who, however loosely,
depend upon the party nomenklatura. In this study
I use CPE in this wider sense while I use the term
Central Party Apparatus (CPA) when talking about the
cohesive top level institutional locale for decision-
making which is made up of the Politburo, Secretariat
and CC Departments and Commissions. The second
force is what I dub the Supporting Communist Intellectual Elite (SCIE),which again can either be regarded in the narrow sense of being made up of the
million or so individuals with Higher Education or,
alternatively, one might wish to add almost double
that number with semi-Higher Educational qualifications. The third force is the remaining overwhelming majority who, although differentiated in occupational and income terms, may quite simply be regarded
as MASSES in relation to the other two [15]. In
the second and third generation of developed socialism
there is normally a growing tendency for individuals
from the SCIE to move into the CPE [16]. This personal advancement is, however, achieved by socialisation into, and subjection to, apparat values, so it
does not prevent recurrent conflicts between the
traditional Soviet-Leninist methods of rule of the
post-revolutionary incumbents at the very top and
the mixed rational scientific and humanist approaches
of what one can loosely call the Communist middle
classes. The latter rightly clamour for status and
remuneration rewards for their special skills but
their frustration with the political rigidity and
blockheadedness of the original CPE is usually
matched by their mutual economic interests in face of
the masses. I view the SCIE and the masses, as
represented by Solidarity and the Workers' Upsurge,

as standing for two quite different conceptions of
reform during the 1980-1981 crisis.   The workers
unleashed a whole range of local and sectional demands, most of which could not possibly be satisfied
under conditions of economic collapse.   Their political programme of workers' autonomy and self-management and a drastic limitation of the PZPR's monopoly
in the direction of greater power sharing and consultation of other social forces was admirable in
human and theoretical terms but again arguably
unrealisable under the conditions of 1980-1981.
The SCIE wanted a diminished PZPR monopoly and greater
social consultation and it presented a more reali-
sable programme of reforms from above to be instituted by the PZPR, especially in the economy, as well
as a whole series of technical and institutional
adjustments designed to make the CPA behave in a more
rational scientific manner.   The matter was complicated as a small but influential wing hived off and
from 1976 formed a Democratic Opposition which inter
alia produced the Polish equivalents of Eurocommunist
programmes and which built up support by pressing for
civil and workers' rights.   In the end both the
orthodox party organisation and the political and
economic spokesmen of the working masses lost out to
the SCIE (which shed its more humane and oppositionist wing) and the peasantry, both of whom had their
interests fairly well served by Jaruzelski's military
rule.
     In this study I examine the Polish crisis mainly
through the prism of leadership developments within
the PZPR and I concentrate on the year between the
Summers of 1980 and 1981 when real pluralist politics
and debate took place.   This aspect holds the key
to an assessment of the capacities of the Polish
Communist system to renew itself by producing a modified form of Communist government capable of avoiding the extremes of zamordyzm and repression on the
one hand and an unacceptable dilution of its leading
role on the other.   The Polish case, especially in
the Spring and Summer of 1981, also throws crucial
light on the possibilities of the party led democratisation of CPs in maturing industrial societies under
conditions of developed socialism.   I beg the reader's
indulgence if this emphasis, and the very real problem of the constraints of space, lead me to neglect
many interesting aspects of important subjects such
as Solidarity, the Roman Catholic Church, the problem of economic reform, the activities of social
groups and the detailed aspects of Polish social
dynamics, but in the nature of things detailed case

studies have to precede any comprehensive synthesis of such a massive subject.

Notes

1. Leszek Kołakowski sets out the argument more clearly than he refutes it in 'Hope and Hopelessness', Survey, XVII, No. 3 (Summer 1971), pp. 37-52.
2. R. Bahro, The Alternative in Eastern Europe (London, New Left Books, 1978).
3. Z. Skuza, TL, 23.12.80.
4. Three of the ephemera, produced for the British mass market, were: The Book of Lech Wałęsa (London, Allen Lane Press, 1982); K. Dobbs, K.S. Karol and D. Trevisan, Poland, Solidarity, Wałęsa (Harmondsworth, Penguin, 1981); K. Ruane, The Polish Challenge (London, BBC Publications, 1982).
5. J. Woodall (ed.), Policy and Politics in Contemporary Poland (London, Frances Pinter, 1981).
6. Observer, 9.11.80.
7. This view of the peculiarly special and tragic character of Poland's history is reflected in, and perpetuated by, the often lurid and dramatic titles of books about Poland in the West. A small sample of the worst sinners of this type: Bridge for the Abyss; God's Playground; A Case-History of Hope; Phoenix in the East.
8. A. Bromke, Poland's Politics; idealism v realism (Harvard UP, 1967).
9. Cf. Theda Skocpol, States and Social Revolutions (London, Cambridge UP, 1979).
10. Every writer on the Polish crisis of 1980-1981 is seriously indebted to Guetta's superb rapportage and analysis. In this he followed in the footsteps of Philippe Ben, who also produced outstanding reports based on excellent sources of information for Le Monde in 1956.
11. For Kuroń's strategy, see his remarkable interview for Le Monde, 29.1.77, his chapter in Z. Erard and M. Zygier (eds.), La Pologne. Une Société en dissidence (Paris, Maspero, 1978) and Ruch Oporu (Paris, Instytut Literacki, 1977).
12. On the need for effective social pressure to prevent political degeneration, M. Tarniewski (pseud.), Ewolucja czy revolucja? (Paris, Instytut Literacki, 1975).
13. Cited in Le Monde, 17.4.81.
14. 'The Second Generation's Socialism', Cumberland Lodge Conference, 1969. Cf. Z. Bauman, 'The Crisis of Soviet type Systems', Problems of Communism, XX, No. 6 (November-December 1971), pp. 45-53.
15. For the detailed official statistics, see Rocznik Statystyczny 1981 (Warsaw, GUS, 1982). See M. Vaughan, 'A multi-dimensional approach to contemporary Polish

stratification', <u>Survey</u>, XX, No. 1 (Winter 1974),
pp. 62-74.

16.   On this interplay, see F. Fleron, 'Co-optation as a
      mechanism of adaptation to change' in R. Kanet (ed.),
      <u>The Behavioural Revolution and Communist Studies</u> (New
      York, Free Press, 1971).

17.   For the stimulating argument that the SCIE is a potential,
      and often actual, ruling class in Eastern Europe, see
      G. Konrad and I. Szelenyi, <u>The Intellectuals on the</u>
      <u>Road to Class Power</u> (Brighton, Harvester Press, 1979).
      For the political impact of the SCIE, D. Lane and G.
      Kolankiewicz (eds.), <u>Social Groups in Polish Society</u>
      (London, Macmillan, 1973);   A. Matejko, <u>Social Change</u>
      <u>and Stratification in Eastern Europe. An Analysis of</u>
      <u>Poland and her Neighbours</u> (New York, Praeger, 1974).

Chapter Two

THE GIEREK QUESTION AND THE CAUSES OF THE
1980 CRISIS

Poland before Gierek; was postwar Poland a crisis-
prone political culture?
        Communist political leadership in Poland has had
to deal with severe crises of revolutionary proportions in 1956, 1970, 1980-1981 as well as major but
shorter ones in 1968 and 1976.   Although there have
been long periods of apparent political stability many
Western political scientists, like Jan Gross, consider
that the PZPR's main task in order to survive in power
was crisis management;   Poland's 'entire history
from 1944 to the present is one of long procrastinat-
ing crisis'.   He suggests, however, that crises in
Poland, as under the Third and Fourth French Repub-
lics, are 'functional'.   They have been the main way
in which the system has unblocked and renewed itself
[1].
        There has been considerable debate in interpret-
ing these events about the balance to be struck between basic political traditions, an underlying and,
in structural terms, unchanging Polish political culture on the one hand and the direct and specific
causes of each individual outburst on the other.
Poland's historical experiences of partition and
occupation by Russia, Austria and Prussia in the nineteenth century, her political and social divisions
and economic backwardness between the two World Wars,
the unparalleled human and economic devastation and
social dislocation which she suffered during the Second
World War and her postwar subordination to the USSR
and a Marxist-Leninist political and social transformation, are the ineradicable experiences which have
scarred the Polish political consciousness.   This
inheritance undoubtedly gives Polish events an edge
which is difficult to convey to the non-Polish out-
sider.   Moreover, the foreign observer is much struck
by the invariable Polish tendency to discuss and

14

interpret current political problems through the
prism of past misfortunes [2].

One should beware of the misconceptions about
the alleged 'ungovernability' of the Poles and of the
unchanging character of Polish national values which
still create a certain popular stereotype in the
West [3]. Nevertheless, there is one valid strand.
The Polish nation survived throughout the nineteenth
century with an a priori hostility and a set of insur-
rectionary values against their foreign controlled
state institutions by developing 'self-defence' social,
educational and economic organisations. Above all,
the Poles turned to the Roman Catholic Church and
developed an almost symbiotic relationship with it.
A tradition was established that Polish civic society
was quite separate from the state and, given the right
conditions, always likely to be a more autonomous
force than in most other European countries. The
Polish state after regaining independence in 1918 was
only partially successful in developing more responsible and integrated civic values and attitudes towards authority. The democratic parliamentary democracy of 1918-1926 was overloaded by too many demands and riven by too many divisions to be successful. Neither its attempt to ride out Poland's divisions in a pluralist fashion nor Piłsudski's military dominated authoritarian clique and system managed
to heal the rift between state and society. The
holocaust of Nazi occupation then destroyed the
Polish state system and either exterminated or scattered the ruling élites. Polish society, subjected
to an unprecedented degree of terror, again turned
inwards towards the family and a variety of social
and resistance self-defence organisations against a
hostile state. The setting up of a pro-Russian
Communist system at the end of the war and its evolution into a Polish form of Stalinism also, until
1976, had the overall effect of strengthening the
anti-state attitudes of much of society.

This historical outline therefore provides strong
evidence for the view that the Polish state has been
a parasite on society with few legitimately accepted
organic links with it. It has often maintained itself by force and has had a somewhat tenuous hold
which could easily be shaken by the generalisation
of specific discontents as the bulk of Poles continued
to view it in a conditional and extractive manner.
The sociologist, Jadwiga Staniszkis, confirms that
the deep polarisation between the state and society
has continued until the present day:

In the Polish tradition the state was always
an 'enemy' state. The only way for Poland
to survive as a society was to build its own
national culture, ethnic code and system
of social sanctions against 'collaborators',
even its own informal educational system.
These act as instruments to isolate society
from the state, to create a distinct substitute
circulation of ideas and support informal
social links (by an elaborate system of social
self-help during political troubles) [4].
Something close to a catholic-national 'counter-
community' has therefore existed in postwar Poland
which the modernising Communist society has only
partially succeeded in assimilating [5]. There has
been a strong latent tendency for it to emerge against
the Communist state during crises. Hence it is
meaningful to talk about confrontations between state
and society in a manner which might strike the Anglo-
Saxon reader as odd. The concept is quite familiar
on the continent, however. One needs only to point
to the well known example of the Communist 'counter-
community' within French capitalist society, notably
in the 'Red Belt' of Paris [6].

In my view this is only a partial explanation
of the Polish propensity towards social revolts
against the prevailing political system. Explanation of the 1980-1981 crisis in terms of a chasm
caused by these historical experiences between the
pays légal dominated by the PZPR and the pays réel
of Polish society represented by the Church, and
Solidarity when it emerged, are an important preliminary statement and the beginnings of an explanation, but no more. Inherited political values are
difficult to eradicate and often outlast institutional
and societal changes for some generations but they
are modified, often drastically, by educational and
socio-economic transformations and consequent changes
in family and other socialisation patterns. The
reassertion of civil society after 1976 was part of
KOR strategy and it can unquestionably be developed
into one of the major strands explaining the rise of
Solidarity in 1980. I argue, however, that broad
historical and national character type of explanations
are less significant than the specific political reasons
why the PZPR was unable to establish its rule over
Polish society more securely [7]

One of the most respected Western academic authorities on Polish politics wrote in 1978 that 'the
Polish People's Republic is in the throes of the most
serious crisis in its entire existence. The present

difficulties reflect not just erroneous policies
but strike at the roots of the system itself' [8].
Bromke's prescient judgement also had the merit of
indicating that the developing crisis was not a
straightforward monocausal affair. It was the simultaneous maturation of many factors, each on its own
sufficient to shake the system, which made the crisis
of Summer 1980 to December 1981 the most fundamental
challenge to Communist power in Poland since its
establishment at the end of the Second World War.
Furthermore, each type of crisis was also extremely
complicated and multi-faceted.

   The economic crisis was not just a matter of bad
financial management which needed some sectional corrective measures. Excessive investment across too
wide a range of over-ambitious industrial plants, an
external hard currency debt to the West which was
allowed to mount up to frightening proportions, and
gross mismanagement in steering the largely private-
peasant agricultural sector presented the Gierek
régime in the late 1970s with a major economic crisis,
but in itself it was not necessarily all that more
unmanageable than earlier crises. It was the political and social consequences of the deflationary
programme and major cut-back in the living standards
gained by the Poles in the prosperous years of 1971-
1974 which ignited all the combustible elements into
one vast general crisis. The economic crisis proper
encouraged the critics of the post-1950 centralised
system of economic planning to re-emerge with a fundamental critique of the Stalinist system and the inadequate post-1970 élitist and technocratic tinkering
about with the system. For the first time since
1956 the call became one for a fundamental overhaul
of the system in the direction of self-managing,
self-accounting industrial enterprises working within
a much reduced framework of political directives.

   At the same time the ever worsening food crisis
reflected a number of factors which are often neglected in the West in favour of spiritual and moral in-
tangibles. Two factors in particular struck me as
a regular observer of the Polish scene in the 1970s.
Firstly, the gastronomic and alcoholic habits of a
bygone agricultural age continued in Poland even
after urban patterns had become predominant.
Secondly, the Poles in the 1970s latched on to food
and drink as a compensation for all their postwar
hardships and sacrifices. Not only did they refuse
to accept any cut-back but a general egalitarianism
and levelling out of differences in consumption patterns between different social groups and the absence

17

of appropriate mechanisms to regulate distribution
generated intolerable demands. Something close to
a state of national pathology - 'a social veto' -
developed over this matter. Although the 'politics
of the stomach' may seem demeaning to the Poles and
too trivial a cause for outsiders, one should remember that food price rises sparked off the wider political crises of 1970, 1976 and 1980. In some respects this factor paralysed Gierek's political will
after June 1976 as he was unable either to satisfy
or to dampen down demand. Nobody starved in Poland
but the frustrated and unrealistic demands and envy,
if not hatred, generated amongst the lower placed by
the conspicuous consumption of the élite as well as
the sense of relative deprivation and continual irri-
tation experienced by the middling sectors of Polish
society are an element in the Polish national psyche
of the late 1970s which cannot be under-rated.
     Under Gierek the PZPR had, so many thought, be-
come the party of the Communist professional, middle
class élite.   Consequently, as Kuroń and Modzelewski
had diagnosed in the mid 1960s, a real, although
muted, class struggle took place over the control
and distribution of the social product [10]:   on the
one hand were ranged the party officialdom backed by
the bulk of the largely University educated general
élite;   on the other was the working class abetted
by a few intellectuals who had fallen out of favour
with the system or younger, more naïve, or more
idealistic, individuals, especially students.
     Above all the PZPR itself had rarely been a
united and effective force.   Its leadership had often
been very factional-ridden.   Personalities and the
clientèle groups which aggregated around them not
only struggled for power but were divided by genuine
quarrels over the best policies for resolving Poland's
manifold tensions and the best means of strengthening
the PZPR's power.   I do not accept the Warsaw café
argument that such opposition groups unleashed crises
in order to overthrow incumbents and to seize power,
except perhaps for the 1967-1968 case.   But there is
no doubt that once real pluralism had emerged in
Communist politics in 1956, early 1971 and after
August 1980 they played on social forces for their
own political ends.   Quite apart from the basic ideological and temperamental split after 1954 between
those who wanted to assert Communist power through
hardline repression and those who saw the necessity
of compromises with national and social forces in
order to ensure Communism's survival, there was a
potential threefold split within the PZPR itself.

Normally the PZPR's hard-core of political incumbents
who controlled all the party, state, economic and
other apparats co-opted the most capable and ambitious
elements from the middle ranks of the party's supporting executive agencies; these middle and lower rank
functionaries would at most act as a political dead-
weight if some reform, such as Gierek's local government reorganisation in 1973-1974, cut across their
interests. The vast bulk of ordinary grassroots
members might leave the party in droves, as in 1956,
but they could easily be replaced once the PZPR re-
established itself. As we shall see, the vast bulk
or the 'outer ring' of the PZPR's membership was placed
in a false position of having responsibility without
power, but this did not have political consequences
until 1980.
    The foregoing catalogue of political, societal
and economic tensions which burst out in 1980 was
the result of a number of basic political facts in
the history of postwar Poland. These are well known
and have been dealt with in detail elsewhere[11].Firstly,
the way in which the Second World War was fought,
with the bulk of the Germans being killed on the
Eastern Front, was paid for by the Western Powers at
the end of the war in Soviet political and military
domination over Eastern Europe. This allowed Stalin
to build up Communist régimes in his sphere between
1944 and 1948. In the Polish case the Communist
takeover was a mixture between the outright imposition of a 'baggage train' government, as in Romania,
and the genuine parliamentary methods of Czechoslovakia
[12]. The Polish CP,which had been reborn as the
PPR in December 1942, in place of the interwar KPP
dissolved by Stalin in 1938, had some genuine sources
of support and a membership of over a million in
October 1948 [13]. The destruction of the Piłsudski-
ite state and its élites and the radicalisation of
postwar politics enabled the PPR to lead a coalition
of socialists, radical peasant and democratic middle
class parties, under near civil war conditions, which
polarised political choices and which carried out
widely agreed reform programmes. The gradual eli-
mination of non-Communist forces from Polish political
life then culminated in late 1948 in the replacement
of the more domestically inclined First Secretary,
Władysław Gomułka, by the Stalinist 'Muscovite',
Bolesław Bierut, in the forced fusion of the PPR and
the PPS and in the establishment of a fully fledged
Communist dictatorship.
    The memory of the 1944 to 1948 model which had
allowed a degree of pluralism and some genuine power

sharing initially, under general but not monolithic
conditions of PPR and Soviet hegemony,however, retained its attraction [14]. Many Poles viewed it
in 1980-1981 as a desirable type of political system
which might be accepted, however grudgingly, by the
USSR as it fell far short of Finland's postwar status
and might permit the Communist hegemony and Soviet
interests to co-exist with the rival pluralism of
Polish society.

It is not my purpose here to outline the political history of Polish Communism in power. In my
view, though, the argument that the Polish Communist
state was an artificial and imposed Soviet creation
is far from the truth and much less significant than
the question of why it failed to build up sounder and
surer foundations over time. While it is undoubtedly
true that there was much anti-Russian feeling in
Poland, this was not directed against Russians as
people, and there was never the same depth of almost
subliminal hatred which was felt for the Germans for
long after the war. It is also not proven that
Polish national, religious, historical and social
class traditions necessarily rendered Poland more
anti-socialist than the other Eastern European
states [15].

Having conceded all the foregoing factors one
should then note that the fundamental reason for
Poland's idiosyncratic postwar cyclical and crisis-
ridden history is the central fact that the Soviet
Stalinist system was never fully established, let
alone developed, in Poland. For a start the period
of full blooded Stalinism was relatively shortlived
from 1948 to 1954, while the terror was far less extensive, both within the PZPR and against society,
than in Hungary or Czechoslovakia [16]. Although
an orthodox form of Soviet Communist rule was instituted and the building of heavy industry through a
centralised command economy given priority, the death
of Stalin in 1953 prevented the Stalinist system from
developing ahead on its own steam. No 'show trials'
took place in Poland and the PZPR was not properly
cowed by the Stalinist hard-core. This had important repercussions later on the amount of factionalism,
corruption, lack of ideological commitment and general
indiscipline which developed within the party [17].
Very limited and half-hearted attempts were made to
collectivise agriculture, while the conflict with the
Church remained a largely political one in spite of
the imprisonment of Cardinal Wyszyński. The Soviet
Collective Leadership's 'New Course' was applied very
slightly in Poland at the PZPR Second Congress in

March 1954 and more firmly after the Third Plenum
in January 1955. What was crucial was that the
limitation of the police terror, the readjustment of
investment in favour of consumer goods and a lighter
rein on intellectuals in Poland did more than just
temporarily hold up the building of a totalitarian
state which was resumed very effectively by the native
leaderships in Czechoslovakia, Bulgaria and the GDR
after 1956. The Polish Stalinist juggernaut was
halted permanently just as it was tooling up. The
Polish political system and the industrial sector
maintained the neo-Stalinist forms assumed in the
late 1940s but Polish society and social groups, as
well as a wide variety of anti-Communist religious
and national values, were never brought fully under
Communist control, let alone eradicated.

The growth of intellectual criticism and of
social discontent, especially among the industrial
working class in 1955-1956, was matched by the reali-
sation by a section of the PZPR élite, after Bierut's
death at the CPSU Twentieth Congress, in Moscow in
March 1956, that the CP would have to become more
reform minded and more inclined towards compromises
with society if it were to ride out and then come to
terms with the massive anti-Stalinist movements in
Polish society in 1956. Only in this way would the
PZPR be able to come out of its bunker, to build
bridges to Polish society and to replace the repression of the Stalinist period with a legitimacy of its
own which would gain it some autonomy from Soviet
control. Their opponents, the Natolin faction of
younger, more Khrushchev inclined politicians and
the most unconditionally pro-Soviet Stalinists,seemed
to lose the argument irretrievably at the Eighth
Plenum in October 1956 [18]. However, the October
Compromise, which set up a modified form of Polish
Communism which lasted for almost a quarter of a century under Gomułka and Gierek, was based on ambiguous and most unstable political foundations. Communism survived in Poland and, subject to some important political window-dressing and trading readjust-
ments, remained a loyal Soviet satellite, albeit one
that was allowed much autonomy in its domestic affairs
by Moscow. The real cost was that the Polish Communists abandoned the attempt to collectivise agriculture and to subinfeudate the Roman Catholic Church.
Socialisation and secularisation were to be carried
on half-heartedly and by stealth. Only the orthodox definition of democratic centralism within the
PZPR and the self-interest of its élite, as well as
the priority given to heavy industry, remained as

21

guarantees that socialism would be built in Poland.

Gomułka rejected the 1956 type of proposals for
the democratisation of Polish political life.   He
only carried out a minor amount of administrative and
economic decentralisation, while reintegrating harder
line officials in his leadership team after 1959 to
the detriment of the more reform minded.   Much was
talked about but in practice little was done about
implementing reform ideas, especially in the economy
where the Economic Council, chaired by Oskar Lange,
produced hardly any effect at all [19].   Hence Gomułka
was responsible for instituting what was later to be
termed 'façade politics', orthodox at the centre and
in Leninist essentials but co-existing most uneasily
with a society where totally different values prevailed and where criticism and intellectual debate
was neither totally suppressed nor implemented to
any degree.

After 1956 various cycles of centralisation and
de-centralisation took place [20].   They were contained, however, within the framework of a hybrid
form of Communism which resulted from the unclear compromise between Gomułka, the PZPR, Polish society
and Soviet power in 1956.   For a quarter of a century Polish Communist leaders had to balance uneasily
between different social groups and between rival
political trends within the PZPR.   The party-society
relationship was characterised by long periods of
apparent PZPR control, when the bureaucratic politics
of the CPA dominated political life punctuated by confrontations, most of which were resolved on an ad hoc
basis but which occasionally developed a fierce inten-
sity and broke out into major political crises, in
1968, 1970 and 1976.   The Gomułka leadership quarrelled with the Church at different times, collided
with groups of intellectuals over various issues and
was finally overthrown by workers' discontent in the
Baltic sea coast towns.

This picture of a Communist Party in control of
the political system but not fully in control of
society is by no means atypical of the early life of
other Communist systems;   for example, the Soviet Union
itself during the New Economic Policy of the 1920s.
What is most unusual about the Polish case is the
longevity during which the PZPR has applied a self-
denying ordinance on the full exercise of its power.
This brings us to the central question of the character of the PZPR and its policies for bringing about
the socialisation of Poland.

Under Gomułka the PZPR became much more representative of Polish society.   It assimilated a wide

variety of patriotic and national traditions and
many of the secular social values.   The party abandoned the attempt to collectivise agriculture outright
and concentrated on encouraging co-operation and
better husbandry through Agricultural Circles.   The
Roman Catholic Church and the PZPR remained locked
in ideological conflict.   They both claimed to embody
the best political values and programme for Poland.
Their confrontations, although raising a lot of excitement, were, however, kept within carefully managed
bounds.   The PZPR preferred to avoid the costs and
dangers of outright conflict, while the Church under
Wyszyński was prepared to render unto Caesar what was
Caesar's in order not to endanger its temporal position.   The national mood in this respect did not
change until the election of Cardinal Karol Wojtyła
of Kraków as Pope John Paul II in 1978, his triumphant
return visit to Poland in 1979 and the Church's support of various groups of intellectual, worker and
student dissidents which developed and flourished
after 1976.   One should also not bagatellise the extent to which Polish cultural life after 1956 became
remarkably free, lively and creative.   It remained
so even in the neo-hardline periods such as the late
1960s and late 1970s.   The latter especially was a
period of partly suppressed energy and dynamism when
numerous 'safety valves', such as the screening of
controversial and biting films, notably those of
Andrzej Wajda and Krzystof Zanussi, were allowed.
Economically, culturally and in tourist travel and
family link terms, Poland became remarkably open to
the Western world and to non-Communist influences,
and above all comparisons.   The Poles fell into a
welter of unrealistic and dissatisfied comparisons
and this factor undoubtedly shortened the fuse which
led to the 1980 crisis in Poland.
        The essence of 1956 for the PZPR was that, while
the Stalinist and Reformist wings were rejected, more
moderate and tactically skilled personalities representing both these tendencies remained within the
system.   The reformism of the 'October' generation
lost ground steadily though, until it was finally
and completely purged in 1968.   The 'Little Stabilisation' of the early 1960s was then complicated by
the emergence of a new nationalist and hard line current.   This originally grew out of the efforts of
Gomułka's main lieutenants, Zenon Kliszko and Ryszard
Strzelecki, to lessen the strain in the PZPR's relations with society by widening the definition of what
was socially progressive in many walks of life, including the interpretation of Poland's history.   A

faction called the Partisans, because of their Second
World War Resistance backgrounds, then gradually
coalesced around the strong personality of Mieczysław
Moczar, the Minister of the Interior from 1964 to
1968. This group had its strongest influence in
the police, a section of the Army and ZBoWiD, the war
veterans' organisation whose influence increased
dramatically in the mid 1960s. But the Partisans'
very mixed and ambiguous ideas, like those of the pre-
war National Democratic ideologue, Roman Dmowski,
also appealed very strongly to a younger, very ambitious and hard-nosed realpolitik minded section of the
intelligentsia and professional classes. The Partisans originally aimed to move Gomułka in their direction, rather than to capture him completely, but
the course of events after the Arab-Israeli War of
1967 allowed them to come within an ace of supplant-
ing him in March 1968.

Gomułka's leadership in the mid 1960s, quite
apart from his own authoritarian predilections and
national-Communist deviations, was therefore distrac-
ted by such pressures on to what at the worst of the
Spring 1968 hysteria appeared to be a chauvinist platform of national unity. Unlike Kadar's policies in
Hungary during the 1960s, the PZPR leadership was
insufficiently concerned with socio-economic reforms
and the improvement of living standards, particularly
as Gomułka himself, scarred by his 1956-1959 struggle
against revisionism as he saw it, was unwilling to
uncork that particular genie again. The economic
reforms of 1964-1965 and 1969-1970 were therefore
very limited and sectional ones and hardly pushed
through with much determination. Gomułka remained
extremely cautious and orthodox in setting economic
priorities. During the 1960s he promoted the further development of heavy industry at the expense of
living standards and consumption, especially housing.
He refused to consider such 'luxuries' as a motor
car industry. His irritability, small minded non-
intellectual horizons, provincialism and autocratic
methods of running the PZPR were much criticised and
derided on his fall. The outcome of Gierek's very
different optimistic and adventurous course now allows us to view him in a new light. The reassess-
ment in Poland of his career started even before
Gierek's downfall [21]. When Gomułka died in
September 1982, at the age of 77, the military régime
hailed him as the most outstanding political figure
of postwar Poland [22].

Gomułka's political blindness, economic incompetence and personal inclinations allowed the

Partisans to stoke up national chauvinist hysteria
as a way of defeating the pressures for reform in
1967-1968. They used Stalinist techniques of scape-
goating, purge and provocation in order to prevent
anything like a 'Prague Spring' from developing in
Poland [23]. Their activities culminated in the
suppression of students and intellectuals in March
1968 and in the exodus of about 12,000 Jews [24].
Their purge of the party subdued the politically reformist currents within the PZPR, while simultaneously
removing the older 1956 generation of both reformists
and neo-Stalinist, pro-Soviet dogmatists [25]. The
repression of a new generation of student protest,
symbolised by Adam Michnik, was to light a long fuse
which did not, however, set the Polish powder keg
alight until 1980. If the Partisans' eventual aim
were a strong hand Communism of the Romanian type,
presumably led by Moczar, they were undercut by the
Soviet invasion of Czechoslovakia. Brezhnev endorsed Gomułka at the PZPR Fifth Congress in November
1968 and he survived until the workers' revolt of
December 1970.
    However, Gomułka's consensus was shattered. He
was forced to co-opt representatives of a younger
political generation. Edward Gierek, the unofficial
'crown prince' since the Fourth Congress in 1964,
was the obvious successor when the PZPR centrol
aktyw and the Soviet leadership, faced by Gomułka's
political bankruptcy and his attempt to suppress the
Baltic sea coast riots by force in mid-December 1970,
decided that they had no stomach for another Kronstadt.
Gierek, who then appeared a much more economically
competent and politically balanced and responsible
nationalist figure, was called in to defuse the social
crisis of December 1970 to February 1971, and to
pacify the discontented groups in Polish society.
The significance of the 1967-1968 events was, however,
that the fanning of nationalist hysteria and the neo-
Stalinist persecution of students, Jews, intellectuals,
reformists and alleged revisionists enabled the Communist leadership to brush SCIE demands for decentralisation and democratisation under the carpet. At
the same time the rejuvenation of the Communist élite
with a group of intelligent, but realpolitik inclined,
strong hand, nationalist minded, technocrats ensured
that some of Poland's key economic and social problems would remain neglected, while those that were
dealt with would be given very centralist solutions.

The Gierek Question; was the 1980 crisis the fault
of individuals, of the régime, of the system or of
society?
The analysis of the causes of the 1980 crisis
was one of the main questions dominating Polish politics after the Gdańsk Agreement. The course of the
debate will be covered in the chapters which follow.
Here,because of limitations of space, one can only
look in outline at some of the basic aspects of
Gierek's decade of rule and their consequences.
Firstly, was the crisis due largely to a whole
host of specific mistakes committed by Gierek and his
advisers during the 1970s which led to an obvious
economic collapse in Summer 1980? An associated
question concerned the economic situation in Summer
1980. Was the problem really as grave and unmanageable as was claimed after Gierek's fall? Could it
have been ridden out by some, admittedly exceptional,
but yet traditional form of austerity and belt-tightening if society had not rebelled? If the latter
were the case a further debate arose during 1981.
What was the balance of responsibility between Gierek's
mismanagement as against the worsening of the economic
situation as a result of the political confrontations,
strikes and other forms of economic dislocation in
the period between August 1980 and December 1981?
In the months which followed Gierek's fall, however, the political conservatives were entirely on
the defensive. The debate was dominated between
those who thought that the previous régime was responsible as against those who ascribed blame to the
whole post-1956 system. The former castigated
Gierek's alleged authoritarian style of political
leadership, the deformations which this caused at
every level of the political and economic systems and
the gap which it created between state and society as
a result. They also denounced the corruption, as
well as the incompetence, of the Communist élite as
in the other type of explanations, which ascribed all
these epiphenomena to fundamental systemic causes.
The third range of criticisms and explanations
can be divided into three categories. Firstly, there
was the argument of Polish nationalists, conservatives
and emigrés, of various hues, that the crisis demonstrated the bankruptcy of Communism per se. Secondly,
there was the diametrically opposed argument of orthodox Soviet inclined Marxist-Leninists that the crisis
was caused by the bourgeois-liberal deviations and
opportunist concessions to the class enemy which
dominated the Polish system after 1956. Thirdly,
there was a complex mixture of different arguments

put forward by reformers, both within the PZPR and
Solidarity, which concern us most in this study.
The detail will be covered later but criticism was
directed at the over-centralised command economy
favouring the development of heavy industry, a manipulatory style of leadership dominated democratic
centralism which stifled intra-party democracy within
the PZPR and the resultant subservience of all the
other apparats, of institutions such as the Sejm and
of the press and subsidiary political parties and
the like.   The Communist reformers, therefore, argued
that the political structure of Communist rule had
been left behind by socio-economic progress and was
no longer adequate to the requirements of a developed
socialist society.
     The above considerations raise the question of
the basic characteristics of the 1956-1980 form of
Communist system in Poland.   On the one hand it was
arguably the most progressive and decent of all Communist systems, not excluding Yugoslavia, which used
the least amount of political terror and which allowed
the greatest degree of freedom and pluralism to its
citizens.   Alternatively, one would have to point
to the stresses and strains which made it so crisis-
prone and which in 1980 culminated in a massive
general crisis of the system.   The 1956-1980 system
was admittedly neither fish nor fowl in comparative
Communist terms, although one can draw parallels with
the Soviet NEP period and some aspects of Bukharin's
political programme and approach in the 1920s.   Was
it therefore doomed because of its political liberalism, as a halfway house, which could neither suppress nor satisfy a vibrant Polish society?

Gierek's Successes in the early 1970s
     One should start, in examining Gierek's respon-
sibility for the 1980 crisis, with the reasons for
the failure of his brand of Communist reformism which
was promised at the PZPR's Sixth Congress in December
1971.   Gierek's failure to emulate Kadar's consis-
tent drive for reform in Hungary after 1961 explains,
at least, some of Polish society's bitterness and
unwillingness to accept anything less than institutional, signed, sealed and delivered guarantees in
1980.
     Gierek was brought to power because of Gomułka's
failure to repress workers' protests in the Baltic
sea coast towns [26].   Official sources admitted
that 45 people had been killed, 1,165 injured and
about 3,000 arrested but the death toll was almost
certainly higher.   Gierek then had to face two months

of industrial unrest culminating in a bitter textile
strike in Łódź which forced him to rescind Gomułka's
price increases and to freeze prices of basic foodstuffs. Much of Gierek's initial popularity was
based on the direct man-to-man approach which he
adopted in early 1971 in facing the Gdańsk and
Szczecin shipyard workers. Equally significantly
circumstances forced him beyond a condemnation of
Gomułka's specific mistakes into a critique of the
autocratic and undemocratic nature of his rule.
Gierek's speech, to the very important Eighth Plenum
on 6-7 February 1971, was an analysis and critique of
all the problems which were to plague his own decade
of power and which were to be levelled against him
in an even sharper form after his downfall [27].
The crisis had developed over many years because
Gomułka's 'faulty style and incorrect method of
leadership' and neglect of social priorities such as
housing and increased real wages had weakened the
bond between the PZPR and the working class. The
need now was for a Five Year, perhaps Ten Year, programme of socio-economic development designed to
raise living standards. Gierek accepted the need
for 'essential guarantees' for greater social consultation and the democratisation of political life but
his promises could mean much or little depending upon
how they were implemented.
     Given the ignominious circumstances of Gierek's
fall it is worth remembering that Polish society
greeted Gierek's early policy of 'Ożywienie' (live-
liness) with considerable enthusiasm and optimism.
This allowed Gierek, who was a skilled political
operator, to dispose of his main political rivals
and to win over the remainder, to set up a fairly
loyal and united party-state leadership with Premier
Piotr Jaroszewicz and to screen and purge the PZPR
membership, all within 18 months of taking office.
By the PZPR Sixth Congress in December 1971 Gierek
had ridden out the social storm and was ready to present a more rounded off and largely economic programme. The 1971-1975 FYP guidelines, to replace
Gomułka's scrapped draft, were ambitious but only in
comparison with the performance of the 1960s. Targets such as projected rises of 18% in real incomes,
of 33% in consumption, of 39% in GNP, of 50% in
industrial and 21% in agricultural production were
realistic and justified [28]. The economy was,
however, imbalanced and the economic boom of 1971-
1974 built on insecure foundations as these targets
were then revised upwards.
     Poland in the early 1970s had one of the highest

rates of economic growth in the world and the country
undoubtedly experienced a short-lived, although intense, consumer revolution.   Gierek reported at the
Seventh Congress in December 1975 that the 'party's
socio-economic policy in the 1971-1975 period was
the systematic improvement of the economic, social
and cultural conditions of life in society'.   Over
a million dwellings had been built, vast improvements had occurred in social, health, educational and
local services while real earnings had increased by
40%, GNP by 62% (10% p.a.), industrial production by
73% and agricultural production by 22% [29].   These
achievements were much higher than the original 1971
targets but were bought at a heavy price.   The
dynamism of the period and the Gierek élite's unwise
sloganeering about becoming the Japan of Eastern
Europe in growth terms produced an explosion of
rising expectations which aggravated the problems of
the post-1975 downturn and presented the leadership
with an almost insuperable psychological-political
problem.   Gierek therefore achieved an important
short-term breakthrough in increasing economic production, consumption and living standards.   The
question was how long could such a high growth rate,
based on foreign borrowing, be maintained and what
would be the political consequences of the downturn.
     Gierek's dash for economic growth was designed
to underwrite his vision of a rich and prosperous,
consumer orientated and economically efficient 'Second
Poland'.   Society was to be run by a rationally
minded and technologically competent Communist élite
open to the best educated and most intelligent individuals.   Class differences would be smoothed by
easy educational and social mobility and by an increasingly modern, urban, secular and non-ideological
life style.   Membership of the PZPR would remain
essential for all actual and aspirant office holders
but it would become the Communist equivalent of the
Church of England.   Decision-making would be heavily
centralised in the CPA but would be made on the basis
of wide consultation of all interested groups, specialists and the best available information.   The
débacle of such hopes should not lead one to underestimate the qualitative changes which Poland under-
went in the early 1970s [30].
     Gierek benefited from the East-West détente to
raise Poland's standing in the world and to increase
her political, economic, cultural and tourist links
with both the West and the Third World [31].   The
Poles found a new national pride and self-confidence
which cured them of many of their previous complexes;

29

this mood was strengthened by such massive national
psychological boosts as their football team's third
place in the 1974 World Cup and the rebuilding of
the Royal Castle in Warsaw.   If anything the pendulum
swung too far with the slogan 'Polak potrafi - a Pole
can do it' taking on an increasingly megalomaniac
tone.

The Roots of Failure

The balance sheet of structural reforms instituted by Gierek was a strikingly short one.   No
basic changes were brought about in the institutions
of Polish political life, either in the PZPR or in
the system of political rule, but changes in Polish
public opinion were catered for in livelier and better
informed news media than in Gomułka's time.   A
plethora of small scale technical improvements was
also introduced in such areas as the functioning of
the Sejm, while institutions were reorganised and sections hived off and amalgamated and new bodies created with bewildering frequency.   Only two major reforms stand out in contrast to the many damp squibs,
such as the educational reform which never materia-
lised after the publication of the much acclaimed
Szczepański Commission's Report Concerning the State
of Education in the Polish People's Republic in 1973
[32].   The reform of the People's Councils in 1972-
1974 was a major administrative change, but any decentralising intention was largely sabotaged by conservative middle and lower level functionaries [33].
The 1973 reform of economic management setting up
WOGs, Large Economic Organisations (Wielkie Organizacje
Gospodarcze) was at best a policy of 'cautious in-
crementalism' [34].   Typically, the WOGs stoked up
wage inflation and expanded their sectoral empires as
weaker party control was replaced neither by rational
market mechanisms nor genuine social control but by
the greater influence of the state administration [35].

Gierek's main strategic political mistake now
seems obvious but it was hardly a surprising one in
the context of the aura of his near infallibility in
the early 1970s.   He failed to initiate the extensive political and economic reforms which were required by the more open and dynamic society which he
envisaged and to emulate Kadar's pattern of reforms.
On the contrary, his largely technocratic approach
was posited on the premise of tight central control
over essentials.   In 1980 it was claimed that such
methods caused less social involvement, increasing
social apathy, the narrowing of control and discussion and an unhealthy emphasis on personal enrichment

at every level, including the top party échelons.
Gierek's problem was how to run a sophisticated, in-
dustrially developed and pluralist society within
the confines of the one-party straitjacket. Economic prosperity allowed him to balance between differing social groups in an atmosphere of moderate
Polish nationalism for a while; but the absence of
structural reforms meant that there were 'no institutional guarantees to prevent the cyclical pattern
of degeneration setting in again' [36].

The second of Gierek's main problems was that he
was unlucky in that his economic boom had barely
started before the 1973 world oil crisis adversely
affected the cost of Polish imports of raw materials
and fodder for the agricultural sector. The latter
made it difficult to maintain the increased rate of
pork production, which because of Polish preferences
constituted 70% of domestic meat production. But
prosperity had come too late to Poland in too much
of a sudden rush and a far wider range of expectations was generated than could be satisfied. Here
I part company with the popular Western view which
concentrates on the pluralist and democratic aspects
of the refusal of Polish society to accept economic
rationality and balance from 1976 onwards. The
economic problem in the 1970s was not merely a technical question of good or bad management; it was
also a political and national-psychological one.
Beneficiaries grudgingly accepted benefits in the
spirit of too little too late. Those who were left
out, and they were a substantial third, at least, of
the population,naturally became even more discon-
ted with their lot. Even more importantly, those
whose lot improved but who fell behind in relative
terms became envious and resentful of the more successful. So the problem was both an economic and
psychological one, as noted by Frances Cairncross:
'The Poles came to enjoy a completely unsustainable
rise in real incomes. It is not surprising that
the Government had found it difficult to break the
habit' [37]. The latter aspect of human behaviour
was noted long ago by Aristotle [38]. He developed
one of the earliest forms of the theory of relative
deprivation, the idea later developed by de Tocqueville,
that revolutions never take place in times of grind-
ing, hopeless poverty but rather in periods of improvement.

The one point about which there is complete
unanimity concerns Gierek's string of economic and
financial mistakes. These have been ably catalogued
by the noted economist, Mieczysław Mieszczankowski [39].

He considers that Gierek took the Polish economy
on to 'the wrong tracks' as early as 1972. The decision to accelerate economic growth was 'a voluntarist violation' of the Sixth Congress resolution
and resulted in a dramatic increase in the accumu-
lation rate from 28% in 1970 to 38% in the mid 1970s.
It was one of the highest rates anywhere in the world
except Japan, an example which enthralled Gierek's
entourage [40]. It fed their hopes that Polish GNP
could grow at 10% over the whole decade, thus resolving their political problems with Polish society.
They refused to heed warnings that this would imba-
lance the economy, make Poland dangerously dependent
upon external borrowing and lengthen the completion
cycle of industrial projects; by 1976, 85% of all
that year's investment was uncompleted. Above all,
the increase in nominal wages, unmatched by improved
labour productivity, fuelled inflation and the consumer psychosis. The spiral of rising prices, originally camouflaged and then open, caused by too
much paper money in circulation chasing too few goods,
was eventually to bring Gierek down and to contri-
bute to the greatest collapse of any postwar European
economy in 1980-1981. Eventually it was only halted,
and even then not fully, by the draconian 3 to 500%
price rises implemented by Jaruzelski's military
junta in February 1982.
     The main source of investment was Western cre-
dit. The foreign debt increased from almost nothing
in 1970 to $2.5 milliard in 1973, $11 milliard in
1976 and, in spite of some post-1976 cut-backs, stood
at about $20 milliard in 1979. Between a third and
a half of Western credits went on buying machines
and technology. The real Polish failure, though,
was to utilise such credits effectively and to produce mechanisms to prevent duplication and to monitor the level of debt so as to keep it within manage-
able limits. The IMF criterion that debt service
should not exceed 25% of the amount borrowed was surpassed by the mid 1970s. It then moved rapidly upwards because of rising world interest rates towards
its uncontrollable take-off in 1980. However, Gierek
continued to favour such large prestige projects as
Huta Katowice and his old political fief of Silesia.
On the other hand, liberal Communists could still
argue convincingly, as late as early 1980, that the
crash investment programme was justified by the
massive social and demographic pressures for improved housing and living standards after 1970 [41].
     These dangerous tendencies in credit and invest-
ment policy were aggravated by a lax financial and

wages and prices policy which doubled inflation over
the decade. The freeze on some food prices after
1971 and the large wage increases required to calm
the situation after December 1970 were partly matched
by increased food and industrial production at first.
Inter alia meat consumption increased by 32% during
1971-1975 but as nominal wages rose by 86% the result
was lengthening queues and shortages which motivated
the attempt to raise meat prices in June 1976. As
the nation refused to accept either increased prices
or cuts in nominal wages and as agricultural and
meat production stagnated after 1975 the inevitable
result was chaos on the meat market.

Gierek's political dilemma came to a head in
1976. The Polish economy working flat out was unable to satisfy the demands upon it and food shortages were aggravated by the bad harvests of 1974
and 1975. The 1971 freeze on food prices, although
circumvented by the surreptitious relabelling of
goods at new prices and price increases on non-essen-
tials, was nevertheless responsible for an absurd
price structure and for an unacceptably heavy subsidy
burden on the general exchequer. What is significant, though, is that the whole Polish nation refused to accept the food price increases of 20 June
1976. I personally doubt whether any consultative
process, however genuine, could have produced a substantially different result and convinced the Poles
that once again the time had come for sacrifices and
belt-tightening. Consultation would inevitably have
meant no price increases. My interpretation helps
to explain why Gierek made no attempt to carry out a
real 'social dialogue' on the food price increases.
The riot at Radom, the factory occupations of the
Płock petrochemical works and the Ursus tractor plant
and the spontaneous nationwide refusal to go to work
was a clear warning and a premonition of the 1980
outbreak [42]. Gierek was realistic enough to give
way immediately in 1976, although most commentators
rarely do justice to his real political dilemma.
On the other hand, there was no excuse for his subsequent do-nothing policy and his failure to impose
economic rationality on the Polish nation through
implementing a Hungarian type of price and market
mechanism.

The workers drew mixed conclusions from these
events. On the one hand the Radom, Płock and Ursus
workers had shown their industrial muscle and had
forced the authorities to surrender even more igno-
miniously than in 1970. On the other hand, their
efficient repression, as in 1971-1972, also

demonstrated that the leadership could still use a
battery of methods,ranging from police and judicial
repression to dismissals from work, transfer of workers' leaders elsewhere and the manipulation of the
mass media (to emphasise the looting rather than the
workers' protest aspect of Radom) in order to break
the organised back of the workers' opposition.

The rapid emergence of KOR after Radom and a
little later of a whole plethora of other dissident
groups showed that a section of the intellectual and
professional classes was trying to rebuild the national alliance with the working class which had defeated the Polish Stalinists in 1956 but which had
been so obviously missing in 1968 and 1970.   The
educated middle classes were highly conditional in
their support of Communist officialdom as they wanted
more consultation, if not participation, in decision-
making, even though some sections had privileged
economic conditions which might be threatened by
workers' demands.   The peasants distrusted Gierek's
policy of 'creeping socialisation' and, although
pleased by the ending of compulsory deliveries, responded to the régime's failure after 1974 to give them
sufficient inducements and safeguards by cutting back
production, especially of pork [43].

Bromke was therefore correct in pointing to the
extremely combustible nature of the ferment in Polish
society from the mid 1970s onwards.   The unreformed
system of political and economic decision-making
was unable to cope.   The absence of either Stalinist
or socialist market disciplines meant that more problems were created than were solved.   Gierek's system
was neither strong enough to impose its will in
many areas (for example, to keep a tight enough control on the Agencies clamouring for foreign credits
and licences) nor decentralised enough to allow enterprises and WOGs to take their own local decisions.
The burying of a real reform programme by 1973 was
therefore paralleled by Gierek's efforts to strengthen the administrative and economic machines to
enable them to face up to the coming social storms.

After 1976 some economic retrenchment was attempted through an 'Economic Manoeuvre' but it was
not pushed very hard.   The really crucial conundrum,
though, is why did Gierek not learn from Radom and
its transparently clear warning?   At the very least
one would have expected some political measures
such as the sacking of the unpopular Premier Jaroszewicz
and that Gierek would widen his political base in
order to spread the risk.   In practice, apart from
appointing Olszowski as CC Secretary in charge of the

economy, Gierek merely resorted to furtively introduced individual price increases and half-hearted
economic retrenchment measures without any genuine
reform or social consultation.   Significantly there
was already one language for the masses and another
for the élite.   So Gierek took refuge in a negative
safety-first stance after 1976 hoping that he could
ride out the social storm.   He attempted to keep up
appearances by presenting an unreal rosy picture of
the economic situation, based on increasingly slanted,
and occasionally suppressed, economic statistics, and
buttressed by what was termed the 'propaganda of
success' [44].
     The period 1976-1980 was characterised by the
unparalleled growth of a plethora of dissident groups
in Poland [45].   Their real aims and significance
and their degree of popular support are difficult to
assess but they can, in retrospect, be seen as having
incubated a wide variety of the forces of contestation which emerged in Summer 1980 [46].   The authorities played a cat and mouse game in harassing the
dissident leaders but no real measures were then taken
to suppress them as Gierek wanted to show his liberalism to his Western creditors [47].   He also regarded this dissident activity, much of which had been
infiltrated by the authorities, and some of which had
been manufactured by the police agencies, as safety
valves for political and social tension.   But there
is no doubt that he underestimated, very badly, their
capacity for encouraging and aggregating latent opposition.   Their potential as battle-hardened information and leadership-core networks during the
crisis which overwhelmed Gierek in Summer 1980,as
well as the support which they received from Polish
emigré organisations, which also became a significant force in the 1970s for the first time because
of their rejuvenation with the 1968 generation, are
factors which only became clearer after the event.
Gierek's tolerant and easy-going treatment of dissident groups was one of the main secret reproaches and
charges later laid against him by the PZPR, Soviet
and socialist bloc hardliners.

Why PZPR Rule had more Weaknesses than Strengths
     The PZPR faced a wide range of problems in exer-
cising its leading role in what after 1956 became an
extremely young demographically, as well as socially
and national vigorous society but two key ones stand
out.   Firstly, while it could pretend to monopolise
power and to control the political arena, its authority was always more open to contestation than in

almost any other long established Communist system.
Peasants, intellectuals, students and workers challenged its rule at various times.   The party had to
walk a difficult tightrope to pacify such groups and
to keep them divided.   The Roman Catholic Church,
with its 6,800 independent pulpits in parishes all
over Poland, an eccelesiastical staff of 20,000
priests and monks in 1977, as well as a legal foot-
hold within the political system with its licensed
press and 5 Znak Sejm deputies, was a formidable
force.
     The second main Communist dilemma was the more
surprising one that, in spite of over 3 decades of
power, the Communist leadership was never able to
turn the PZPR into a wholly reliable instrument for
Communist rule in Poland.   There is reliable evidence regarding the split and faction ridden character of the PZPR leadership, especially in times of
crisis.   From its inception in 1948, through the
fusion of the PPR (1942-1948) with the PPS, the PZPR
also faced great difficulties in recruiting and maintaining a large, stable, ideologically reliable and
socially sound membership.   At its unification the
PZPR had 1.5 million members but this fell to 1.15
million in 1952 as a result of the Stalinist screen-
ings, while the 1.34 million members of 1955 had
dwindled to just over a million in 1958 because of
the defections and expulsions of the 1955-1957 crisis.
The PZPR only resolved its numerical weakness after
that increasing from 1.15 million (3.9% of the population) in 1960 to 2.32 million (7.13%) in 1970 to
2.36 million (6.94%) in 1975 and numbered 3.08 million (7.7%) in January 1980.   Party membership was
scrutinised and purged with different levels of
severity at various times (1949-1952, 1967-1968,
1971-1972 and 1981-1982).   There have also been
periods of dramatic voluntary withdrawal from the
party (1955-1956 and 1980-1982) [48].
     Communist leaders as well as facing problems
with the size and stability of PZPR membership have
also found it difficult to maintain an adequate working class element.   This diminished from a high
point of 60% of the PZPR membership in 1952 to just
over 40% in 1960.   It then fluctuated at around that
level, being 40.8% in 1975.   The peasant percentage
fell from 17% in 1952 to a mere 9.6% in 1975.   In
practice the non-manual section of the PZPR, which
increased from 20% in 1952 to 42% in 1958 and 1970,
reaching 44.5% in 1975, became the crucial element.
At the PZPR Eighth Congress in February 1980, just
before the crisis broke out, the PZPR was composed of

The Gierek question

1.42 million workers, 290,000 peasants and what,
one presumes, were 1.37 million non-manual professionals, retired people, apparatchiks, Army members
and the like [49].   The formal statistics, however
doctored, could barely camouflage the fact that, in
many respects, the PZPR under Gierek unashamedly
became the party of the Polish élite and white collar
class.   In the settled post-1971 period the co-option
of the brightest and the best as well as the most
ambitious and the most servile proceeded apace.
Gierek's membership purge of 1971-1972 largely replaced the workers brought in by Gomułka with his
younger generation of workers.   Special efforts were
made to produce a strong PZPR implantation in the 200
odd largest enterprises which were kept in direct
contact with the CC.   The attempt to tie this
clientèle group in the larger workplaces in support
of the regime backfired in the late 1970s.   The overall level of working class membership, though, remained at around 40% for the whole decade.   The PZPR
was not untypical in this respect and the Kremlin
expressed no concern on this score until Gierek's
failure to maintain political stability became apparent.   More importantly, then, one should in a moment
examine the thesis that Gierek rather became the
prisoner, or at least the spokesman, according to
taste, of a new type of politico-bureaucratic élite
and its subsidiary beneficiaries.
      The shelving of serious reform proposals, cer-
tainly by the time of the First PZPR National Conference in October 1973, was accompanied by Gierek's
increasing reliance on his 'inner circle' of Politburo and Secretariat cronies.   These included the
new faces who had emerged into prominance at the
Seventh PZPR Congress - notably Jerzy Łukasiewicz,
Alojzy Karkoszka, Tadeusz Wrzaszczyk, Zdzisław
Żandarowski, Józef Pińkowski and Tadeusz Pyka.
After Gierek's fall there was much talk of his
'Silesian Mafia' but this was a permanent feature of
the whole decade.   Edward Babiuch was always Gierek's
right hand man and unofficially Second Secretary.
Even those who fell into temporary disfavour, or were
told to take temporary back seats in order to allay
criticism (like Kazimierz Barcikowski and Jan Szydlak)
did not fall very far and bounced back in February
1980.   Others, like Zdzisław Grudzień, minded Gierek's
political base in Katowice, a stronghold to which he
bolted back after his fiasco over the food price
increases in 1976.
      My own hunch is that Gierek retreated into his
political bunker after 1976 as he was too shrewd and

well informed not to be aware of the growing signs
of crisis all around him.   The bon mot by the writer
Jerzy Putrament in 1981 that Bierut was an average,
although decent enough, individual with excellent
advisers, that Gomułka was an outstanding personality with poor advisers, while Gierek combined
Bierut's intellect with Gomułka's advisers, was witty
but inaccurate and politically tendentious as far as
it concerned Gierek.   After Gierek's fall everyone
claimed to have foreseen the inevitability of the
1980 crisis.   The testimony of the Committee of
Experts (which included Paweł Bożyk, Włodzimierz
Wesołowski, Alojzy Melich and Sylwester Zawadzki)
called to report on the economy in 1977 makes it
clear that Gierek was warned in remarkably prescient
terms of the dangers of attempting to cure the economic situation by cutting living standards and of
dealing with social tensions by administrative means
[50].
     Gierek claimed at the Eighth Congress that the
PZPR's social and economic successes during the 1970s
had 'strengthened social acceptance of the ideals of
socialism and the uniting of the nation with the
party' [51].   Six months later Poland was in the
grip of a revolutionary upheaval and Gierek was dismissed in disgrace.   Some might consider this sufficient condemnation of Gierek's mistakes and of the
quality of his political leadership.   On the other
hand, the argument may also be presented that Poland,
because of her peculiar political culture and social
autonomy, cannot be governed successfully by normal
neo-Soviet methods as in Bulgaria or the GDR.   Why,
then, have periods of reform Communist rule been so
relatively short - 1956-1958 and 1971-1973 or so?
The answer does not, I think, lie in the old chestnut
of Soviet pressure inducing a return to hardline
policies, as has been most convincingly demonstrated
by Jedlicki in the case of Gomułka after 1956 [52].
Certainly the threat of Soviet military intervention
does not seem to have braked either the reform of the
nationalist factions within the PZPR or the activities of social groups outside the party either before
the 1980-1981 crisis or even less during its course.
     My argument is that an important range of expla-
nations should be sought in the dynamics of domestic
Communist political processes.   Prima facie, post
1955 developments suggest that new leaderships bring
in new men at various levels of the party, state and
other apparatuses.   The new leaders gradually succumb to bureaucratic and formal methods of internal
party democracy and in the running of their respective

bailiwicks. After a while they start really believing their own slogans. At that point they are
really only talking to themselves as nobody without
a vested interest pays any attention to their official propaganda. Such Communist élites develop
their own interests, political and material. Whatever the subjective intentions of the leader they
restructure and guide his policies in their preferred directions; it takes an extraordinary amount
of political vision and courage by the leader to see
beyond the cocoon surrounding him of a few hundred
key political notables, officials and advisers.
Naturally the political élite after the initial
leadership changes desire as little personnel turnover as possible and feel themselves threatened by
major reforms or policy changes. In H.G. Skilling's
terms pluralist and neo-democratic Communism in
Poland always faced overwhelmingly strong internal
PZPR pressures for a return to consultative authori-
tarianism [53]. According to such a hypothesis
the functionaries became a formidable pressure group
in favour of unadventurous conservative administration after 1975. The lonely, apparently all-power-
ful eminence of the leader (Gomułka, 1964-1970;
Gierek, 1974-1980) seen in this light increasingly
looks like an optical illusion if one regards it in
terms of his capacity to get things done. The
cyclical pattern of post-1955 Polish politics is one
of Ascherson's key themes, and rightly so. The concept has been well known since Władysław Bieńkowski
dissected the reasons for the simultaneous expansion
of the formal power and actual ossification of the
CPA in the 1960s [54].

The institutional methods of Gierek's rule and
the detailed political history of his time have been
examined elsewhere [55]. An analysis of the top
PZPR personnel in the Politburo and Secretariat de-
monstrates the steady ascent, during the whole of
the 1970s, of a wave of individuals who had achieved
positions in the CC Departments and Commissions in
the late 1960s. Babiuch (Head of the crucial CC
Organisation Department, 1965-1970), Kania (Head of
the Administration Department, 1968-1971), Olszowski
(Head of CC Press Department, 1963-1968), Żandarowski
(Head, Organisation Department, 1970-1977) and
Żabiński (deputy Head, Organisation Department, 1971-
1973) were only the most prominent exemplars of a
new wage of what appeared to be well educated, post
revolutionary, second generation officials [56].
Success within the CPA not only led to the Politburo
and Secretariat for some but also opened up the way

to promotion to key positions in the KW organisations
as well as in most of the other apparats, excluding
the military, police and planning ones.   If Gierek
became a prisoner of this self-recruiting and self-
promoting apparatus he was not an unwilling one.
There is no doubt that he tired after his early years
of vigorous and dynamic rule.   What was worse was
that his diminishing political impetus could hardly
be corrected by the now elegantly dressed but politically grey apparatchiks who surrounded him.   They
listened with awe to their Great Leader but could not
help him either to formulate or to implement a decisive and relevant party programme after 1974.

Judgement on Gierek

One may conclude with the following judgement on
Gierek.   He offered the Poles, but did not implement,
a reform programme which crystallised at the Sixth
Congress, and which resurfaced again unavailingly
at the death of his régime.   He promised prosperity
based on the modernisation of the economy, more pragmatic and efficient political and economic management and a more flexible response to social needs,
especially housing and education.   Much of this he
delivered in the first half of the 1970s; but he
could not continue the expansion into the late 1970s
for the reasons outlined in this chapter, and so came
into conflict with the growing demands of a politically untamed Polish society.   At the time no one
dissented from the necessity for the strategy of massive economic growth based on imported Western technology and credit.   Everyone felt that this was
dictated by Poland's growing demographic demands and
urbanisation and by the housing, employment and
social needs which accompanied them.   Franciszek
Szlachcic, a Politburo member from 1971 to 1974, confirmed that 'the objective source of many tensions in
our postwar history, and in particular the crisis,
is the rapid increase in population' [57].   Szlachcic
was also correct in diagnosing the neglect and mismanagement of agriculture, the unchecked and unco-
ordinated growth of industrial investment and of the
balance of payments deficit as Gierek's main mistakes.
It was also true that Gierek and his supporters were
carried away by the economic boom of 1971-1974.
They underestimated the effect of the 1973 world oil
crisis on their import prices, trading prospects and
interest rates.   As Szlachcic said: 'Euphoria,
gigantomania and façade politics took control over
common sense'.   The judgement on Gierek is therefore unquestionable.   However understandable his

motives, he was guilty of a whole host of economic
mistakes.

In Communist terms Gierek was a decent, moderately intelligent and realistic liberal-conserva-
tive; a Louis-Philippe figure, whose compromises
satisfied neither the ultras nor the reformers in
the PZPR, he knew the limits to reform set by the
PZPR apparat and Soviet power. He was also painfully aware of the combustible nature of Polish
society and of the great constraints circumscribing
the PZPR's leading role in Poland. The stand-off
between the PZPR and society from the mid 1950s onwards had produced the following consequences: a
politically schizophrenic party composed of individuals who were opportunistic enough to know where
advancement lay but not dedicated enough to struggle
for the Communist cause; a nation with a largely
instrumental and extractive view of the state's functions, whose moral guide was the Roman Catholic
Church not the PZPR, who looked West not East and
whose national cohesion was more likely to express
itself against rather than in support of the state.
Does all this justify Gierek's mistrust of the spontaneity of the Polish people and his relative passivity in the late 1970s? My answer explains why
Gierek was not as bad as he was painted after August
1980, but the wide range of specific political and
economic mistakes made by Gierek and his team more
than justified their belated removal in 1980.

The Poles had shown in 1970 and 1976 that they
would not tolerate any open economic cut-back without
wage compensation. But exogeneous factors and economic rationality demanded such steps. Would such
measures have been accepted, as was claimed in 1980-
1981, if the Poles had been told the real economic
facts and if a democratic process of consultation
had replaced the normal round of apparat manipulated
meetings and press coverage? Gierek clearly, for
good or ill, did not believe this. He would have
lost his political support and personal prestige and
laid himself open to the attacks of his enemies within
the party. But Gierek overestimated the time which
remained to him. On the other hand, the sheer scale
of the crisis which overthrew him and his associates
now suggests that the implementation of the PZPR
Sixth Congress programme supported by some additional
Hungarian type reforms would have been a far smaller
risk, in the long run, than his early 1970s dash
for economic growth and his late 1970s political
Canutism. The demands and pressures which overloaded, but which did not quite short circuit, the

Polish political system in 1980-1981, however, also
suggests that only an extraordinarily long and con-
sistent run of brave, intelligent and even lucky
policies could have contained the pot-pourri of
national, social, worker-protest, religious, demographic, consumerist, societal and reform socialist
pressures which exploded in mid 1980.

Notes

1. J.T. Gross, 'Thirty years of crisis-management in
    Poland' in T. Rakowska-Harmstone (ed.), Perspectives
    for Change in Communist Societies (Boulder, Colorado,
    Westview Press, 1979), pp. 148-150. Cf. D.C. Pirages,
    Modernisation and Political Tension-Management; A
    Socialist Society in Perspective; Case-study of Poland
    (New York, Praeger, 1972).
2. In recent years almost any outburst of social tension has
    induced the authorities to license the distinguished
    historian, Stefan Kieniewicz, to discuss the lessons of
    the 1831 and 1863 Uprisings as an obvious historical
    warning of the limits set to reform and national re-
    assertion by postwar Soviet domination. Cf. 'W oczach
    narodu i historyka', Polityka, 18.10.80.
3. The case for a varied and changing pattern of Polish
    national characteristics was presented by the Poznań
    historian, Jerzy Topolski, 'Fakty czy mity?', Polityka,
    27.2.82.
4. 'On some contradictions of Socialist Society', Soviet
    Studies, XXXI, No. 2 (April 1979), p. 185.
5. On the consequent compromises, see J.R. Fiszman, Revolu-
    tion and Tradition in People's Poland (Princeton UP, 1972).
6. See R. Tiersky, French Communism, 1920-1972 (New York,
    Columbia UP, 1974).
7. Cf. P. Lewis, 'Obstacles to the establishment of politi-
    cal legitimacy in Poland', British Journal of Political
    Science, XII (April 1982), pp. 125-147.
8. A. Bromke, 'Poland at the crossroads', World Today,
    XXXIV, No. 4 (April 1978), p. 147.
9. P. Osnos. 'The Polish Road to Communism', Foreign Affairs,
    56, No. 1 (October 1977), p. 211.
10. Jacek Kuroń and Karol Modzelewski, An Open Letter to the
    Party (Socialist Review Co., London, n.d.).
11. Most notably by Z. Pełczyński in his coverage of postwar
    Poland in R.F. Leslie (ed.), The History of Poland since
    1863 (Cambridge UP, 1980). An early official Gierek
    version was WŁ. Góra, Polska Rzeczpospolita Ludowa,
    1944-1974 (Warsaw, KiW, 1976).
12. See S. Lotarski in T. Hammond (ed.), The Anatomy of
    Communist Takeovers (New Haven, Yale UP, 1975).

13. A rise from 555,888 in January 1947. PZPR Rezolucje,
    Odezwy, Instrukcje i Okólniki Komitetu Centralnego,
    1/1947-XII/1948 (Warsaw, KiW, 1973), p. 287.
14. Gierek shifted the cut-off point for non-dogmatic his-
    torical analysis from 1944 to 1948. Cf. F. Ryszka,
    Polska Ludowa, 1944-1950 (Wrocław-Warsaw, Ossolineum,
    1974).
15. The historical school, inspired by Mickiewicz, Słowacki
    and other nineteenth century patriotic writers, which
    popularised the irreducibly catholic and national pat-
    riotic special destiny of Poland, was symbolised in
    recent times by the writings of Oskar Halecki, A History
    of Poland (London, Dent, 1961). One should not confuse
    the original with Anthony Polonsky's superior revamped
    version (London, Routledge and Kegan Paul, 1978).
16. W. Brus, 'Stalinism and the People's Democracies' in
    R. Tucker (ed.), Stalinism. Essays in Historical Inter-
    pretation (New York, Norton, 1977).
17. The main historical overviews of Polish Communism are:
    M.K. Dziewanowski, The Communist Party of Poland. An
    Outline of History (Harvard UP, rev. 2nd ed., 1976);
    J.B. de Weydenthal, The Communists of Poland (Stanford,
    Hoover Institution Press, 1978).
18. See K. Syrop, Spring in October; the story of the Polish
    revolution, 1956 (London, Weidenfeld and Nicolson, 1957);
    G. Sakwa, 'The Polish October', Polish Review, XXXIII,
    No. 3 (1978), pp. 62-78.
19. See J.M. Montias, Central Planning in Poland (Yale UP,
    1962).
20. See H-J. Stehle, The Independent Satellite. Society and
    Politics in Poland since 1945 (New York, Praeger, 1965);
    R. Hiscocks, Poland, Bridge for the Abyss? (London,
    Oxford UP, 1963); N. Bethell, Gomułka. His Poland and
    his Communism (London, Longmans, 1969). A comprehen-
    sive examination of one aspect of the post 1956 balance
    between control and pluralism is G. Sakwa and M. Crouch,
    'Sejm Elections in Communist Poland', British Journal
    of Political Science, VIII (1978), pp. 403-424.
21. Le Figaro and The Times, 7.2.80.
22. See his obituary in Polityka, 4.10.82.
23. One of the main themes of J. Banas, The Scapegoats; the
    exodus of the remnants of Polish Jewry (London, Weidenfeld
    and Nicolson, 1979).
24. See A.R. Johnson, 'Poland; the end of the post October
    era', Survey (July 1968), pp. 87-98; A. Bromke, 'The
    Party and Poland's political crisis', World Today
    (February 1969).
25. G. Sanford, 'Jews and the Polish power-struggle', Soviet
    Jewish Affairs, XI, No. 3 (1981), pp. 72-76.
26. For a liberal reform Communist analysis, M.F. Rakowski,
    Przesilenie grudniowe (Warsaw, PIW, 1981).

The Gierek question

27.   VIII Plenum KC PZPR, 6-7 lutego 1971r (Warsaw, KiW, 1971).
      Its proceedings were also covered in a limited circula-
      tion issue of Nowe Drogi (May 1971).
28.   6th Congress of the Polish United Workers' Party (Warsaw,
      1972), pp. 246-247.
29.   VII Zjazd PZPR, 8-12 grudnia 1975r Stenogram z obrad
      plenarnych (Warsaw, KiW, 1975), pp. 13-42.
30.   The optimism and achievements of this period are conveyed
      by J. Maziarski, The Polish Upswing, 1971-1975 (Warsaw,
      Interpress, 1975). Compare A. Bromke and J. Strong
      (eds.), Gierek's Poland (New York, Pergamon, 1973).
31.   See Foreign Minister Olszowski on 'Polish foreign policy
      in an age of détente', Polish Perspectives, XVIII (March
      1974), pp. 3-12.
32.   Raport o stanie oświaty w PRL (Warsaw, PWN, 1973).
33.   R. Taras, 'Democratic Centralism and Polish Local Govern-
      ment Reforms', Public Administration, LIII (Winter 1975),
      pp. 403-426.
34.   P.G. Hare and T. Wanless, 'Polish and Hungarian economic
      reforms - a comparison', Soviet Studies, XXXIII, No. 4
      (October 1981), pp. 495-498.
35.   P. Lewis in Woodall, Policy and Politics, p. 93.
36.   G. Sakwa, 'Poland under Gierek', European Review, XXII,
      No. 4 (Autumn 1972), p. 26.
37.   'Polish queue joke gets longer', Guardian, 13.8.80.
38.   Aristotle's Politics (New York, Random House, 1943),p.212.
39.   'Kryzys gospodarczy-przyczyny i drogi wyjścia', Nowe
      Drogi (December 1980), pp. 133-154.
40.   Symbolically, Zdzisław Rurarz, one of the foremost apo-
      logists for 'accelerated' growth in 1972, 'chose free-
      dom' as ambassador to Japan in December 1981.
41.   M.F. Rakowski, Guardian, 30.1.80.
42.   M. Turski, 'Ostatnie poważne ostrzeżenie Radom 1976',
      Polityka, 27.6.81 and 4.7.81.
43.   For a biting critique of Gierek's agricultural policy,
      Zygmunt Kozłowski, 'Rolnictwo PRL na ślepym torze',
      Kultura (Paris, September 1980), pp. 64-75.
44.   For the swansong to Gierekian optimism, see Z. Szeliga,
      Polska; Dziś i jutro (Warsaw, KiW, 1978); also
      Pięć esejów o Polsce współczesnej (Warsaw, Interpress,
      1979).
45.   A. Bromke, 'The Opposition in Poland', Problems of
      Communism, XXVIII, No. 5 (September-October 1978),
      pp. 39-42.
46.   Kultura (Paris, October 1980), pp. 59-65, published a
      comprehensive list of 44 uncensored publications appear-
      ing in Poland from 1976 onwards.
47.   For a fascinating insight into the CPA view on dissidents,
      see CC Secretary Werblan's briefing of April 1978, pub-
      lished by the Catholic dissident publication, Spotkania,
      No. 4 (July 1978), pp. 258-263.

48. On these aspects, see G. Sanford, 'Polish People's Re-
     public' in B. Szajkowski (ed.), Marxist
     Governments (London, Macmillan, 1981), III, pp. 564-565.
49. VIII Zjazd PZPR, 11-15 lutego 1980r (Warsaw, KiW, 1980),
     p. 60.
50. 'Raport Doradców' and interview with Bożyk, Polityka,
     29.11.80.
51. VIII Zjazd, pp. 13 ff.
52. W. Jedlicki, 'Chamy i Żydy', Kultura (Paris, December
     1962), pp. 3-41.
53. 'Background to the study of opposition in Eastern
     Europe', Government & Opposition (Summer 1969), pp. 294-
     324.
54. Motory i Hamulce Socjalizmu (Paris, Instytut Literacki,
     1969).
55. See G. Blazyński, Flashpoint Poland (Oxford, Pergamon,
     1980); M. Simon and R. Kanet (eds.), Background to
     Crisis. Policy and Politics in Gierek's Poland (Boulder,
     Colorado, Westview Press, 1981).
56. G. Sanford, 'Gierek's downfall and the response of the
     Polish United Workers' Party to Social Crisis', Paper
     presented to the annual conference of the National
     Association of Soviet and Eastern European Studies
     (Cambridge, 1981), pp. 11-13 and Appendix 2.
57. Szlachcic testimony to the Grabski Commission on
     Responsibility, TL, 28.5.80.

Chapter Three

THE COLLAPSE OF THE POST-1956 SYSTEM

It is often assumed now that the question to
be answered is not so much why a crisis broke out
in Poland as only why it broke out in Summer 1980
and why it took the form which it did with the transformation of industrial strikes into Solidarity?
A mass national organisation, Solidarity, was only
partially a TU but initially and at the end of its
life it became a vast nationwide movement of protest
and national renewal as well.   In this chapter I
examine the PZPR's reaction to two quite separate
strands: firstly, to the Workers' Upsurge of July
to September, and, secondly, to the wave of French
May 1968 contestation and social protest which it
sparked off among the rest of society.
At the Eighth PZPR Congress in February 1980
Gierek narrowed his leadership base by dropping
independent individuals such as Olszowski, Tejchma
and Kępa.   Premier Jaroszewicz was made the régime
scapegoat for the economic situation and replaced
by Edward Babiuch, Gierek's main lieutenant and
unofficial PZPR Second Secretary during the 1970s
[1].   Gierek wanted to produce a united direction
which could impose unpopular moderate economic
austerity measures.   However, Gierek showed no
public recognition of the need for major changes in
political and economic directions.   His Eighth Congress speeches showed that he thought he could ride
out the situation by slight changes to his old
methods as long as he maintained his party base
secure and kept up appearances in order to keep
society quiet [2].
The post-Eighth Congress policy was one of moderate economic retrenchment without reform or popular participation.   Gierek seemed decided to run
a tighter ship within the PZPR as well as to exert
greater control over the state apparatus which had
undoubtedly benefited in 1976-1980 from the PZPR's

lethargy and loss of will after Radom.   The economic problem was, however, so serious that it mes-
merised Gierek and diverted his attention away from
what, with hindsight, we know to have been the
greater danger of an outburst by society [3].   By
the Summer, though, officials were revealing the
enormity of Poland's foreign debt for the first time
as the aim was now to convince the Poles of the need
to increase imports, to cut exports and to freeze,
if not actually cut, wages.   The Sejm therefore
modified the 1980 NPS-G by cutting import targets
by $800 million (a mere 2% of the total) and by rais-
ing export targets by $400 million [4].   The new
Gierek-Babiuch line was stated most sharply by the
noted publicist, Jerzy Urban, who chose an odd moment to make his peace with Gierek after having been
in disfavour.   He argued that the Poles were living
beyond their means.   Wage-increases would stoke up
inflation and threaten real wages.   'Wage demands,
however justified, constitute the cutting off of
the branch on which everyone is sitting,' declared
Urban at his most Thatcheresque (Polityka,26.7.80).
Gierek's spokesmen naturally attempted to blame
Poland's economic problems on such external factors as rising world interest rates and the post-
1973 increases in oil and raw material prices
(Kleer, Polityka, 9.8.80).   They also attempted to
balance the disasters of the late 1970s against the
achievements of the earlier part of the decade [5].
This special pleading was most unconvincing as it
offered no way out except a period of renewed austerity.   The political dilemma, though, was that
the pressure of demographic factors and rising expectations had impelled Gierek into the imprudent
policy of dynamic expansion in the first case so the
economic problem, although grave, was in many respects primarily a political and psychological one.
     The above considerations are often neglected
in considering the causes of the 1980 outbreak.
Many commentators, influenced by the euphoria of
the time, considered that Poland's economic situation was so tragic that a social outburst in Summer
1980 was both inevitable and necessary and probably
morally right as well.   But the economist's view
is well stated by Nuti: 'Price increases were not
only a sound economic measure, in view of the widening inflationary gap ... but indeed overdue.   Also,
the scarcity of meat has been somewhat overstated.
Meat consumption in Poland increased rapidly from 43
kilograms per head in 1960 to 74 kilograms in 1980'
[6].I can only offer the personal view that,if Polish
society had accepted Gierek's moderate austerity

programme, Western bankers would probably have maintained sufficient confidence in him to keep his ship afloat;. Poland's problems in terms of international comparisons were not unique and paralleled by another 20 to 30 countries, notably Brazil, Mexico and Turkey. The Polish people, at the price of a few years of belt-tightening, would have been spared 16 months of nerve racking political tension, the greatest economic and consumer collapse in post-war Europe and perhaps even the loss of the relative political liberties which they had enjoyed, but not valued sufficiently, between 1956 and 1980.

The Workers' Upsurge overthrows Gierek: the PZPR loses Control of Society

What sparked off the political and economic crisis was, as so often before, an attempt to raise meat prices. Meat by 1980 benefited from a subsidy of the equivalent of £1.5 milliard per annum. In 1977 a system of commercial shops had been instituted which sold the best meat at about double the ordinary prices; by 1980 this accounted for about a fifth of all meat sales. On 1 July the Government carried out an indirect price rise, without prior consultation, by transferring the remaining types of better quality meat to them. These surprise tactics fooled no one. A wave of strikes broke out immediately,starting at the Ursus tractor factory near Warsaw, and other factors in Gdańsk, Tczew and Mielec [7]. The strikes continued sporadically right across the country, varying in scale, significance and demands for the next 6 weeks until they reached their climax in Gdańsk in mid August.

Kania revealed in late August that strikes had broken out in 533 factories in all 49 provinces and had involved 640,000 workers [8]. Whole towns, such as Mielec and Żyrardów, had been paralysed by general strikes, as had Lublin by a transport strike and Warsaw itself by a bus stoppage in mid August which followed a rubbish collectors' strike. Western journalists in Warsaw had been informed of these developments by Jacek Kuroń, who set himself up as KSS-KOR's spokesman [9].

Gierek attempted to rally the managers of the largest factories at a secret meeting on 11 July. On 18 July the Politburo promised the Lublin strikers a special commission headed by deputy-Premier Jagielski to examine their grievances, but the workers held out for larger wage-increases. Gierek's possibilities for manoeuvre were very limited as repression in individual cases might have sparked off a national revolt. The only road open for him was

to try and settle each strike individually and to
hope that the strike wave would blow itself out and
be resolved by purely economic concessions and some
symbolic scapegoating of factory managers and party
officials.   In July alone at least 300,000 workers
in 100 factories had struck so the Politburo drew
the appropriate conclusions on 23 July.   It issued
clearer instructions as to the necessity of preventing the spread of strikes through economic concessions.   The party's authority in the factories was
crumbling rapidly, though.   In the elections to the
Lublin railworkers' union Executive, for example, in
late July at least half the candidates were indepen-
dents nominated directly by the workers themselves.
Another sign of the times was that the railmen's 35
demands, including free elections to TUs, foreshadowed
many of the later Gdańsk political and social demands.
What the PZPR really thought at this time is unclear.
CC Ideology Secretary Jerzy Łukasiewicz reiterated
Gierek's stock line as late as a press conference on
13 August;   the strikes were purely economic in
character and had no political significance.   One
can surmise that there was already a group of
pragmatists, headed by Kania, within the Politburo
who awaited the outcome of events.   The liberals,
such as Rakowski, who were willing to introduce socio-
economic reforms, were as yet to be found much further down the leadership levels.
     The chain reaction of strikes right across
Poland was marked by the following crucial characteristics.   Firstly, the workers remained within
factory limits so the tactic of the 'occupation' or
'Polish' strike was the inevitable outcome [10].
The Communist leaders knew how easily, as in Poznań
in 1956 and the Baltic sea coast in 1970, demonstrations could flare up into uncontrollable riots.
They therefore made every effort to contain discontent within the factories themselves.   Secondly,
industrial protests and strikes, although spontaneous, quickly took on the organisational form of
Workers' Commissions, a type of Soviet adapted
to modern Polish conditions.   Official union
functionaries invariably had no influence over the
striking workers,whose demands were voiced by individuals thrown up at random by the strike movement
itself.   In other words, the Polish working class
experienced something akin to a 6 week gestation
period before the great Baltic sea coast strikes
erupted in mid August.   During this time a vast
amount of tactical experience had been amassed and
networks of individuals had been forged through
collective action.   The noted, long-time,reform-

minded sociologist, Stanisław Ehrlich, analysed the
balance between spontaneity and organised activity
in August 1980 as follows:

> The leaders and few dozen strong KOR aktyw
> did not call up these events but they fore-
> saw and inspired them (the workers took the
> very concept of independent TUs from KOR
> writings) and in a few centres they helped
> the organisers of the [workers'] councils
> and above all they became an information
> network [11].

Ehrlich therefore considered that KOR had neither
the means nor the members to reach all bar a few
crucial factories and that they had almost no influence on the peasants, while their contacts were
strongest among students and young intellectuals.

Lastly,more than mere economic discontent was
at stake. As was foreseen most presciently by a
significant article in the Guardian (30.7.80),
'Poland's "Summer of 1980" may produce far more sweeping and more enduring changes in the country's political and economic life than Czechoslovakia's "Spring
of 1968"'. The report noted that, although the
Polish Government refused to rescind the price increases, no attempts were being made to repress the
strikes. Managers were negotiating at plant and
shop floor level with the unofficial strike committees set up by the workers to bypass the official
unions. The June-July settlements had started with
10-15% wage increases and had peaked at around 20%
in some cases. This had prevented the workers from
taking to the streets, but workers' demands were
only partially about pay and factory conditions.
They were also directed against the whole centralised Communist system and in particular the unres-
ponsiveness of the official unions to workers' wishes.
Socio-economic discontent was also matched by the
significant factor that 'the party liberals believe
that there is a genuine crisis in the régime'.

The course of events in the Lenin Shipyard in
Gdańsk,which caused the downfall of Gierek's régime
and which led to the emergence of Solidarity, is
well known and hardly needs to be recounted here [12].
What one might note is that the shipyard and its
dock area was a marvellous site for a mass occupation strike. The workers there were also moved by
personal memories of the deaths of their colleagues
in December 1970. Secondly, their example was followed, in spite of the cutting of communications by
the authorities, by most of the factories on the
Baltic sea coast from Szczecin to Elbląg. It
turned very rapidly into a regional strike which

was only a step away from becoming a national one.
Thirdly, Klemens Gniech, the shipyard's director,
between 14 and 16 August almost managed to convince
the strikers to settle for a pay rise of 1,500
złoties per month, a no-victimisation pledge and the
reinstatement of Anna Walentynowicz. It was a close
call as the situation then escalated both in terms
of regional spread and in the shift from largely
economic to social and political demands. With the
formation of the first Inter-Factory Strike Committee (MKS) in Gdańsk on 16 August and the tabling of
16, later expanded to 21, largely political and social
demands, which included the right to strike and to
form 'free TUs', what Ascherson calls 'the real
struggle for the future of Poland began' [13].
One should stress the historical significance of the
appearance of the MKSs. The MKSs ensured that the
régime would be unable to use force and would be
forced into direct negotiations with the strikers
which it was bound to lose. They also provided
the framework for the future evolution of Solidarity,
a national MKS writ large, which ensured that the
outside possibility of 'free TUs' assuming a local
or enterprise organisational form was buried right
from the outset.
    Gierek's reaction to the industrial unrest of
Summer 1980 had, as we have seen, been to attempt to
isolate each strike and to deal with it as much as
possible through bread and butter concessions while
managers were instructed to play on the divisions
between the workers themselves. In order to maintain the official pretence that all was normal, the
mass media ignored the industrial unrest until mid
August; even then they referred to it euphemisti-
cally as 'work stoppages' (TL, 15.8.80). Instead
they stressed the seriousness of Poland's economic
situation and many statistics on that score were now
revealed for the first time.
    The Gierek leadership did not attempt any general
initiative until Premier Babiuch's major televised
speech of 15 August. Babiuch defended the post-
February belt-tightening measures, although he admitted that the authorities were to blame for not
informing the Poles sufficiently, and in good time,
of the gravity of the economic situation. His
priority remained the amelioration of the country's
balance of payments (TL, 16-17.8.80). Babiuch was
right in economic terms but quite unconvincing politically. Wałęsa was reported as saying that
'Babiuch's sweet voice can no longer convince anyone', while Andrzej Gwiazda declared that 'the authorities will no longer be able to ignore demands

for the democratisation of public life' (Dziennik
Polski, 18.8.80). Gierek therefore moved in with
a crisp and direct speech on 18 August which even a
month previously would have been hailed as a mile-
stone. He claimed to understand the reasons for
social discontent but condemned the harm done by
strikes. Economic demands such as the freezing of
meat prices, food imports, price controls and measures to help the poor could all be considered.
Gierek declared that he wished to negotiate compromises with the strikers. However, 'activities
harming the political and social order in Poland
cannot and will not be tolerated. This is indicated by Polish raison d'état' (TL, 19.8.80).
Gierek's attempt to rally the CPA and its supporting
élites and to overawe society by threatening repri-
sals against the anti-socialist groups who were using
the Baltic strikes for their own ends were, however,
overwhelmed by the rapid press of events.
    The Presidium of the Council of Ministers imple-
mented the measures announced by Gierek on 21 August.
More significantly, the head of the party-state commission negotiating with the Gdańsk strikers, Tadeusz
Pyka, was replaced by the senior deputy Premier,
Jagielski, while yet another deputy Premier,
Kazimierz Barcikowski, was despatched to Szczecin.
Pyka had attempted to break up the MKS 'Wybrzeże'
by negotiating separately with the 161 individual
factories which composed it. But only 17 agreed to
preliminary negotiations and even they broke them
off on 20 August when Pyka overplayed his hand by
demanding that they leave the MKS first. The strikers were also reinforced on 23 August by the arri-
val of a group of sympathetic 'experts' from Warsaw
[14]. They included Tadeusz Mazowiecki, Editor of
the Catholic monthly, Więź (The Link), Professor
Bronisław Geremek, a medieval PAN historian, Jadwiga
Staniszkis, a sociologist, and Waldemar Kuczyński,
an economist.
    On or about 21 August the Politburo decided to
accept the Gdańsk MKS as a competent negotiating
partner which represented the workers. This was
tantamount 'to the recognition by the authorities
of the principle of free collective bargaining
for the first time in a Communist state' (Sunday
Times, 24.8.80). Jagielski's dramatic and tense
week long negotiations with the Gdańsk MKS, headed
by Wałęsa, which began on 23 August and which culminated with the signing of the Gdańsk Agreement on
31 August, have been recounted in full elsewhere
[15]. I want to concentrate here on the less well
known story of how the crisis was viewed and responded

to by the PZPR, inasfar as one can piece the story
together from official documents, the actual decisions taken and the internal logic of events.
  The PZPR leadership was hardly united in facing
what an English journalist called 'the unthinkable
nightmare' of 'opposition to the workers' state'
from the working class itself (Sunday Times, 24.8.80).
Dobbs also considered that the Communist leadership
was divided between hardliners who wanted to re-
double the propaganda campaign, to arrest large numbers of dissidents and to force a decisive showdown
with the strikers and those, mainly outside the ranks
of the top leadership, who now accepted the need
for sweeping reforms. To this simple classification
one should add the pragmatic, centrist majority in
the Politburo who already looked to Kania to steady
the PZPR boat. The flavour of the thinking of the
Gierek conservatives is conveyed by reading
Łukasiewicz' confidentially circulated letter of 19
August to PZPR militants which was reproduced by the
Gdańsk MKS: 'The demand to form so-called free
unions is being put forward not out of concern for
the improved representation of workers' interests
but in order to gain within their framework the
institutionalised possibilities of conducting
counter-socialist activities directed against our
party and our people's state' [16].
  Gierek's appeal for social peace on 18 August
was interpreted by the PZPR liberals within the intellectual supporting élite as indicating his renewed commitment to reform. Some, such as Rakowski,
the Editor of Polityka, had reverted to the ideas of
1971 and presented reform arguments in favour of decentralisation at the PZPR Second National Conference
in January 1978. Rakowski analysed the economic
situation even before Gdańsk in remarkably forth-
right terms, concluding that it had become 'an in-
coherent mechanism, directives function faultily,
occasionally in defiance of common sense' (Polityka,
5.7.80). The scale of the industrial unrest now
led him to argue that a way of reforming the Communist system from top to bottom would have to be found
as its overthrow would endanger the peace of Europe
by provoking Soviet intervention (Polityka, 2.8.80).
The inquest on Gierek among the liberal Communist
intelligentsia therefore started even before his
fall (cf. Pajestka, Polityka, 30.8.80).
  By the Fourth Plenum on 24 August it was clear
that Gierek was incapable of ending the Baltic sea
coast factory occupations. His promises of economic concessions and reform and the implied threat
of either domestic police repression or Soviet

intervention were quite ineffective.   The arrest of
leading dissidents was also too little too late.
The evidence suggests that the rejection of the
option of repression stemmed from Gierek's own inclinations, the caution and disunity of the PZPR
central aktyw and perhaps even a Soviet veto.   These
factors ruled out a Polish Kronstadt although, in
purely realpolitik terms, one can speculate on the
consequences of the bombing of the Lenin Shipyard or
its storming by the tanks of the Polish Army before
23 August.   That the latter manoeuvre succeeded
relatively painlessly in December 1981 is no indicator that it would have done so under the very different conditions of August 1980.   It was ruled out
entirely when the PZPR leadership decided to negotiate seriously with the Gdańsk strikers and to purge
its own leadership.   One can accept the judgement
of the Polish Communist leaders and their Soviet advisers that forcible repression in August 1980 entailed an unacceptably high risk of sparking off a
national uprising, or at least a Baltic regional
one.   Political measures, however drastic, would
therefore have to be resorted to, as, unlike Hungary
in early November 1956, the central institutions of
Communist rule were still in place and functioning,
albeit in a weak and demoralised manner.   The preliminary security measures were therefore not followed up.   The PZPR committed itself irreversibly
to a different tack for the next 16 months.
    Gierek lost the bulk of his closest lieutenants
and his Politburo majority at the Fourth Plenum
(Nowe Drogi, September 1980).   Edward Babiuch, the
Premier, Jerzy Łukasiewicz, the Ideology Secretary,
Jan Szydlak, the CRZZ Chairman since February 1980,
and Tadeusz Wrzaszczyk, the Planning Chairman, were
dismissed from the Politburo and, where appropriate,
from their state posts as well.   The two Politburo
candidates were also sacked: Pyka because of his
failure in Gdańsk and Żandarowski because as CC
Secretary in charge of party personnel he had made
many enemies.   Gierek's main critic, Stefan
Olszowski, was returned to both the Politburo and
Secretariat, while Pińkowski, a little known economist, became the new Premier.   The rise of somewhat younger, but absolutely safe, party men can be
chronicled in the almost mechanical step-by-step
advancement of an ambitious ex-Youth Movement Chairman and Opole KW First Secretary, Andrzej Żabiński,
who now became a Politburo candidate.   Most demonstratively, Tadeusz Grabski was co-opted on to the
CC and soon became a deputy Premier.
    In this way Gierek was stripped of his main

supporters, although he remained as 'a lame duck'
First Secretary for a few more days.   A good clue
to his eventual successor was that Stanisław Kania,
who already in late June had given the keynote speech
at the Third Plenum on the Health Services,now again
dominated the Fourth Plenum with his bleak report on
the national situation [17].   He revealed that about
a quarter of a million workers belonging to 260 enterprises were on strike in the Baltic region.   This
was 'the most massive and long lasting strike wave
in the history of People's Poland' with very deep and
varied causes which had built up over many years.
Kania rejected hardline calls for a stand against
the workers: 'There is no reason to use force
against striking workers and there never will be
any such reason.'   Kania also made it clear that
the Jagielski and Barcikowski commissions would continue to negotiate in order to provide a decent outcome to the strikes and factory occupations.
      The Fourth Plenum debate was a short one as few
individuals were willing to speak out before the situation clarified itself [18].   A number of party
officials - such as Tadeusz Fiszbach (Gdańsk KW
First Secretary), Stanisław Miśkiewicz (the KZ Secretary in the Warski Shipyard in Szczecin) and Jan
Łąbecki (his equivalent in the Lenin Shipyard) -
criticised Gierek's handling of the situation.
They drew reformist conclusions from their experiences with their striking workers.   Fiszbach argued
that the genuine social and economic protest meant
that the PZPR should handle the crisis by 'forming
institutional guarantees to prevent the aggregation
of mistakes'.   Łąbecki, in a heavily censored
speech, stated that the workers were protesting
against careerist and corrupt officials, not against
the socialist order.   Olszowski, bidding to replace
Gierek, outlined his brand of Communist reformism.
He called for an economic and financial reform and
wanted to build up the credibility of the party
state through democratisation in order to change
what he termed 'a theatrical form of public life'
in which all institutions had been manipulated by
the power holders.   Rakowski agreed with Olszowski
that this was 'the most severe political crisis in
the 35 years' existence of People's Poland'.
Gierek himself merely made a humble self-criticism
of his mistakes.   He accepted secret elections
within TUs.   He admitted that he had lost society's
support as he had banked everything after the Eighth
Congress on being able 'during the next few years
to re-establish equilibrium in the economy and to
increase its effectiveness'.

The collapse

The Council of State, meeting on the same day
as the CC, carried out widespread changes by decree
in the Council of Ministers (Biographies, TL,25.8.80).
Pińkowski replaced Babiuch as Chairman, Pyka and
Wrzaszczyk were replaced as deputy Chairmen by
Grabski, Aleksander Kopeć and Henryk Kisiel, the
latter also becoming Chairman of the Planning Com-
mission. Józef Czyrek became Foreign Minister,
while Marian Krzak took over the poisoned chalice of
Poland's finances. Maciej Szczepański,'Bloody
Matthew' (about whom more later), was replaced as
Chairman of the Committee on Radio and TV by Józef
Barecki, the Editor of Trybuna Ludu since 1972.
New men also took over the State Prices Commission
and GUS, the latter being entrusted to a non-party
SGPiS Professor, Wiesław Sadowski, who was charged
with restoring credibility to official statistics.
All these sweeping party and state changes had
no effect on the strikers. Remembering Gierek's
1971 promises, and their leaders fearing for their
necks in any future stabilisation, they held out for
cast iron written agreements and two institutional
guarantees: the right to strike and to organise
'independent and self-governing TUs' (NSZZs)
were to underpin the system and to provide checks on
the PZPR and the state machines which it controlled.
Jagielski's negotiation of the Gdańsk Agreement
agreeing to this, as well as to a wide variety of
economic, social and political demands, and
Barcikowski's similar achievement in Szczecin, defused the immediate confrontation [19]. Many
questions were, however, left open which caused
disputes in the future between Solidarity and the
PZPR. Firstly, the Gdańsk negotiations had been
bedevilled by controversy over the party's leading
role. It was not clear whether the NSZZs would
concur that the condition which had been agreed of
working within the constitution meant accepting the
party's hegemony. Article 2 of the Gdańsk Agreement, on the surface, seemed clear enough but
Jagielski's victory in formulating it was a Pyrrhic
one, as events were soon to show. The NSZZ also
accepted the socialist economic order and that they
would 'defend the social and material interests of
employees and do not intend to play the role of a
political party'. Secondly, the detailed and
sweeping package of varied political, economic and
social concessions, agreed to by Jagielski on the
PZPR's behalf, was bound to produce recurring bitter
conflicts over the manner and time scale of their
implementation - let alone as to whether they were
justified, or even feasible. Such issues as the

working week, increased wages and special benefits
for the lower paid and those with large families had
been conceded at a time of grave economic crisis.
Disputes over these topics as well as poisoning the
political atmosphere did much to aggravate inflation and consumer demand and to build up the 'queuing
psychosis' which later did so much to render sen-
sible politics difficult in Poland.
    The public, and apparently sincere, acceptance
of the strikers' conditions was arguably the greatest
humiliation which any ruling CP has ever had to accept. The historic significance of the Gdańsk
Agreement was that it set out 'the principle of a
social group's being allowed to organise itself in
a body that would operate outside the direct control
of the party and the state' [20]. Observers were
struck at the time by the profound transformation
in the functioning of the one party system and also
the extent to which the PZPR had 'become artificial
... to the main impulses of Polish life, although it
still staggered on as a ruling bureaucracy with a
challenged and hesitant authority backed up by
Soviet power' (Frankland, Observer, 31.8.80).
    The PZPR attempted to save face by arguing that
it had responded in a correct Leninist manner to a
justified workers' protest which had adopted constitutional methods within a socialist framework. Its
post-Fourth Plenum line was that the Summer strikes
had shown that the bond between the party and the
working class had been broken. The main task now
was to rebuild it through a dialogue with society.
Official commentators still stressed, though, that
it was up to the PZPR to define what could be discussed, such as the role of TUs and the mass media,
and to preserve the sacrosanct aspects of its leading role and the question of Poland's position in
the USSR's security zone. The PZPR nevertheless
accepted 'the need for introducing deep changes in
the functioning of democratic mechanisms' (Wojna,
TL, 27.8.80). After the Fourth Plenum the official
media started reporting in detail the main issues
and disagreements being negotiated in Gdańsk [21].
The Council of Ministers also started work on implementing the decisions arising from the party's new
course, such as increased meat imports, the renewed
rationing of sugar and the withdrawal of Polish
produced goods from the PEWEX hard currency shops.
    After hearing Kania's report at its Fifth Plenum
on 30 August, the PZPR CC confirmed the decision to
agree to the signing of the Gdańsk and Szczecin
Agreements in the form negotiated by Jagielski and
Barcikowski. We do not know if there were any

formal dispute or debate as only a short paragraph-
long communiqué of the plenum's proceedings was ever
published [22].

However, the strikes had not been limited solely
to the Baltic, as strikes took place all over
Poland in solidarity with the Baltic workers.
Cardinal Wyszyński's sermon at Jasna Góra on 26
August calling for social peace and responsible actions was publicised by the authorities in a form
which drew an Episcopal Press Bureau protest that
the official version was 'neither integral nor au-
thorised' [23]. Radicals were already disappointed
with the Church's political moderation and social
conservatism. The signing of the Gdańsk Agreement,
however, did not prevent the spread of strikes to
the coalmines of Silesia in late August. After
negotiations between deputy-Premier Kopeć, Żabiński
and Mining Minister Lejczak and the Silesian MKS
the miners had their right to strike and to associate in NSZZs confirmed in the Jastrębie Agreement
of 3 September [24].

The compromise and ambiguous character of the
Gdańsk Agreement was evident. Wałęsa declared:
'We have not achieved everything, but we have achieved
a lot, and the rest we will obtain in the future
because we have our free and self-governing TUs'
(Dziennik Polski, 2.9.80). On the other hand, the
Social Agreements, although welcomed by the Eurocommunist and Yugoslav CPs, met with a critical reaction from the Soviet, Czechoslovak and East German
ones who failed to report their more embarrassing
aspects. Only Nepszabadsag, the Hungarian CP paper,
gave a full and factual account. The indications
were that there was no direct threat of Soviet intervention in spite of their dismay at the concession
of the right to strike and to organise free TUs.
This was perhaps because, as a senior Polish official was reported as saying, 'the party is the key
to the whole situation. As long as it holds together we feel that we are safe' (Dobbs, Guardian,
4.9.80).

Although the mass media had opened up dramatically during the previous week it was still firmly
under party control. Polish Communists had always
stressed, in private conversation with me during the
1970s, that the main mistake in the Prague Spring
had been their noisy mass media and that they would
now allow this to happen in Poland. Official
sources claimed that the successful outcome in
Gdańsk confirmed the PZPR view 'that the only possible way out of the crisis is the road of agreement
with the working class'. They considered that the

social and cost of living aspect of the Agreements
represented 'a reasonable compromise', that the organisational form of the TUs would have to be discussed and embodied in a new law while the question
of socialist democracy was something which could be
dealt with once the situation had settled down
(TL, 1.9.80).

The PZPR Leadership retreats into its Bunker

The Workers' Upsurge did more than just overthrow the Gierek leadership.   It presented both an
ideological and organisational challenge to the
Soviet form of Communism in Poland which had already
been adapted in a major way in 1956.   In particular,
the development of MKSs, a regional federation of
Soviets in their fullest form, presaged the emergence of a similar national organisation, Solidarity.
The dilemma faced by the Polish working class in
Summer 1980 was that only such a wider organisational
form, which aggregated the various enterprise level
discontents together, could force the Communist authorities to concede the right to strike and to free
TUs.   The workers' leaders considered these to be
the main institutional safeguards to ensure autonomy
for the workers from the state.   They were also
the mechanisms to force consideration and acceptance
of specific workers' demands.   They constituted
the best guarantees that the reforms would not be
clawed back when the Communist system recovered its
strength, as had happened to the workers' councils
after 1956.

In the excitement and the press of events of
August 1980 few paused to consider the consequences.
Such a development was welcomed by the Eurocommunist
CPs and the European democratic Left but the Soviet
experience with the Workers' Opposition in 1918-1922
and the symbolism conjured up by the word Kronstadt
cast a grim shadow over the long term viability of
the Polish experiment.   Ideology, self-interest
and their strategic position within the Soviet bloc
naturally inclined the Polish leadership against
free TUs.   The only question was whether they could
be forced to live with them.   At Gdańsk the authorities surrendered because they hoped that the MKS
would fall apart once it had gained its socio-economic demands.   After that the PZPR leadership hoped
to restrict the new free TUs to the level of individual factories or, at worst, regions or whole
industries, and to maintain a counterpoise in their
official unions.   Both these calculations were
proved wrong in September-October when the Communist
authorities really lost control over events and

retreated into their political bunker to think out
their long term strategy. They failed at every
level to prevent the spread of the Baltic plague
over the whole country. Solidarity emerged as a
nationally organised movement while the official
unions were for the most part whittled down to
mere husks.
    The long term tragedy about Summer 1980 was
that it was a political stand-off in brute power
terms. The Communist leadership was defeated and
forced into a major tactical retreat but it was
neither smashed nor convinced of the rightness and
irreversibility of what had happened. In consequence
it could bide its time,mount various delaying actions
against Solidarity, rally to SCIE reform Communist
conceptions and counter-attack about a year later
after the Ninth Congress. By then Polish society
had been worn down by the economic collapse and by
a never ending series of national and local confrontations.
    The PZPR central aktyw,composed of the Politburo,
Secretariat, CC Departmental Heads and KW First
Secretaries, met at the party HQ on 2 September to
assess the situation. It was indicative of Kania's
growing role that he presented the report while
Premier Pińkowski reported on the work of the Council
of Ministers. The following day the CRZZ, under
its new Chairman, Romuald Jankowski, the Metalwor-
kers' Union Chairman, called for national unity and
accepted the principle of democratic election to
union committees with no limitations on the number
of candidates. The PZPR would naturally have preferred to renew their official unions on self-
governing lines but they were now resigned to the
formation of new unions where this was demanded by
the workforce itself. The conditions were that
such bodies should respect the constitution and the
party's leading role. They should not attempt to
become political forces but should concern themselves solely with the defence of the economic and
social interests of the workers (TL, 5.9.80).
    All these developments made Gierek's position
untenable. We do not really know how serious his
heart attack was, although 5 eminent doctors certified that he had suffered 'a grave disturbance of
the heart's functioning' (TL, 6-7.9.80). The Sixth
Plenum therefore met without him on the night of
5-6 September, under the chairmanship of Henryk
Jabłoński, the Head of State. Kania, who replaced
Gierek, was 'the Kremlin's favourite' for the succession (Zorza, Guardian, 8.9.80). He had drawn
attention to himself by presenting the CC reports

at the Third, Fourth and Fifth Plena and had played
an increasingly important and balanced pragmatic
role during the Summer which gained him the support
of the PZPR Central Party aktyw.   Olszowski, his
main rival, had been out of the centre of power as
ambassador to the GDR since the Eighth Congress.
He had also been the CC Secretary in charge of the
economy from 1976 to February 1980, so his aggressive reformism did not cut much ice with his CC
colleagues, although they must have been impressed
by his skilled political footwork in distancing
himself from Gierek.   Moscow might also have coun-
selled that he be kept in reserve in the event of
Kania, like Ochab in 1956, proving to be no more
than a stop-gap.
       Kania was born on 8 March 1927 in what is now
Krosno province in South-eastern Poland of poor peasant origins.   He joined the PPR, worked for the
Communist League of Rural Youth (ZMW) and eventually
became the deputy Secretary of the League of Polish
Youth (ZMP) in Rzeszów.   Kania had little formal
schooling, so at the height of the Stalinist period
he was sent to a course at the PZPR's Central Party
School which he completed in 1952.   After that
Kania became Head of the Rural Youth Department at
ZMP's Warsaw HQ, from which he moved in 1958 to become Head of the Agriculture Department and then
Secretary in the PZPR's Warsaw KW organisation.
In 1968, thanks to Babiuch's patronage, which tied
him to Gierek's fortunes, he became Head of the very
important CC Administration Department.   In the
1970s Kania became one of the most important men in
Poland, especially after Szlachcic's fall in 1974;
but he did not develop either a personal following,
a strong party image or a well known profile among
the Polish public.   In April 1971 he became a CC
Secretary with responsibilities which widened out
during the 1970s from control of domestic security
matters to relations with the Roman Catholic Church
and the organisation of Wojtyła's visit in 1979.
Kania became a CC candidate in 1964, a full member
in 1968, a Politburo candidate in 1971 and a full
member in 1975 (official biography, TL, 6-7.9.80).
       Kania had implemented Gierek's very liberal
and tolerant line,by Communist standards, with the
dissidents whom he harassed but did not exterminate
in the late 1970s.   He maintained an acceptable
modus vivendi with the Church and with the intellectuals who, in spite of the alleged sins of the
much maligned Łukasiewicz, flourished as nowhere
else in the Communist bloc.   Kania had never held
a Government or managerial post but, like Gierek,

he seems to have been a somewhat more flexible and
less bloodthirsty <u>apparatchik</u> than his first generation predecessors. He was reported as saying, at
the time of the tabling of the 21 Gdańsk Demands,
that a counter-revolution was taking place but that
force was ruled out as the PZPR 'only had political
instruments to deal with it' [25]. He also told
the Gdańsk KW Executive that the strikes had been
caused by defects in the PZPR's policies and administration and that 'today the widest area of
understanding is a necessity in order to maintain
quiet in the country' [26]. However, he also considered that the original intentions of the strikers
had been transformed into 'activities directed against
the fundamental principles of political and social
life' in People's Poland. Anti-socialist elements
were causing chaos and would have to be resisted
(Życie Warszawy, 19.8.80).
    Kania's lack of formal education, dull perso-
nality, oratorical mediocrity and a career spent
entirely within the PZPR as a rural youth, agricultural and security specialist produced a somewhat
grey effect. At the time his unassuming personal
humility contrasted well with Gierek's and Olszowski's
more determined postures and seemed to cast him in
the same mould as Kadar in Hungary or Zhivkov in
Bulgaria. Kania also started as barely a <u>primus</u>
<u>inter pares</u> within the PZPR leadership. The
party was fragmented into numerous and diverse
clientèles who looked to a variety of personalities.
Kania and Olszowski therefore had to work in tandem
right from the start and it was not until December
that the leadership base was widened by the emergence of Moczar and Grabski and more reforming personalities. No clear policy line, however, emerged
for a whole month until the renewed Sixth Plenum in
early October. In this period the PZPR tottered
momentarily on the brink of collapse at grassroots level and Kania remained almost invisible to
society within his CPA bunker. In addition, the
September Plenum did not give Kania a workable
majority by appointing his political friends to the
Politburo. It merely promoted individuals such
as Żabiński and Barcikowski to full Politburo members
who had acquiesced in his elevation, while the Secretariat was widened by the inclusion of Gierek's
critic, Grabski, another Żabiński type Youth Movement official, Zdzisław Kurowski and Kania's friend,
Jerzy Wojtecki, the Head of the CC Agriculture
Department. Kania, in a very modest acceptance
speech, which later was (rather oddly) read out for
him on radio and TV, merely stated that the massive

social protest had been directed not against socialism 'but against distortions, against mistakes in
our policy'; he admitted that the party had made
grave economic and social mistakes. His keynote
was that 'democracy was not a gesture by the authorities' but a sincere commitment to regaining the
workers' confidence by fulfilling the Social Agreements [27]. One can also accept the sincerity of
Kania's declaration that he had never expected the
party to entrust him with such an awesome responsibility. That Kania's appointment was supported
by the Soviet leadership, who wanted a free man
without a political clan or clear policy line behind
him, is also clear enough from Brezhnev's warm message of congratulations (TL, 8.9.80).

The first public debate on Gierek's stewardship
had begun a few hours before his fall with the extremely lively Sejm session of 5 September [28].
The Sejm confirmed the sweeping Government changes
carried out by the Council of State decree of 24
August. Premier Pińkowski then presented a very
long and dull report setting out the preliminary
guidelines for economic recovery and the Government's intention to implement various aspects of the
Gdańsk Agreement. The previously passive deputies,
on hearing of Gierek's heart attack and of the con-
vocation of the Sixth Plenum, sensed the growing
power vacuum and found their tongues. Żabiński,
trying to direct this groundswell on behalf of the
PZPR deputies' club, declared that the authorities
would have to explain to the nation why the justified Sixth Congress Plan for Poland's development
'had undergone distortion and deformation in the
course of its implementation'. He concluded that
the 1970s presented 'a globally negative balance'.
Professor Jan Szczepański, an influential non-
party member of the Council of State, stressed
that there could be no democratisation of social
life without that of the party, which would have to
change its recruitment policy. Karol Małcużyński,
a well known journalist who had incurred Gierek's
disfavour in the late 1970s, mounted a bitter attack
on the régime's mass media policy. 'The propaganda
of success,' he declared, popularising the term,
became an irritating nonsense because of the glaring contrast between what the authorities said and
what the public knew. Sylwester Zawadzki, a senior
Professor of State Law, carried out a similar exercise on 'the bureaucratic distortions of the late
1970s and the social protests which they occasioned'.
On 4 September the Politburo set up a commission, headed by the CKKP Chairman, to investigate

the affairs of 52 year old Maciej Szczepański,
Gierek's close friend and speech writer from his
time as KW First Secretary in Katowice, 1957-1970.
Szczepański was dismissed as Head of Radio and TV
and Western journalists were regaled with leaks concerning his alleged lurid sins, such as that he
maintained a bevy of black prostitutes and had built
himself a palace.   The change in top leadership,
unlike 1956 or 1970, was received largely with indif-
ference by the Polish public.   The general view was
that Gierek had sincere good intentions but that he
had proved incapable of mastering the intricacies
of Polish political life.
     Ascherson argues that the September Sixth Plenum
established a Kania-Olszowski condominium which carried out what he terms 'a two track policy' [29].
The former, backed by major figures such as
Barcikowski, Jagielski and Jabłoński, concerned himself with the fulfilment of the Social Agreements,
the implementation of the various institutional reforms (TUs, censorship, and so on) and with the renewal of the PZPR.   However, in this division of
labour Olszowski was involved in preventing this
process from getting out of hand, especially in the
mass media, which he controlled as CC Secretary.
Aided by such allies as Grabski and Żabiński, he
favoured necessary reforms to be implemented from
'above', especially economic ones.   After the
fiasco of his leadership ambitions in September the
political centre moved so quickly as to turn him,
the moderate reformer of the 1970s, into a qualified conservative concerned with discipline and the
maintenance of the party's leading role.   These
attitudes gained him increasing support from late
Autumn onwards among the party functionaries.
Ascherson is rather mystified by the twists and
turns of PZPR policy after August.   Periods of
close collaboration with Solidarity were interspersed
with recurring confrontations of increasing inten-
sity and danger from the Solidarity registration
crisis to Bydgoszcz in late March 1981.   All the
earlier ones, at least, ended with defeat for the
PZPR and the dissipation of such social confidence
as had been gained by its responsible and reform-
minded behaviour in August.   As a result political
tension was stoked up and the economic disaster was
aggravated.   Whereas Ascherson explains this situation in terms of divisions within the party stemming
from 'the muddles produced by Olszowski's control
of many party levers and Kania's support in the CC'
and irresponsible anti-Solidarity activities by
local officials, I take a somewhat different view.

The collapse

Firstly, as we shall see, the CC membership knew that it would be held collectively responsible for the mistakes of the Gierek period; its composition would have to be changed drastically as part of the process of calming social indignation and of making a clean start. The timing of the calling of an Extraordinary PZPR Congress to do this and to produce personnel whose credibility would not be undermined by having been in office during the mid to late 1970s therefore became a key factor in the political equation. The old CC, right from the outset, was bound to be highly conditional in its loyalty to a full renewal programme and to Kania's apparent commitment to it. Although quiescent in September through fear of revolutionary tumbrils and Hungarian 1956 type lampposts and undercut by the reform dynamism of the October Sixth Plenum, it made a comeback in November. Its support, although wavering and divided, if anything then went in Olszowski's and Grabski's direction. Secondly, the political deal struck at Gdańsk, Szczecin and Jastrzębie was a very ambiguous one on both sides. The Communist leadership had, both for Soviet bloc reasons and the linked factor of its hegemonic role, accepted them only as long as the following premises were accepted. Independent TUs would have to be purely economic, not political, in their activity and they would have to be organised on a factory or, at most, industry wide basis. The possibility of the emergence of Solidarity as a massive national catch-all blanket organisation was something which the PZPR leaders had preferred not to think about in late August. The presence of outside advisers and KOR activists, not to mention KPN ones, was also something which they were not willing to tolerate in the long run. The more pragmatic leaders, however, realised that some time, perhaps even years, might elapse before the party would be able to move against such undesirable forces and expel them from the factories. So at the very top a division of labour did perhaps emerge, symbolised by Olszowski and Kania. One should not, however, underestimate the unity of the Communist élite in their basic perception that, while massive reforms and democratisation at local levels (such as factories and Universities), the bottom communal level of local government and social bodies (such as housing and other co-operatives) was possible, and some even thinking on Gierek's early 1970s lines even thought desirable, there was no possibility of accepting Solidarity in the shape which it emerged in September. The USSR and Poland's hardline neighbours, Czechoslovakia and the

GDR, would not accept this because of fear of ideological contamination and the encouragement which
this would give to their own dissidents and reform
Communist factions.   Very few Polish Communist
leaders actually accepted the need for such a
guarantee of democratisation in such a form as it
ran contrary to all their Leninist principles and interests.   The internal Communist debate was hence-
forth to be dominated largely by the following arguments.   Firstly, how could the PZPR renew itself
in order to calm society and to become an effective
political force again?   Secondly, was the question
of the speed and the extent to which this rejuvenated
party should block Solidarity demands for power sharing
and its efforts to dismantle the neo-Stalinist system
of political and economic control and of the administrative, police, judicial and censorship apparats
which underpinned it?   It was also appreciated that
Solidarity was bound to champion the whole mess of
local and social grievances which inevitably surfaced once the political centre had been weakened
and discredited and once the strike weapon had
become an everyday form of pressure upon the local
and factory administrations.

The attempt to produce a new reformed and democratised political framework safeguarding a rejuvenated PZPR's leading role was bound to be a difficult and delicate exercise calling for much political
judgement and restraint on all sides.   In my view,
this was the best that could be achieved so I make
no apology for ignoring the more radical programmes
outside the Marxist-Leninist framework.   My enterprise will be to show the detailed steps by which
Poland failed to institutionalise the 'historic
compromise' between Polish society and the Communist
state which was hoped for in August 1980.   My final
premise is therefore that, although dedicated
adherents of the Soviet model and a variety of hardliners existed in some numbers in Poland, the
essential modicum of goodwill towards reform and
democratisation, as stated above on PZPR terms,
also existed both within the general Communist élite
and especially among its ordinary membership.   It
also dominated the intellectual and professional
classes who, however quarrelsome and divided they
might have been on details, were one of the basic
supports of the Communist system despite their dis-
like for the narrow rigidity of traditional CPA
methods of rule.   I am therefore not convinced that
the PZPR leaders adopted a politique de pire from
the outset;   that is, that they attempted to destabilise the post-Gierek system and to aggravate the

economic morass to such an extent that Soviet intervention or a domestically applied State of War would
become necessary.

With hindsight one can blame or praise Kania
for being such a trimmer, with the consequences which
followed, according to one's ideological commitments.
Western socialists hoping for a democratised socialist system with a decentralised state and economy
and self-managing factories controlled by free TUs
are justified in blaming Kania for his failure to
profit from the demoralisation of the PZPR apparat
in September-October 1980. He could then have
placed himself at the head of the party and social
reform movement and called the Extraordinary Congress within a few weeks of Gdańsk in order to clear
out the leaders and officials of the Gierek period
and to produce a Politburo and CC genuinely committed to reform. But it is clear that this is not
what Kania and his Soviet allies wanted. The pressure for reform had come from society and was to
affect the grassroots rather than the top levels
of the party, as had occurred in Czechoslovakia in
1966-1968.

What the PZPR leaders really thought and wanted
was very revealingly expressed by Żabiński in early
1981 in a briefing for his top security men in
Silesia which the local Solidarity acquired and reproduced [30]. Żabiński, of course, spoke in a
simple and brutal way because of his audience but
the gist of what he said undoubtedly conveyed the
gut feeling of the CPA. He made it clear that the
PZPR leaders had been overwhelmed and only thought
of survival in August 1980: 'The aim was to quench
the strikes, calm the nation and consider the situation later'. The problem, which he freely admitted,
was that the working class supported the class enemy
and its slogans of free TUs because Gierek had
neglected the social goals of socialism. PZPR
tactics should now be to reduce KOR and clergy influence in Solidarity and to increase that of the
party, to corrupt the Solidarity leaders by giving
them a taste of power and privilege and, above all,
to break up the national character of the movement
by playing upon the splits between different types
of workers. Żabiński envisaged a subtle and long
term political struggle, stretching out over many
years, leading to a party controlled unification of
the union movement, although he conceded that free
TUs at factory level might be acceptable.

Kania played a very quiet back seat role during
September and did not once appear on radio or TV to
address the nation. He left all the running to

Premier Pińkowski, who announced package after package of reforms stemming from the Social Agreements.
Throughout September the PZPR was in a state of total
disarray, while its shell-shocked leadership only
reacted passively to the important social developments before the October Plenum.   Firstly, the organisation of free TUs, especially Solidarity,
spread all over Poland at a great rate.   Secondly,
the Workers' Upsurge in the factories acted as a
catalyst and spread to all the other stratas in
society, beginning with the students, intellectuals
and Universities and going through the white and then
blue collar professions to the peasants.   Thirdly,
the normally passive and manipulated ordinary mass
membership of the PZPR also caught the contagion
and became a major force in its own right.   Caught
in the crossfire between society's indignation with
the PZPR and the leadership's initial policy of in-
filtrating Solidarity with party members in order to
gain control, a substantial section, perhaps about
a third of all PZPR members notably among the workers, eventually joined Solidarity.   They did so
not to implement the leadership policy of entryism
but the better to join in the national process of
renewal.   Although many members left the party
the bulk of the remainder, unlike 1955-1957, stayed
on to await events.   Lastly, the collapse and discrediting of the old leadership disorientated and
paralysed the PZPR functionaries at all levels.
Most apparats waited to see which way the wind would
blow next.   Some long established functionaries,
knowing that their jobs were most at risk, refused
to go quietly and attempted to hold back the rising
tide in their bailiwicks.   Others, depending upon
their circumstances, hoped to catch the new currents
and to achieve promotion in the jobs to be vacated.
More rarely they genuinely came to realise that ac-
commodation with the workers was the best way out for
the party.
     The new leadership's first party task was to
meet and to attempt to rally the middle level apparats
and most committed militants.   This took place in
a string of meetings between the leaders and the
major provincial Executives between 9 and 22 September,
a dialogue which revealed the various responses to
the crisis within the party.   First of all Kania,
accompanied by Jagielski and Andrzej Jedynak, the
rising Minister of Heavy and Agricultural Machinery,
heard the reformist tones of the Gdańsk aktyw on 8
September.   The progressive KW First Secretary,
Tadeusz Fiszbach, told them that the party had been
right to agree to the Social Agreements.   It should

now join in the workers' debate over the causes and
consequences of the crisis in order to draw the
right conclusions. The workers considered that
past leaderships had failed to do so in 1956 and
1970. The new qualitative element was the maturity
of the working class whose protest, although expressed in a dramatic form, had not gone out of
control and had been resolved by a negotiated compromise (TL and Życie Warszawy, 9.9.80). The following day Kania heard Żabinski tell the Katowice
aktyw that the need was now for revised social
priorities and self-management. Kania very sensibly took a reserved line and again awaited what
was said to him, but he already began to set out the
themes which were to be developed at the October
Sixth Plenum. Poland had arrived at a new stage
of her development. After 36 years of building
socialism it had become 'not only a socio-economic
system but a state of national consciousness recognised by millions of Poles'. There was no alternative to the peaceful resolution of conflicts,
while the revised forms of the party's leading role
would be discussed at the renewed Sixth Plenum.
Kania defended the need for TU unity but admitted
quite bluntly that the party had only accepted free
TUs because this was what most factory workforces
wanted (TL, 10.9.80).
     The other leaders were as busy as Kania in
meeting the KW organisations to take stock of the
party after Gdańsk. Their message for the public
was that the Government would not be able to fulfil
the Agreements if strikes continued but they already
had to face the anger of the party militants.
Grassroots resentment at having to defend policies
and leaders whom they had long criticised intra
muros surfaced at the Warsaw City Plenum. There
was also much bad tempered discussion about how
accurate information could be ensured, how intra-
party and societal democracy could best be achieved
and how the party's leading role could be sharpened.
The counterpoise in Warsaw was provided by orthodox
Marxist-Leninists such as Eugeniusz Duraczyński, a
Second World War historian and PZPR Secretary in
the PAN cell. He stressed that anti-socialist
elements were not only acting outside the party but
also within its ranks. He wanted a purge of members
opposed to 'real socialism'. Duraczyński spoke
a year too early. In September 1980 the overwhelming call by PZPR militants was for the expulsion of
corrupt, opportunist and incompetent officials responsible for the mistakes of the Gierek era (TL,
13-14.9.80).

The collapse

All the foregoing activity was assessed at a
meeting of KW First Secretaries presided over by
Kania on 15 September.   The fateful decision was
then taken not to renew the Sixth Plenum until it
had been prepared more carefully and until the political situation had crystallised somewhat.   This
apparat fear of political spontaneity was to charac-
terise Kania's policy, especially in regard to the
holding of the congress.   In practice this meant
that the PZPR opted for its own restricted view of
reform, defined and controlled by itself, which meant
that little common ground except similar sounding
slogans was to exist between it and Solidarity.
The reality was, however, camouflaged by a meeting
of the FJN where its Chairman, Jabłoński, called for
national reconciliation and reiterated the popular
theme that there had been 'no victors or losers, only
Poland won' as a result of Gdańsk (TL, 16.9.80).
Relatively few leadership changes took place
within the PZPR between the two meetings of the Sixth
Plenum as the CPA was naturally preoccupied with
other problems.   Most notable was Grudzień's replacement as KW First Secretary in Katowice by Żabiński
on 19 September.   Jerzy Zasada, who had dominated
the political life of Poznań for the entire 1970s,
was also replaced the same day by Jerzy Kusiak, who
had been ambassador to Romania.   A few days later
three important CC Department Heads were appointed.
Józef Klasa, who had shown considerable liberalism
as KW First Secretary in Kraków (1971-1975), was
recalled from his political shelter as ambassador
to Mexico to oversee radio and TV and to counterpoise Olszowski, who was CC Secretary in that sector.
Walery Namiotkiewicz, Gomułka's erstwhile secretary,
went to Ideological Training and Kazimierz Rokoszewski,
another hardliner, ensconced himself in the important Cadres Department.   The other changes mainly
involved the mass media: Zdzisław Balicki, a relatively unknown journalist from Wrocław, taking over
the Radio and TV Committee, an Olszowski nominee
from the CC Press Department, Wiesław Bek, took over
the Editorship of Trybuna Ludu, while Barecki became
the Government press spokesman.
The first, and in fact only, major political
speech designed to rally the PZPR and to lift its
spirits came from Stefan Olszowski in Bydgoszcz on
19 September.   Doing his utmost to sound like a
real party chieftain, in contrast to the almost invisible Kania, Olszowski traced out many of the
policies required for the reform programme which the
PZPR was developing.   Olszowski condemned Gierek's
mistakes but very cleverly evaded responsibility for

them. He stressed that the Social Agreements laid
obligations on the workers as well as on the Government and promised an economic reform, the renewal
of the TU movement and the introduction of self-
management. He warned corrupt managers and officials that they could expect no mercy and concluded
with an appeal to the Poles' sense of political
realism. The Polish-Soviet alliance was 'the fundamental guarantee of the stability of our position
in the world' but Poland would only count to the
extent that the nation proved capable of resolving
its domestic problems (TL, 20-21.9.80).
        The above intra-party developments were, how-
ever, much less publicised and noticed than the work
of the Council of Ministers and a whole plethora of
committees which were set up at this time. Mixed
Government-Solidarity Commissions headed by
Barcikowski and Jedynak were set up to oversee the
implementation of the Gdańsk and Szczecin Agreements.
On 24 September Barcikowski, Kopeć and Jagielski met
Wałęsa and other Solidarity leaders in the Government offices to discuss problems arising out of the
Agreements. Later that day Wałęsa told Western
journalists that Solidarity did not want to run the
economy but only to check up on economic management
and to ensure that the Agreements were fulfilled.
A Committee on Economic Reform, chaired by Pińkowski
with Olszowski as his deputy and eventual successor,
started on its long slog on 17 September, which led
to the publication of its preliminary and much
criticised proposals in January 1981. A few days
later a 23-strong Mixed Government-Solidarity and
specialist committee was set up by Council of State
decree to draft the TU Bill under Sylwester Zawadzki's
chairmanship. On 25 September the Mixed Government-
Roman Catholic Church Commission met for the first
time in a decade. It had earlier been agreed to
transmit Sunday mass over the radio for the first
time since the war. To the public it seemed as
though the lawyers and the clerks had moved in to
produce the dry and practical formulas and uninspir-
ing compromises which are always necessary to turn
high ideals into reality.
        The issues in Polish politics were confused and
unclearly expressed in September as all sides tried
to find their bearings in the completely transformed
political landscape. The Planning Chairman, Kisiel,
estimated the costs of the Summer strikes, very con-
servatively, at about the equivalent of £500
million and that economic production in August had
fallen 10% in comparison to the previous August
(Polityka, 20.9.80). Government policy, though,

was changing investment priorities away from heavy
industry to the domestic and export markets and the
raw material, agricultural and food sectors, to
encourage light industry and to freeze investment
projects with long completion cycles (TL, 9.9.80).
Officials faced an important psychological block in
their efforts to explain to the Poles that the
economic situation was so bad that their rebellion
might bring political, social and even moral benefits but that protest against worsening economic
conditions was merely whistling in the wind; only
hard work and social and industrial peace for many
years to come could improve their lot.   On the
other hand, the average Pole aware of the increasing
food shortages and lengthening queues hastened to
off-load his zŁoties and to convert them into goods
as quickly as possible, thus worsening the general
retail situation.   At least three contradictory
responses emerged as the full facts of Poland's external debts and economic problems were revealed.
The first, both within the PZPR and society, was to
fuel the demands for the condign punishment of those
responsible.   Secondly, mainly among Solidarity
militants and their Western apologists, but also
among some party reformers, the idealistic feeling
developed that a burst of national unity and renewal
would release the pent-up energies of the Polish
people, who together would overcome any mere economic problems in no time at all [31].   Lastly, a
large number of Poles refused to accept that life
could cheat them in this unfair way.   They sought
simple explanations in terms of Soviet exploitation
and PZPR Machiavellianism and hoped that the West
would bail them out.   Many Poles found it impossible to break the lifelong habit of having a purely
extractive attitude towards the socialist provident
state and were disorientated by its failure.   Nevertheless there was no absence of prescient warnings
that 'the country stood on the brink of perhaps the
most dangerous economic, biological and political
catastrophe in its history' [32].

Solidarity emerges and Society joins in; the Wrong Turning?

The most fateful development in September which
dominated the course of Polish politics for the next
16 months was not, however, what was happening in
the party or what the Government was doing.   Cru-
cially the Workers' Upsurge and the Communist collapse at Gdańsk encouraged the spread of contestation among the whole range of other professional
and blue collar social groups in Poland.   The

working class protest was thus generalised into a
nationwide phenomenon.   It was for a while as though,
in Szczypiorski's words, 'the totalitarian structure
of power, the whole system of single party dictatorship, was falling like a pack of cards' [33].
The effective break-up of the CRZZ, the emasculation
of the official unions, which in general were left
as organisational husks which had lost the bulk of
their membership,and the emergence of Solidarity as
a massive force replicating the MKS 'Wybrzeże' experience on a national scale, therefore took place
under circumstances which went far beyond the Workers' Upsurge.   Putting the matter very schematically, Polish society escaped from the control of
the PZPR leadership and this included substantial
sections of its own party membership.   The traditional Polish 'counter community' was reborn in a
new shape and organised its national self-defence
organisation in Solidarity against the Communist
system.   But its aims were most unclear and contradictory except for the workers' autonomy programme, which had been hammered out through the
experience of the Summer.   The more coherent programmes of socialist reform or national revolution
attributed to it by self-interested politicians and
academics originally had little basis in fact.
The reality was that Poland entered on a 16 month
period of general protest and contestation of all
authority, similar in a much more extended way to
what France had undergone in May 1968 [34].   As in
the 18th century, the Poles formed a federation in
Solidarity and carried on what they so expressively
call a 'rokosz' or rebellion.   The process, as then,
was aggravated by the national tendency for individuals to blame each other and to 'settle accounts'
[35].
     The above explanation in terms of traditional
Polish political culture partly stems from the analysis of Jadwiga Staniszkis, whose ideas have had a
very significant influence on Western thinking on the
subject.   A fiercely intelligent sociologist, who
participated as an expert in the Gdańsk negotiations,
she had earlier made her name by gloomily forecast-
ing disruptive social trends.   Politically she was
in the grey interstices between KOR and the most
radical Communist intelligentsia [36].   Her abstract
sociological generalisations and theoretical propo-
sitions, expressed in opaque language which maintained
academic forms and distance, concealed a real ideological commitment to a politically motivated general
theory of the crisis facing Polish society and of
the need for its democratisation.   Her diagnosis

The collapse

was that 'corporatist techniques of protest-absorp-
tion deepened stratification' [37]. They were responsible for the economic crisis, social discontent
and the depoliticisation, corruption and bureaucratisation of the party, which in turn mobilised
both the workers and the party rank and file into the
great outbursts which began in the Summer of 1980.
So far one can agree that this is an interesting
partial view of one of the causes of the crisis,
particularly as economists like Brus had long presented the case for reform in the economic sphere
[38]; similarly, Waldemar Kuczyński had argued that
the socialist economy also needed rational and pre-
dictable 'rules of the game' which could only be
ensured by 'a real constitution' guaranteed by a
sovereign society [39]. What is more ideologically
based and unprovable is her assertion that the workers and party grassroots were motivated not so much
by straightforward economic discontent and anger
with local officials as by the desire for radical
structural changes. Equally controversial is her
argument that these pressures were kept in check by
the moderate Wałęsa Solidarity leadership as part
of the functioning of what popularly became known
as the 'Self-Limiting Revolution' after August
1980 [40].
     The above concept, although it conveys the ab-
sence of social support for the Soviet form of Communist rule in Poland, is, however, both self-serving and absurd: the former because it was thought
up by intellectuals and politicians who wanted to
dignify the national protest at the economic downturn and to use it to justify and to shield their
domestic reformist strategies; absurd because Soviet
power would not have restrained its recourse to repression for so long if the situation had been a
camouflaged equivalent of Hungary 1956 with Communist
power really breaking down. The picture of revolutionary lava being blown out of the Polish volcano
and being shovelled back into it by 'Self-Limiting'
mechanisms is an intellectually stimulating one
but, considered in retrospect, it has little heuris-
tic value. All labels are necessarily incomplete
parodies of the truth but the term 'Limited Revolution' is perhaps a sounder and apter one as it avoids
the former's value judgements.
     The Council of State laid down the procedure
by which new TUs were to be registered by the Provincial Court in Warsaw in a decree of 13 September.
Clause 4 empowered the Court to examine whether the
proposed NSZZ's statute 'was contrary to the PRL's
constitution and to other legal regulations' [41].

Disputes could be referred on appeal to the Supreme
Court but it was widely believed that such a procedure would enable the authorities to define what was
anti-constitutional;   in this way they could limit
the organisation of what they might consider hostile
forces.   The first dozen or so NSZZs registered by
the Warsaw Court were mainly official controlled
branch unions in new dress who had applied some cosmetics but were still run by the same people.   However, all over Poland independent workers' representatives were meeting to replace official nominees,
to change the statute of their official union and to
apply for registration as an NSZZ [42].

The main September developments were the emergence of Solidarity, its initial conflicts with the
régime, the continuation of massive industrial unrest
all over Poland and the mobilisation of intellectual
and professional circles.   Taking the organisation
of Solidarity first, one is stuck by the incredible
speed of its emergence.   By mid September about 85%
of the Trójmiasto workers had joined NSZZs and the
incipient Solidarity set up its HQ in the Hotel
Morski.   The Mazowsze NSZZ was formed on similar
lines in Warsaw and elected Zbigniew Bujak from
Ursus as its Chairman [43].   The birth of NSZZs
representing industrial groups such as dockers,
printers and steel workers encouraged teachers, journalists and film and theatre people to think on similar lines.

The signing of the Gdańsk, Szczecin and
Jastrzębie Agreements only brought industrial peace
to the regions concerned.   Unrest spread to other
industrial centres in spite of the Government declarations that the Baltic and Silesian concessions
applied to the whole country.   The most serious and
symptomatic was perhaps a strike involving 18,000
workers in the Mielec aviation factory.   KW First
Secretary, Leon Kotarba, was reported as saying that
'there is no place in Mielec for TUs not controlled
by the CP' (Dziennik Polski, 10.9.80).   Rumours that
Kotarba was planning a loyalty oath binding workers
to the official unions aggravated the situation.
They led to 45 demands being tabled by the strikers
demanding Kotarba's resignation as well as those of
70 departmental heads in the factory, a pattern
which was to be repeated very often during the following 6 months.   Other demands were for religious
instruction in schools and the broadcasting of mass
over the radio.

Local workplace developments provided the pressure for national ones and for the organisation of
Solidarity as a national movement.   270 delegates

from 31 industrial towns met in Gdańsk from 17
September onwards to found the National Committee of
Free Trade Unions (NKK-WZZ) and to pass a model
statute [44]. Developments moved so fast that by
the time of the Second Delegates' Conference on 23rd
the 40 free TUs, on paper at least, represented 5
million workers. Here the really fateful decision
was taken to form a countrywide NSZZ called Solidarity
whose statute was now confirmed. Wałęsa headed a
30-strong delegation to have it registered in Warsaw.
    After handing over the registration document
to the Warsaw Court, Wałęsa had an unsatisfactory
conversation with Jagielski on 25 September.
Solidarity therefore decided to call a one hour warning strike on 3 October. The Government was given
until 10 October to show why Solidarity should not
proceed on to a general strike. The Communist
leadership, however, took a contrary tack and
through Barcikowski on 30 September accused Solidarity
of wanting 'to maintain social tension and to push
the country into chaos' (TL, 1.10.80). The stage
was thus set for the Registration Crisis, which will
be examined in the next chapter, and which was to
rumble on until mid November.
    Working class developments sparked off similar
trends among the intellectuals and all from PAN
academics to students demanded independent unions.
As usual in Communist reform periods picturesque
figures emerged voicing strong views in striking
language, such as Stefan Bratkowski. He wanted
the PZPR Congress to be convened immediately in
order to resolve the political situation in both party
and country. He considered that the party under
Gierek had patronised 'thieves and embezzlers'.
It had been ruled by an oligarchy while the ordinary
members had been treated as vassals. The PZPR
should become a democratic organisation and not
just 'an association for the defence of the mistakes
of the leadership', working on the principle of
'every 5 years a congress and every 10 a catastrophe'
(Dziennik Polski, 15.9.80). The ZLP had already
on 9 September, even under Jerzy Putrament's conservative chairmanship, called for the abolition of
the so-called 'Black List' of writers, the limiting
of censorship and the establishment of an independent Cultural Council to oversee Poland's cultural
life [45].

The PZPR Membership parts company with its Leaders
    If Poland seemed to be in a state of general
crisis it was because once the power of the PZPR
central leadership weakened a whole series of diverse,

unconnected and often competing pressures and grievances broke through to the surface. Szczypiorski's
analysis that 'the mono-party was paying now not
only for the last 10 years of Gierek's dictatorship
but for all the periods of the party's domination'
was more justified than his romantic view of the
unparalleled moral unity which he, and so many Western commentators, claimed to discern [46]. But,
irrespective of the correct sequence between cause
and effect, once the lid had been taken off Polish
society almost every social group presented its
grievances and attempted to assert itself in a way
which involved the symbolic defeat and humiliation
of the authorities. The process started in July-
August with the workers, while September saw similar
movements among the intellectual and white collar
classes. Above all, what are colloquially known
as the PZPR doły (literally lower depths), the outer
circle of about 2½ million or so ordinary members,
also started to move. These were the grassroots
of the party who were not in the magic circle of the
half million or so PZPR leaders, full-time functionaries, individuals holding office as a result of
party patronage, backed up by the most committed
militants who together composed the PZPR aktyws who
were the de facto rulers of Poland at every level.
     The attempt to capture the NSZZs through a
policy of party entryism, if ever it were a calculated policy, had clearly failed by the time
Solidarity emerged formally but by then it was too
late to reverse the trend. In spite of the statutory banning of party officials from Solidarity
committees about a third, and certainly no less than
a quarter, of the PZPR's membership eventually joined
Solidarity. At peak it comprised no less than a
tenth of its total membership and was highly influential in such places as Silesia. The doły, largely
workers, however, joined Solidarity for very different reasons from those expected by the PZPR
leadership. Yet another formidable disintegrative
element was added to the continuing dissolution
of the Communist system.
     In August-September 1980 the collapse of the
authority of the CPA and its equivalents at provincial, municipal and factory level meant that the
ordinary party members in their POPs were left
without instructions or clear rallying points.
Contrary to popular Western belief, criticisms and
discontents were often expressed at POP level during
the 1970s. This had little political effect, however. The POP Secretaries and the lowest level
party functionaries who directed their work were

able to screen and select the inputs which were
allowed to go up the vertical levels of the party
hierarchy according to their perception and appraisal
of the instructions which filtered down to them from
the top leadership. It was not so much that the
grassroots membership was manipulated as that it
was cut off from any influence on decision-making
according to mechanisms which are more obviously dis-
cernible in CPs in West European democracies,and
which have been most tellingly elucidated by Annie
Kriegel in her study of the pre Union of the Left
French CP [47]. On the other hand, although,like
everyone else in Poland, the do$\not{l}$y were allowed to
grumble, to criticise lower level officials and to
make extravagant proposals for Poland's further development in their cells, they were also placed in
a false position; they had to defend Gierek's
obvious failures in their workplaces and were enjoined to attempt to convince their colleagues of
matters which they often knew to be manifestly false.
Such a dilemma was described in a very graphic report
of why a skilled lathe operator from Opole, called
Albin Terka, had decided to leave the PZPR (Polityka,
4.10.80). Terka had defended Gierek's policies in
front of his factory colleagues, although he had
spoken out in his POP. He now wanted to know why
he had been ignored and what mechanisms had 'caused
party life to function separately here at the grassroots' from the leadership's decisions. Sentiments
such as Terka's animated the vast mass of PZPR membership who, after much wavering, unlike him, decided
to continue as activists within the party and often
within Solidarity as well. The criticism of manipulation by an irresponsible, if not incompetent
and corrupt, political leadership was soon to form
the basis for the groundswell of demands for inner
party democracy - open discussion, reliable information, the genuine election and rotation of party
officers, the separation of party and state office
holding and a host of similar suggestions - which
Kania accepted as recevable at the October Plenum.
     The economic downturn after 1976 showed the
dangers of Gierek's party recruitment policies,
which in some respects had made the PZPR the party
of the new social and professional élites.   In the
early 1970s Gierek purged much of the working class
membership recruited by Gomu$\not{l}$ka.   He replaced it
with a younger, more skilled, better educated, less
ideologically motivated and more consumer orientated
generation.   He hoped that it would have the com-
petence as well as the personal standing to extend
PZPR influence in its workplaces.   The paradox was

that their general support for the socialist system,
and even for the pattern of inequalities fostered
by Gierek, became less important in 1980 than their
specific extractive discontents with a system which,
after 1976, failed to satisfy their expectations of
further consumer prosperity and ever expanding
promotion prospects.   This is a partial explanation
of why they did not want a revolution but why they
behaved in a revolutionary manner in Summer 1980.
They desired a profound overhaul of the system which
had disappointed their expectations and the punishment of those who had benefited from traditional
methods of Communist corruption.   All this explains
why such rank and file PZPR members, especially
industrial workers, found little difficulty in
August-September 1980 in establishing common ground
with their non-party colleagues against the class
of political and managerial incumbents [48].   The
theory of the 'non-antagonistic antagonisms' stemming from the conflict between the proletariat's roles
as a ruling and as a working class was developed;
this explains the bureaucratisation of the party state,
the étatisation of the TUs and the consequent deformation of the class character of the system [49].
     Kolankiewicz has argued that Gierek's 'selective
incorporation' of a key section of the working class
in the 200 odd largest factories, which after the
WOG reforms were in direct contact with the CC Secretariat, ensured that 'every factory would become
a fortress' but of a concentrated and increasingly
class conscious working class,not of the leadership
as Gierek had intended [50].   The additional incorporation of skilled workers in the party also proved
another stick for Gierek's back.   The former were
a potential leadership core against the official TUs,
while the latter, as in the case of Terka, proved
psychologically dissatisfied with formal office
holding or status without real power.   Not all
could be bought off with occasional benefits and
boosts to their personal vanity.   In a simple-
minded sort of way they came to feel that there was
nothing wrong with Gierek's slogans, particularly
his 1971 ones, except his failure to implement them.
The puppet shows and façade politics of the Gierek
system should be replaced by a real and genuine implementation of socialist values in order to break
down the dichotomy, what Wajda called the 'moral
schizophrenia', between personal and public life
which the politically realist generations had accepted until about 1968.   This reaction was not uniform,
though, among the professional classes who belonged
to the PZPR where one often found a sophisticated

awareness of the realities of Communist politics in Eastern Europe. This was linked with an instinct for self-preservation, which translated itself in a form of political _attentisme_ and of going along with prevailing trends as often as the more striking individual examples of passionate commitment to the post-Gdańsk reforms.

One needs to conclude this chapter with a quick look at the international dimension of these Polish events. The Western reaction was uniformly favourable, especially on the level of public opinion. This was shown in AFL-CIO financial aid for Solidarity and a $670,000 American loan for foodstuffs. The Soviet reaction to the emergence of autonomous social organisations and Solidarity, which threatened the PZPR's hegemony, was initially very restrained in public. The Kremlin leaders knew that their main task, once they had swallowed the tactical need for the Gdańsk Agreement, was to shore up Kania's leadership in order to allow him and the PZPR CPA to weather the immediate social storms. They therefore granted Poland a 10 year credit worth $260 million as a result of Jagielski's Moscow visit of 11 September. The Kremlin then took stock of the situation to see how social protest in Poland could first be contained, then weakened and divided and finally overcome. One can presume from the course of events that Kania and his Politburo colleagues had no objection to this and did not for one moment consider the alternative policy of using the social effervescence to liberate themselves from Soviet control. The social upheaval had been so massive that the Polish CPA, having been pushed back into its political bunker, was not inclined to take any major risk that might lose it Soviet protection. It therefore banked everything on surviving and on using its own domestic political and other resources to save its system and its rule.

Notes

1. SSS, VIIth Sejm, 29th sitting of 28 February 1980, for Jaroszewicz's resignation and Babiuch's acceptance speeches.
2. VIII Zjazd PZPR, 11-15 lutego 1980r. Podstawowe dokumenty i materiały (Warsaw, KiW, 1980).
3. On the full parameters of the causes and character of the economic crisis, see the magisterial analysis by D.M. Nuti, 'The Polish Crisis; Economic Factors and Constraints' in The Socialist Register, 1981 (London, Merlin Press, 1981).

4. SSS,VIIIth Sejm, 4th sitting of 23 June 1980. See
    Contemporary Poland, XIV, No. 13 (July 1980, pp. 21-31;
    Chęcinski, Polityka, 26.6.80.
5. 'To co najwazniejsze', Nowe Drogi (July 1980), pp.28-35.
6. Nuti, 'Polish crisis', p. 123.
7. For a participant's account of the Ursus strike, ICPA
    News Bulletin, 12.8.80, pp. 4-5.
8. Nowe Drogi (September 1980), p. 18.
9. 'For Polish strike facts, dial KOR', Sunday Times,
    10.8.80. For the KOR statement of 8 August, ICPA
    News Bulletin, 12.8.80, pp. 2-4.
10. Cf. J. Reynolds, 'Communists, Socialists and Workers.
    Poland, 1944-1948', Soviet Studies, XXX (October 1978),
    pp. 516-539.
11. S. Ehrlich, 'Rebelia w systemie i praworządności',
    Kultura, 29.3.81.
12. See W. Giełzyński & L. Stefański, Gdańsk. Sierpień 80
    (Warsaw, KiW, 1981). N. Ascherson, The Polish August
    (London, Penguin, 1981), Chapter 5. M. Dobbs, 'Inside
    the Lenin Shipyard', Sunday Times, 17.8.80. J-Y. Potel,
    The Summer before the Frost (London, Pluto Press, 1982).
13. Ascherson, Polish August, p. 150.
14. On the role of these experts and her account of Gdańsk
    events, J. Staniszkis, 'The evolution of forms of work-
    ing-class protest in Poland; sociological reflections
    on the Gdańsk-Szczecin case, August 1980', Soviet Studies,
    XXXIII, No. 2 (April 1981), pp. 204-231.
15. See P. Raina, Independent Social Movements in Poland
    (London, Orbis Books, 1981), Chapter 19. Ascherson,
    Polish August, pp. 145-177. Giełżyński & Stefański,
    Gdańsk. Sierpień 80, op. cit. Consult the 'Calendar
    of Strike Events' in Kultura (Paris, October 1980),
    pp. 66-75.
16. Biuletyn Solidarność, No. 2, 24.8.80.
17. 'Informacja Tow. Stanisława Kani ', Nowe Drogi
    (September 1980), pp. 18-22.
18. Ibid., pp. 23-64.
19. The official Polish version of the 3 Social Agreements
    is Protokóły porozumień Gdańsk, Szczecin, Jastrzębie ...
    (Warsaw, KAW, 1981). The Gdańsk and Szczecin Agree-
    ments appeared in Życie Warszawy, 2.9.80. English
    translations can be found in Ascherson, Polish August,
    pp. 280-295, and Contemporary Poland (November-December
    1980), pp. 86-99.
20. J.B. Weydenthal, 'Workers and Party in Poland', Problems
    of Communism, XXIX, No. 6 (November-December 1980, p.12.
21. 'Stanowisko komisji rządowej wobec postulatów strajkujących
    załóg Gdańskich', TL, 28.8.80.
22. Nowe Drogi (September 1980), p. 65.
23. Kultura (Paris, October 1980), p. 156; English trans.
    of sermon, Contemporary Poland (September-October 1980),
    pp. 77-85.

24. Text in TL, 4.9.80; Contemporary Poland (September-October 1980), pp. 100-104.
25. 'Profile of Stanisław Kania', Sunday Times, 7.9.80.
26. Kultura (Paris, October 1980), p. 154.
27. Nowe Drogi (September 1980), pp. 69-73; English text in Contemporary Poland (September-October 1980),pp.52-56.
28. SSS, VIIIth Sejm, 5th sitting of 5.9.80. Pińkowski, cols. 8-26; Żabiński, cols. 27-31; Szczepański, cols. 49-54; Małcużyński, cols. 80-86; Zawadzki, cols.107-111.
29. Ascherson, Polish August, p. 185.
30. Wolny Związkowiec, 5.3.81, published in Dąbrowa Górnicza. Reproduced in ICPA News Bulletin, 17.4.81.
31. For a typical paen of praise to the realism, flexibility and wisdom of the Poles in achieving the Social Agreements, see B. Dróżdż, Życie Warszawy, 2.10.80.
32. Witold Bardzki, 'Nowy list z Warszawy', Kultura (Paris, September 1980), p. 63.
33. A. Szczypiorski, The Polish Ordeal (London, Croom Helm, 1982), p. 119.
34. Cf. B. Brown, Protest in Paris. Anatomy of a Revolt (Morristown, NJ, General Learning Press, 1974).
35. The theme was developed by Krzystof Teodor Toeplitz, 'Od sloganów do konkretów', Polityka, 13.11.82.
36. A role which gained a fierce attack on her after the imposition of the State of War; A. Pawłowska, 'Władza nie znajduje się na ulicy', TL, 13-14.3.82.
37. Staniszkis, 'Evolution of forms ...', op. cit., p. 230.
38. W. Brus, Economics and Politics of Socialism (London, Routledge & Kegan Paul, 1973).
39. W. Kuczyński, 'Planning and economic reforms under socialism', Soviet Studies, XXXI, No. 4 (October 1979), pp. 505-522.
40. See her interview,'Samoograniczająca rewolucja', Kultura, 22.3.81.
41. TL, 15.9.80; English text, Contemporary Poland (September-October 1980), pp. 105-106.
42. For a description of what this meant at grassroots' level in Lublin, ICPA News Bulletin, 3.10.80, pp. 2-3.
43. On the birth of Mazowsze and other NSZZs, see ICPA Information Bulletins, 1.10.80.
44. Free TU sources claimed that over 3 million people in 3,500 factories either had, or wanted to, join the NSZZ. ICPA News Bulletin, 3.10.80, p. 5.
45. ZLP declaration in Tygodnik Powszechny, 21.9.80.
46. Szczypiorski, Polish Ordeal, p. 118.
47. A. Kriegel, The French Communists. Profile of a People (Chicago UP, 1972). For an official view on POPs, see J. Wacławek, Podstawowa Organizacja PZPR (Warsaw, KiW,1976).
48. Mieczysław Krajewski, 'Nowe doświadczenia, nowe treści', Literatura, 18.9.80.
49. 'Motory i Hamulce', Życie Warszawy, 23.9.80.
50. G. Kolankiewicz, 'Bureaucratised political participation and its consequences in Poland',Politics,I,No.1 (Apr.81).p.3

Chapter Four

COMMUNIST POWER-STRUGGLE AND SOCIAL CONFLICTS
(OCTOBER 1980-FEBRUARY 1981)

Poland had since 1956 been a very pluralist and
idiosyncratic Communist system because of the roles
conceded to the Roman Catholic Church, the private
peasantry who dominated agriculture and the intellectuals whose lively disputes and contestation
humanised Marxism-Leninism and gave it a more open,
more Western, more defensive and more Polish form.
The workers'uprisings of December 1970, July 1976
and Summer 1980 now suggested that a fresh type of
pluralism, that of independent and self-managing
workers' organisations, would have to be accommodated
within the post-August system if stability were to
be achieved.   The Marxist-Leninist hard-core in
Poland and their Soviet backers might have accepted
'free trades unions' and workers' councils if they
had become purely economic bodies eschewing political
ambitions and if, above all, they had been organised
on a factory or, at most, industry-wide basis.
But Solidarity developed very rapidly into a nationwide organisation with a frighteningly large potential
membership of almost half the adult population.
Its broad 'umbrella' character inevitably meant that
various KOR, KPN, KIK and other elements who wanted
to transform the political system radically also
would work and become influential within it.   The
PZPR central aktyw had not foreseen, or perhaps had
preferred not to think about, such a frightening
outcome in August.   By the time this became
clearer in late September the political dam had
broken irrevocably and the PZPR leadership could
merely attempt such holding operations as the attempt
to reshape Solidarity through its control of the
process of legal registration.   The fact was that
the acceptance of the sort of Solidarity which was
emerging from September onwards would also have
implied that the PZPR would have to transform itself
internally in a more democratic direction and

function within a pluralist system on the lines
envisaged by the more Eurocommunist CPs, such as
the Italian or the Spanish.   In utopian terms of
socialist development this was viewed by many as a
highly desirable development.   The political
reality, however, was that this would almost
certainly have led to an unstable type of power-
sharing which very probably would have led to the
erosion of the PZPR's hegemony and its eventual
replacement by a Finnish-type of democracy.   The CP
would become only one political force among many,
and not the directing force in domestic politics,
although the USSR would have considerable say in
this sphere and even more on the country's external
relations.
     The Polish Communist power-realists did not for
one moment believe that the Democratic Movement's
conception that Polish society would self-limit
itself if the party would move from monopoly rule to
a form of lesser domination was feasible or even
sincerely meant.   They considered that such a
process would inevitably produce either anarchy or
a national insurrection and that, at best, it was
merely a trick to squeeze them out of power and to
dismantle the instruments of their rule.   Quite
apart from these considerations there was a crucial
external factor.   Would the Kremlin accept such a
dramatic change in the post-Second World War Yalta
settlement?   If so, could new forces be found
within Poland to support and work the new order and
to satisfy the opposing requirements of Polish
society and Soviet power?   Everything about Poland's
history and present political culture suggested that
the installation and maintenance of such delicate
balances and finely tuned political mechanisms
demanded a tradition of self-restraint and political
compromise which would be quite beyond the Poles.
Quite apart from this, the economic collapse and
consumer war of all against all of 1980-1981 was a
fearsome joker in the pack which, in my judgement,
rendered highly unlikely the achievement of common
ground and peaceful, negotiated intra-system
compromises between the pragmatic conciliators in
both the Solidarity and the Communist camps.   The
optimistic view that only such a Social Contract
could contain the eruption of mass popular economic
discontent by directing attention to the political
and social sectors, where something could be
achieved in the short and medium term, was an
attractive western-liberal and reform-socialist
abstraction, but always likely to be proved utopian
by the hard realities of Communist power-politics

in the Soviet-dominated sphere of Eastern Europe.
    From the beginning of the Polish crisis in
Summer 1980 to the closing of this chapter in
Poland's history by the declaration of the State of
War in December 1981, Western analysis of the subject,
especially in the mass media, was dominated by
speculation about direct Soviet or Warsaw Pact
military intervention, as occurred in Czechoslovakia
in 1968.   In the event this proved a red herring as
we now know that the local representatives of the
Warsaw Pact in Poland, the Polish Army and their
supporting police forces, proved quite sufficient
and reliable enough at the end of the day to carry
out such an operation on their own.   Prior to this
the emergence of Solidarity and a series of nail-
biting confrontations between it and the régime,
as well as the dramatic extent to which the PZPR
grassroots and other organisations assumed an
independent life of their own, all had seemed to
suggest that the spread of pluralism and the
diminution of the PZPR's hegemony was inevitable.
Much of this period was dominated,however, by the
consequences of great governmental weakness and
this blurred the crucial fact that the key to
Poland's evolution still lay with the top échelons
of the PZPR leadership aktyw and their ability to
renew themselves and to ride out the political storm.
As the use of force had been shelved in August the
Kremlin, together with Kania, evolved a policy of
gaining time; of taking the sting out of the August
developments by appearing to accept the validity of
the workers' critique and by promising reform.   It
was the Kremlin's confidence in Kania's capacity to
implement such a policy that led them to support
him unreservedly, at first.   They nevertheless
applied military and political pressure and economic
inducements when appropriate, and maintained their
ideological condemnation of the Polish heresy in
order to dampen down similar stirrings within their
bloc.   One should also add that many uncommitted
Poles, and even the more intelligent Solidarity
supporters, always considered that the PZPR's
internal evolution was the crucial factor in saving
Poland from Soviet tanks or complete social and
economic chaos.
    The power-struggle which centred around the
Polish Question after August 1980 was therefore an
extremely complicated four-sided one, particularly
as none of the forces in play was itself monolithic.
The Soviet leadership wanted to achieve political
stability in Poland but was determined to minimise
the economic and military costs involved and the

repercussions on the rest of the socialist world.
The great conundrum was whether, and at what point,
they might consider some reform in Poland to be an
unacceptable, because irreversible, dilution of the
principles of Leninist rule within their sphere of
control.   The PZPR naturally wished to maintain
its hegemony but its more intelligent and pragmatic
members realised that much of the compromised Gierek
élite would have to be sacrificed, that considerable
structural reform in the economy was essential and
that a modus vivendi with Solidarity and the post-
August realities would have to be achieved in the
short run.   On the other hand, they hardly needed
Soviet encouragement to strengthen their determination to prevent the piecemeal dismantling of the
essential props of Communist rule in Poland, the
central and provincial PZPR apparats, the police,
the Judiciary, the Army and the mass media [1].   As
long as the central core remained solid they knew
that the CPSU would back them and that the new
uncompromised directing personnel at every level
would constitute a powerful force which in its own
self-interest would attempt to erode the area of
pluralism which had been conceded in August.   The
third major force was Solidarity, which claimed a
formidable figure of ten million supporters by
December 1980.   It was, however, bound to reflect
the various centripetal and conflicting pressures of
its diverse membership.   It was also always torn
between those who, like Wałęsa, favoured a gradualist
policy of establishing themselves and co-existing with
the system by concentrating on largely economic
demands, and those who wanted to confront the régime
in order to institutionalise and safeguard Solidarity
by forcing the PZPR to accept it in its post-September
form.   This difference over tactics also reflected
the basic clash of orientation between the 'Free
Trade Unionists' and the various nationalist, Catholic
and reform-socialist political trends which now became
incorporated within Solidarity.   Lastly, the Roman
Catholic Church and Polish society generally may
have seemed to play more passive political roles
but the former's mediation between régime and
Solidarity was important, while the recurring
outbursts of spontaneous and uncontrollable
discontent and protest by society could never be
underestimated by both the PZPR and Solidarity
leaderships.

The PZPR promises Reform and Leadership Change
      The resumption of the Sixth Plenum was postponed
until 4-6 October because of Politburo divisions and

the disquiet of the provincial party apparats who
were now caught in the eye of the storm. Kania's
line, supported most strongly by Barcikowski and
Jagielski, was to announce a reform programme in
order to regain the political initiative for the
PZPR and to pacify Polish society by fulfilling the
more practicable parts of the Social Agreements.
This was opposed behind closed doors by Olszowski,
who set himself up as the apparat spokesman. The
pogrobowcy (pall-bearers) of the Gierek régime, such
as Waszczuk, Wojtaszek, Kowalczyk and Karkoszka,
who had acquiesced in Kania's elevation, now also
held back reform moves if only because these implied
a drastic renewal of leadership personnel which put
them most at risk. They mounted initiatives
designed to stem the organisation and spread of
Solidarity. The result was numerous confrontations
starting with the Registration Crisis of October-
November 1980, the Narożniak affair in Warsaw in
late November, the 'free Saturdays' controversy in
January 1981, a whole list of local outbursts, some
of which had significant national repercussions,
such as Częstochowa in mid-November and the massive
regional confrontations in January, of which Bielsko-
Biaƚa, Jelenia Góra and Łódź were only the most
extensive. Although these crises eventually moved
the PZPR on to a more extensive purge of corrupt and
discredited officials of the Gierek period, to a high
rate of leadership change and to an apparent acceptance of full-scale reform and democratisation in
both Party and State by Spring 1981, one needs to
bear the following questions in mind in this chapter.
Why did it prove impossible for the PZPR to seize
the political initiative within two months of August
by calling an early Extraordinary Congress in order
to clear out the old CC and Politburo and to produce
a leadership which would have sufficient credibility
and commitment to reform to enable it to work with
Solidarity and to integrate it in the new system of
Communist rule? We now know that the Ninth Congress
was held too late in this respect. By then most of
the goodwill between the PZPR and Solidarity had
been exhausted and the economic disaster arguably
rendered rational and pluralist politics impossible.
So did Kania's failure to do so stem from
pusillanimity and a lack of nerve and political
vision? Or, more likely, did it reflect the fact
that the only guarantor of Communist rule in Poland
for the USSR and its hardline socialist allies,
Czechoslovakia and the GDR, remained the party apparat
whose personnel could be rejuvenated but which would
have to be preserved in essentials, as would the

Army and police?
    The period between the renewed Sixth and Eighth
Plena (early October 1980 to early February 1981) was
therefore dominated by three main strands. Firstly,
a bitter ideological and factional dispute took
place within the top PZPR levels over the speed at
which the Social Agreements should be fulfilled,
the extent to which Gierek's officials should be
dismissed and punished and the best strategy and
tactics for either limiting the spread of Solidarity
or of transforming and incorporating it in a workable
and acceptable manner within the system. Secondly,
the organisation and development of Solidarity, the
emergence of its leadership and its internal disputes,
is a fascinating subject in its own right which will
doubtless find its historians elsewhere. Thirdly,
the whole period was dominated by a whole series of
political and socio-economic conflicts, only some of
which were direct régime-Solidarity confrontations.
Many of them in November 1980, and again in a fuller
way in January 1981, were a whole range of regional
and sectional outbursts, partly caused by and partly
the cause of a massive weakness of central power.
    The renewed Sixth Plenum took place just after
the one hour Solidarity warning strike of 3 October
over its registration and ranks amongst the PZPR's
most important. Seventy CC members out of 252
spoke, while another 23 had their written contributions enrolled on the record in a process of
collective Communist soul-searching which was aptly
described as '48 hours of psychodrama' [2].
    Kania's keynote speech was his major programmatic
exposition, comparable in significance to Gomułka's
in October 1956 or Gierek's in February 1971. It
therefore merits detailed examination [3]. Kania
admitted that the PZPR was facing 'the gravest crisis
in the history of People's Poland' and that its main
task was to regain society's confidence. Poland
would remain socialist and a full member of the
socialist community not only for geopolitical reasons
but primarily because socialism in Poland was 'a
state of need for millions of people'. Kania's
hackneyed but important face-saving theme or, in my
view, alibi which opened up the way for the various
necessary reforms was that the workers' protest had
not been directed against socialism but against
distortions and mistaken policies.
    As to the causes of the crisis, Kania demolished
Gierek's economic policies most magisterially. The
1971 decisions in favour of accelerated economic
development and rising living standards were
undoubtedly popular and justified; but dreadful

mistakes occurred in their implementation, especially
in the overshooting of the Sixth Congress investment
targets by a third and in the voluntarist favouring
of large and economically irrational capital projects
such as the Huta Katowice steel-mill in Gierek's
Silesia (distant both from ports and Soviet supplies
of iron-ore). In the second half of the 1970s
agriculture was neglected, living standards were
allowed to rise more than justified by increasing
labour productivity and 'all reason was surpassed
in the country's indebtedness'. Excessive urbanisation, which shifted two million Poles from the
countryside during the 1970s, weakened its produc-
tive capacities and aggravated the housing, social
and consumption problems of the cities. Over-large
wage differentials developed as well as corruption,
economic speculation at all levels and an unhealthy
desire for hard currency fostered by PEWEX shops.
Planning mistakes were aggravated by the refusal to
listen to criticism and counter proposals and by the
stifling effect of 'the propaganda of success' blared
forth by the mass media. Gierek neglected an
economic reform in favour of the disastrous attempt
to balance the economy by raising prices. His
early success enabled him and Jaroszewicz to
establish and maintain an autocratic, arrogant and
closed style of leadership. This left much of the
CC and Politburo helpless in face 'of the faulty
style of mechanisms of action of Party and state
institutions', concluded Kania at his most obviously
self-serving.
Having polished off Gierek, Kania turned to the
key problem of Autumn 1980, about which he was much
less convincing: 'The guarantees, insuring us in
future against political, economic and social distortions and against crises ... We know that in
order to overcome the crisis we must pose and
resolve the problem of guarantees' [4]. In the
short term the difficult economic situation could be
alleviated by rationing, by increased imports of
foodstuffs and raw materials, especially from the
USSR, by drastic cuts in Government expenditure and
by reducing investment, although two-thirds of the
projects under construction could not be completed
in under three years. In the longer term an
'extensive reform of the system of directing and
managing the economy was essential'. Kania felt
that social self-management and the leading role of
the Party did not conflict but mutually supplemented
one another. The PZPR had accepted 'free trades
unions' because this is what the workers wanted but
primarily because Solidarity had promised to respect

the constitution, to accept the PZPR's leading role
and to work within the socialist order.   Kania
trotted out the standard clichés of all reform
periods, such as 1956 and 1971, about raising the
role of the Sejm and People's Councils, of Workers'
Self-Management Conferences (KSRs), of the allied
ZSL and SD parties and of the FJN, but he also
promised an educational reform and accurate information in the mass media.

Kania's more significant passage concerned the
return to Leninist principles in the internal democratic processes of the PZPR.   Proposals concerning
the secret election and rotation of party officers
at lower levels, the direct election of party
central leaders and the striking of a better balance
between Democracy and Centralism by defining the
duties of the Politburo, Secretariat and First
Secretary and the means by which the CC could
exercise effective control over them could be considered.   Communist officials who had misused their
offices for private gain in the last decade would
be investigated by NIK and the CKKP.   Party-state
relations should be guided by the maxim that 'the
party directs and the Government governs'.   The
principle which had been abused in the Gierek period
was that the party should take the strategic policy
decisions but not get submerged in administrative
and economic details.   Finally, Kania accepted the
need for an Extraordinary Congress but it should be
prepared very carefully.   He promised that the
leadership would decide the issue at the next plenum.

The vigorous and often bitter discussion which
then followed represented a collective letting off
of steam by the CC which had accumulated over the
previous decade.   The content of the contributions
is too varied and detailed to be more than just
sketched in here [5].   Firstly, there were strong
personal attacks on the previous leadership and
the policies.   Olszowski called for the removal
from the CC of all those responsible for the crisis
and for a 'concerted, united and efficacious' lead
in order to rally the bulk of the party militants
who were disorientated but who were not to blame
for the Gierek team's poor planning, excessive and
misapplied investment and rigging of party meetings.
Moczar, with his NIK files bulging with reports of
incompetence and corruption, argued that the party
could only go over to the offensive if it cleansed
itself at every level of 'dishonest and demoralised
and, occasionally, even corrupt elements'.   He was
perhaps best placed to know which individuals had
been compromised by association with the likes of

Kazimierz Tyrański, the director of the MINEX Trust, whose sensational trial was just beginning (Karkoszka,Glazur, Jerzy Olszowski).   Secondly, other individuals, such as Józef Tejchma, the ex-Minister of Culture,who had been sent into pleasant exile as ambassador to Switzerland after the Eighth Congress, analysed the reasons for the failure of Gierek's centralised mechanisms of rule.   Self-management in agricultural circles, in housing and other types of Co-operatives and in the trades unions and factories had become a fiction with the consequence that large sections of the population had become apathetic.   In intellectual life the directives for book publishing and the mass media had run counter to the desire of an educated and cultured society for co-decision by groups and individuals and for a balanced dialogue with the authorities based on a more truthful information policy.   Tejchma called for the CC to control the Politburo more effectively in future, for their respective powers and functions to be delineated by statute and for party officials to be elected and rotated.   Thirdly, the individuals under attack, notably Łukasiewicz, Grudzień and Wrzaszczyk, accepted in their autocritiques that they had made mistakes, but defended themselves manfully against being held wholly to blame for the crisis.

Personal apologias, although a significant development in Communist political practice, were, however, less important than the main debate at the plenum.   Although camouflaged, it was an argument between a reform group who genuinely, although with varying degrees of commitment, wanted to come to terms and to live with Solidarity and the post-August realities and those who wanted to curtail and even reverse what had happened.   Taking the latter group first, whose arguments were under-standably muted in public and which had to be read between the lines, especially as they covered them-selves by joining in the attack on Gierek as heartily as everybody else, one should note the following.   Romuald Jankowski, the new CRZZ Chair-man, accepted the mistakes of the old unions and the secessions from them, but he argued that a central federation would be necessary sooner or later.   Władysław Kruczek, his predecessor during the 1970s, called for a renewal of the official unions and claimed that he had always been excluded from Gierek's ruling circle within the Politburo. Jerzy Bielecki, the director of the Żerań car factory, accused the Mazowsze Solidarity of wanting to change the structure of People's Poland.   Kowalczyk, who

was about to lose his job as Minister of the
Interior, claimed that foreign intelligence networks
were attempting to convert the NSZZs into 'an anti-
socialist opposition'.   Werblan considered that all
the three great crises of 1956, 1970 and 1980 could
have been avoided if suitable policies had been
adopted in time.   In a very intelligent manner he
tried to steer the debate from the need for structural
reform of the system to that of correcting the mistakes of poor leaders and individuals [6].
     Although the plenum was fairly united in its
condemnation of Gierek's régime and his mistakes
and in its analysis of the causes of the crises an
important split in emphasis appeared at this time
between three very different types of reformers.
A small but growing core of committed reformers
found their spokesman in Tadeusz Fiszbach, the Gdańsk
KW First Secretary, who presented the fullest
exposition of the reform case.   The crisis, according
to his analysis, was so deep because there was a
universal demand for 'legal-political guarantees
safeguarding the functioning of the state from
deformations'.   The party would not overcome this
particular crisis through smooth declarations and
political cosmetics, as in the past.   The way out
was for the CC to work out 'a programme for the
democratisation of life as well as for allowing
society to participate in forming and controlling
the authorities, which would ensure a real approach
to socialist social justice in our collective life'.
The more pragmatic centrist reformers backed Kania's
more reserved analysis.   Jagielski and Barcikowski,
whose signatures had been placed on the Gdańsk and
Szczecin Agreements, pleaded for more investment in
agriculture, for an immediate and far reaching
economic reform and for the development of self-
management institutions throughout society.
Pińkowski outlined the various measures already
taken to stabilise the situation and indicated that
economic management needed to be decentralised.
Jaruzelski, as usual, took a politically gnomic
stance on behalf of the military but he warned that
domestic upheavals weakened the Warsaw Pact.
Rakowski produced the most elegant and subtle
and moderate reform line.   The correct policy was
to avoid the extremes of confrontation with or
surrender to Solidarity.   The long term aim should
be 'the assimilation of the new movement into our
socio-political system'.   Such a policy would in
due course distinguish the socialist elements in
Solidarity, who were willing to work within the
reformed system, from its outright opponents.   He

echoed Jagielski's argument that the unity of the
trade union movement could not be rebuilt by
administrative measures and that the workers' confidence could only be regained by good economic
management and by taking their views into account.
The last group of ostensible reformers is more
difficult to categorise, but individuals such as
Olszowski and Grabski wanted to gain control of the
apparat by purging and scape-goating Gierek's
discredited functionary class without mercy. If all
went well they hoped that this might suffice as a
substitute for a restructing of the party's rule,
although they envisaged very far reaching reforms
from above, especially in the economy, and promised
more efficient, technocratic management of society
on GDR lines. For the moment they confused the
political situation through their demagoguery, such
as Grabski's attack on Kania's report for not going
far enough, although they were to grow in influence
as the crisis continued.

The personnel changes effected by the plenum
were minor ones and nowhere near as great as expected.
They reflected a gradual shift in favour of Kania's
pragmatism but the plenum's recriminations revealed
the disunited and rudderless state of the party and
its disintegration into rival and quarrelsome
factions who permitted themselves public language
which had not been heard in 1956, let alone 1971.
One could already identify numerous political currents
such as the Fiszbach pro-Solidarity trend, the
Rakowski party reform intellectuals, the Kania-
Barcikowski-Jagielski pragmatic centrists, the
Olszowski-Grabski technocrats, who were soon to fuse
with Moczar's resurgent but toned down national
bolshevism, the remaining Gierek functionaries, who
were most under threat and a whole plethora of less
discredited hardliners and orthodox Marxist-Leninists
of various hues ranging from Jerzy Putrament to
Andrzej Werblan.

Gierek's remaining Politburo supporter,
Zdzisław Grudzień, was replaced by two relative new-
comers who became candidates. Władysław Kruk, the
KW First Secretary in Lublin, had had to deal with
the first major industrial unrest in July, while
Roman Ney, the Rector of the influential Mining-
Metallurgy Academy in Kraków (AGH), unprecedentedly
came straight into the Politburo from outside the
CC. Barcikowski replaced Żabiński as a CC
Secretary, while the youth functionary, Stanisław
Gabrielski, became a Secretariat member. The
really unusual personnel developments concerned the
composition of the CC itself, which is rarely

changed very much in between congresses.   Fifteen full new members (<u>inter alia</u> Gabrielski, Masny, Miśkiewicz Ney, Opałko) and 8 candidate members (Romanik, Siwak), many of whom, as new men, were to play important political roles, were appointed in place of the 10 Gierek supporters who were now dismissed.   The question of Gierek's responsibility was postponed, using the excuse of his state of health, but his main lieutenants were disgraced from the CC in terms which set out their personal responsibilities for the crisis.   Babiuch and Żandarowski were blamed for a lax recruitment policy and for the distortions in the party's internal life. Łukasiewicz was held to have shaped an ideological and propaganda line which was 'divorced from reality'.   Szydlak and Wrzaszczyk were castigated for voluntaristic economic and planning mistakes, while Pyka was made the scapegoat for the first phase of the Gdańsk negotiations.   Two KW First Secretaries, Kulesza from Leszno and Alfred Kowalski from Piła, were told to resign in view of the corruption charges levelled against them.   The more serious cases of Szczepański and his deputy on the Radio and TV Committee, Eugeniusz Patyk, were dealt with in a separate resolution which dismissed them from the CC and called for their investigation by the appropriate judicial and state controlled bodies as well as for their expulsion from the party, which was effected on 7 October.   Szczepański also had his parliamentary immunity lifted the following day so that criminal proceedings could be instituted against him.

The Sixth Plenum in sum struck a balance between the need to present a credible reform and democratisation programme to society and that of slowly changing the composition of the PZPR leadership and disentangling it from Gierek's decade of rule without demoralising it any further.   Although the PZPR's leading role was not being openly threatened the August-September developments were, however, perceived as a fundamental threat to Communist rule in Poland.   Once Gierek's consensus had been shattered the central and provincial leaderships formed conflicting currents and factions which, in the absence of a dominant leader like Gomułka in 1956, totally paralysed the party's capacity for an effective and united response to the crisis.   The one thing that could be agreed was to condemn Gierek and his entourage unreservedly at the Sixth Plenum and to blame him for the crisis.   The problem, though, was that, while Kania, Barcikowski and Jagielski claimed to support the implementation of

the Social Agreements, they either could not, or
would not, discipline their local officials, who,
perhaps backed by Olszowski and Moczar, were doing
everything possible to sabotage their fulfilment [7].
Only Fiszbach had pleaded for a dynamic reform policy
based on a whole-hearted acceptance of the positive
aspects of the post-August realities.   The silent
majority on the CC feared to oppose the Agreements
openly but multiplied warnings against anti-socialist
activities and elements which threw further doubts
on Kania's sincerity.   Party immobilisme could
therefore be partly explained in terms of the
internal balance of forces within the PZPR which
prevented the setting of a date for the Extraordinary
Congress which would clear out Gierek's CC.   All
that Kania could do, given these political factors,
was to move the party gradually in a reformist
direction by changing the leaderships at provincial
and factory level and by weakening the Politburo
conservatives at the Seventh Plenum.   This aspect
was always to lag behind what was required to make it
really credible in the eyes of Polish society.
The fear of losing control of rapidly moving developments also prevented the PZPR from committing itself
in principle to reform policies such as an Economic
Reform while allowing the specialists to argue over
the technical details later.   The Sixth Plenum at
best represented a promising start.   It was not
followed up because of the PZPR's immobilisme and
attentisme, which allowed inbroglios such as
Solidarity's registration and the disputed wage-
rises to turn into catastrophic and long drawn out
confrontations which the party was bound to lose after
after having surrendered at Gdańsk.

    The Sixth Plenum decisions were next aired by
the Sejm on 8 October when Pińkowski announced
sweeping ministerial changes [8].   Tejchma was
recalled to the Ministry of Culture, Moczar took over
an extended and refurbished NIK, now independent of
the Premier's control, to which it had been subordinated in 1976, and the hardliner, Kowalczyk, found
a temporary refuge as deputy Premier after losing
control of the Ministry of the Interior to his
deputy, Mirosław Milewski.   Pińkowski presented a
depressing report on the economic situation, while
Henryk Kisiel, the Chairman of the Planning Commission, outlined the draft 1981 NPS-G which envisaged
a budget deficit of 24 milliard złoties.   It some-
how hoped to protect living standards and to reduce
Poland's external debts by cutting industrial and
Government spending.   As usual during a crisis
situation, Sejm deputies produced hard hitting

speeches which impressed foreign journalists, if
not Polish public opinion.   The Sejm also developed
a greater range of activity both in its plenary
sessions and its committees.   A ministerial Question
Time was re-introduced on 21 October which was
extended into a two and a half hour session on 19
November.   The questions were naturally very
specific and detailed economic, social and cultural
ones and did not normally touch on the main
political issues.
    The October Sixth Plenum was, as usual, followed
by the leaders' meetings with the provincial party
committees.   The calls there were for a rapid con-
vocation of the Extraordinary Congress and for a full
analysis of the causes of the crisis and how to overcome it.   There was also a chorus of condemnation
of the voluntarist and manipulatory style of leadership which had ignored the warnings and criticisms
of the ordinary party militants.   These themes were
repeated to Kania at one of 'the fortresses of
socialism', the Huta Warszawa steel mill, where he
learnt that 50 PZPR workers had handed in their
party cards since August.   The workers told him
quite bluntly that the 3 million PZPR members were
a live intellectual force prepared to defend
socialism but not the official caste which had used
socialism as a pretext for misappropriating public
funds.   Kania merely repeated the Sixth Plenum
themes but his main accent was placed firmly on the
need to work out a programme for resolving the crisis
before the Congress as 'without such a programme
there is no purpose in calling the Congress' (TL,
9 October 1980).
    The CPA slowly resumed its normal round of work;
for example, all the PZPR provincial Economic
Secretaries met with Olszowski and Żabiński on 13
October at PZPR HQ to discuss how to stabilise the
economy and how to fulfil the Social Agreements.
The next day the Politburo met to discuss the Sixth
Plenum decisions, to consider the food and consumer
shortages and to extend the membership of the
Committee on Economic Reform (TL, 15 October 1980).
In a sign of the times some journalists ventured to
criticise the laconic and uninformative communiqué
on its proceedings, but the main lines of leadership
thinking were set out clearly enough by an official
publicist a few days later [9].   Although the
analysis stated on the stock lines that the crisis
was not so much the fault of the system as of the
previous leadership, and that reform was now both
possible and desirable, Krasucki's initial purpose
was to allay fears that all reforms would sooner or

later be swept into the bag labelled 'enemies of socialism'. People who had protested sincerely against Gierek's mistakes were quite different from outright enemies who had declared war on socialism such as Moczulski and the KPN and who had no interest in any reformed version either. The matter was more complicated in the case of Kuroń and Michnik as their justified criticisms from the late 1970s onwards were only a cover for their right-wing revisionist and leftist utopian ambitions which were designed to build KOR in as a permanent feature of the new system. Their strategy in the 'second stage' after the Summer outbursts would be to use the pre-Congress preparations and discussions to infiltrate various social organisations in order to wrest them from party control; their tactics would be to multiply the criticisms of the mistakes and deformations of the past in order to escalate demands, to increase tension and chaos and to demoralise loyal PZPR members [10]. The analysis was couched wholly in realpolitik terms of KTO KOGO and was a good indication of how difficult it is for a communist leadership to accept the good faith of an adversary or the merits of any proposal emanating from outside its own circle.

Krasucki's polemic may perhaps have been an indirect reply to the Declaration of the Founding Committee of NSZZ Solidarity in Jastrzębie-Zdrój, which, although not published until somewhat later [11], attempted to convince the CPA that it had freed itself from anti-socialist elements and that it was only making tactical use of the critical intelligentsia. The NSZZ stressed its determination to work within constituted limits and to be the sort of force on which the PZPR could base itself in order to overcome the deformations of socialism which had crept in in Gierek's time. All this was evidence of the extent to which some sections of Solidarity in the Silesian region had been taken over success-fully by the disciplined and well organised Silesian Communists, a quarter of whose members (100,000) joined Solidarity and who played a prominent part in its leadership despite the formal ban on PZPR officials holding office in the new union [12]. The supporting Communist intellectual élite's réplique at this time was perhaps best expressed by Daniel Passent,who argued forcibly that 'the fundamental condition for rebuilding the authority, prestige and effectiveness of our state is its democrati-sation' [13].

By the third week in October Kania had changed the First Secretaries in 7 provinces (Katowice,

Poznań, Toruń, Wrocław, Kalisz, Bydgoszcz and
Konin) as part of the gradual policy of systematically
clearing out the old Gierek team confirmed at the
Sixth Plenum. Some, such as Zdzisław Grudzień and
Ludwik Drożdż, who had built luxury villas for
dignitaries in Wrocław on what was aptly nicknamed
'the Directors' Ranch', had compromised themselves
financially and went quietly. Before long, the new
men in turn cleared Gierek's supporters off the KW
Executives. Żabiński did so in Katowice in early
October, when he had 13 Executive members and 3 KW
secretaries dismissed.
    Significant leadership changes also affected
the minor parties and social organisations. The
SDP at its Extraordinary Congress elected a new 70-
strong council and the outspoken Stefan Bratkowski,
who had been in disfavour since as far back as 1973,
and who had patronised DiP, as its new Chairman.
Bratkowski was built up as something of a cult figure
by Western journalists because of his reform personae.
Although not an outstanding intellect, he proved a
forceful personality, whose well-timed interventions
assumed considerable significance on various
occasions during the following year. He considered
that the Gdańsk Agreement, the DiP Reports and the
Sixth Plenum 'in no way went beyond the revolution
of common sense' [14]. The ZSL decided in early
November to convene its Eighth Congress a few weeks
later and in the interim dismissed four of its
Gierekite notables. Similar changes had earlier
occurred on 20 October within PAX, whose leader,
Ryszard Reiff, had succeeded the infamous Bolesław
Piasecki on his death in 1979 [15]. Reiff attempted
to make his new policy of improved relations with
the Catholic hierarchy credible by sacking three of
Piasecki's closest lieutenants (Hagmajer,
Przetakiewicz and Rutkowski) as well as his intelligent and uncompromised rival, Janusz Stefanowicz.
    On 3 November the ZBoWiD Executive Council met
to elect Moczar as its Chairman in place of Piotr
Jaroszewicz, a position which he had already held
until he had lost his power-struggle with Gierek in
1971. In his partially censored speech (cf. TL,
4 November 1980), Moczar called for the cleansing
of the PZPR of opportunists as well as of those
responsible for the mistakes of the Gierek period.
He contrasted the purity of the War-Veterans' war-
time struggles and their irreproachable commitment
to the socialist order with the irresponsible and
anti-socialist elements whose escalating demands
'could lead the country to a national catastrophe'.
He welcomed the advent of Solidarity, giving it the

benevolent advice to rid itself of what he termed
its harmful elements.   He also wanted the War-
Veterans' Ministry set up by Gierek dissolved as it
had limited ZBoWiD's autonomy.   Moczar thus made
his political comeback by signalling his unreserved
loyalty and utility to the socialist order in Poland
and the Soviet alliance.
     At a meeting with academic and student repre-
sentatives on 29 September Kania reserved his position on the SZSP demands of 17 September for
University autonomy, the free election of Rectors
and Deans by Senates and an independent students'
organisation.   He indicated that the crisis which
had broken out in August was far from over and
attempted to rally the mature student apparatchiks
led by the SZSP Chairman, Gabrielski, into greater
efforts to keep students and young academics in
line (TL, 30 September 1980).   In this area, as in
the economic field, the authorities had already
been undercut by the foundation of an Independent
Association of Polish Students in Gdańsk in late
August which spread so quickly all over Poland that
it was constituted as a national body (NZSP) in
Warsaw on 22 September.   Jabłoński at the cere-
monial inauguration of the academic year in Olsztyn
on 1 October did, however, promise greater autonomy
for the universities and for student bodies (TL,
2 October 1980).   Jabłoński's warning against
troublemakers did not deter the Flying University
(TKN) from profiting from the collapse of PZPR
control and the changed atmosphere to extend its
activities among both independent students and
Solidarity supporters [16].   On the other hand,
student contestation did not explode in a major
way until some weeks later.
     Polish intellectual life had never been dull,
but it really bloomed after August in terms of what
was being written and published and was marked by a
notable call for literary vigour and diversity which
sparked off a typically Polish debate [17].   There
were also growing demands for the loosening and
revision of censorship.   The Polish intelligentsia
gained an additional psychological boost with the
attribution of the Nobel Peace Prize to Czesław Miłosz,
a long-time emigré writer who had settled in France
since 'choosing freedom' in 1951 [18].   Miłosz,
although widely read, hardly had the literary style
which would have made him a best-seller but his
work had never been published in Poland as he was
politically most associated with a Cold War
analysis of how intellectuals adapt to life in a
totalitarian system.   The Captive Mind is much

acclaimed but, like much of Miłosz's work, it can
also be regarded as precious and obscure [19].
Nevertheless, Miłosz's Nobel Prize was universally
regarded as a notable victory for the Polish
counter-community. The authorities were forced to
accept yet another erstwhile 'enemy of socialism'
and the rapid publication of some of Miłosz's poems
and other writings.

The Confrontation over Solidarity's Registration
        Although the PZPR had conceded the right to
organise free trades-unions in late August, it
probably hoped to exercise a major influence on the
form which they would take by retaining control of
the registration procedure by the Warsaw Provincial
Court. They had also stipulated that the new
unions accept the PZPR's leading role and declare
their loyalty to socialism. This issue led to the
first great confrontation between the régime and
Solidarity over the question of the latter's registration which rumbled on from late September to mid
November. But the major contention only masked a
wide range of subsidiary disputes. The national
warning strike on Friday, 3 October, which was backed
up by the threat of a 24-hour general strike scheduled
for 20 October, was just as much over two other issues
arising out of the Social Agreements. One was the
demand for an immediate, across the board wage-
increase of 800 złoties by the agreed date of 30
September instead of the average 650 złoties
promised by the Government for October; the other
was Solidarity's demand to put its case over on the
mass media. By late September Solidarity was already
made up of 47 regional sections but the control of the
Gdańsk National Co-ordinating Committee (KKP) over
them was somewhat tenuous. Bogdan Lis, a major
KKP spokesman, therefore argued that the warning
strike benefited the Government as 'without it we
would have had a series of wildcat strikes across
the country' [20]. The problem was that the
authorities had made the fatal mistake of rejecting
a uniform across the board wage-increase as they had
hoped to be in a stronger position after the Gdańsk
strike finished. Their policy of local negotiations
at individual plant or industrial sector level was
also designed to shape the new free trades-unions
into enterprise level ones. The policy backfired
as the negotiations in September between hapless
Ministers without clear instructions or authority
and suspicious workers' representatives under continual pressure from their own grassroots merely
produced a messy and irrational pattern of agreements

which satisfied no one.

The Government's reaction to the catastrophic economic situation, marked by dramatic falls in production, a bad harvest (20 per cent less potatoes and 30 per cent less sugar-beet than in 1979), an inflation rate of 12 per cent which was being worsened by the huge 20-odd per cent increases in the wage-fund and by a debt of over $20 milliard, was, however, extremely timorous. Rather than reform the economy and strive for an effective Social Contract with the workers it merely borrowed a further $2 milliard in order to buy extra food, it changed its investment priorities and cut exports. It also sought Soviet aid during Planning Chairman Baibakov's visit to Warsaw on 11 October. On the other hand, voices such as Urban's put the case that the Social Agreements could not be fulfilled because of Poland's economic difficulties and that the new unions had better decide whether their economic demands were designed to overthrow socialism or whether they were willing to accept the sacrifices that co-responsibility entailed [21].

The bulk of official union members, usually over 80 per cent, decamped to Solidarity in spite of régime efforts to form refurbished branch unions distinct from both Solidarity and the old official unions. The Presidia of the Council of Ministers and the Chairmen of the main branch unions discussed these problems on 27 September. The former stressed the costs of the industrial disruption, while the latter emphasised the need for specific undertakings with set time limits for the implementation of the more justified workers' demands (TL, 29 September 1980). The wave of strikes continued independently at plant level, however, where the ferment produced a welter of confused, and often extreme, political and economic demands. By mid October the Machine-Engineering Ministry alone had been inundated with no less than 5,600 postulates from workers in its sphere (TL, 14 October 1980). In general, strike disputes were defused by mixed Government-Solidarity commissions, as in the case of the Wrocław railwaymen in late October, who produced 44 postulates to cover their bitter grievances which had accumulated over many years.

The Solidarity warning strike of 3 October received near 100 per cent backing in the Baltic region, Poznań, Wrocław, Silesia and designated factories around Warsaw. It was also remarkably well controlled, as Wałęsa braked attempts to continue the strike in Poznań. For the moment, Wałęsa felt that it was sufficient that 'we have shown that we exist and that we will not allow ourselves to be done over' [22].

The negotiations over registration, wages and access to the mass media bogged down after the Sixth Plenum but Solidarity continued to expand and to organise itself. Guetta noted that almost all the workers in large factories, including Communist militants, had joined. In towns such as Wrocław and Gdańsk Solidarity had implanted itself in all the professional sectors while, most significantly for the future, the movement was spreading into the countryside. 97 per cent of all the Nowa Huta workers had joined Solidarity, whose rapid expansion in the Kraków area was aided by the conciliatory policies of Krystin Dąbrowa, the forty year old KW First Secretary [23]. 'In a calm which is always absolute the whole of Polish society is in the process of organising - in the interior of the system which it does not contest - a formidable counterforce which modifies its character,' reported Guetta with a pardonable rhetorical flourish (Le Monde, 15 October 1980).

The registration crisis was a fundamental one which went far beyond nit-picking over the detailed wording of Solidarity's statute. The PZPR leadership wanted Solidarity to do more than merely recognise that a Communist system existed in Poland and that it would have to put up with it as best it could. It wanted Solidarity to pay ideological homage to its Communist principles so that the authorities could in future define and limit its organisation and activities to what it considered appropriate. In particular, it wanted to present Solidarity to its socialist allies as the fruit of a renewal of the trade-union movement which did not entail any break in ideological continuity. This was unacceptable to Solidarity in its post-Gdańsk exhilaration. Its determination was if anything steeled, in a very Polish way, by the struggle of nerves with the régime over this and other issues. Both sides had their allies as well. The Warsaw Pact Foreign Ministers convened in Warsaw on 19 October, while the same day Cardinal Wyszyński supported Solidarity. A stalemate was thus reached as Rakowski reiterated that the PZPR would stand firm [24]. The increasingly angry mood of Solidarity's supporters ruled out any public climb-down by the KKP which gained time on 20 October by postponing the threatened strike until 4 November.

The Warsaw Court on 24 October accepted Solidarity's statutes but Kościelniak, the presiding judge,

unilaterally, and most improperly according to correct judicial procedure (which was either to accept
or to reject the statutes in their entirety), added
to Paragraph One the disputed clauses which had
caused all the trouble; the trade-union 'bases itself on the principle of the socialist means of
the ownership of production which by themselves constitute the fundamentals of the socialist system
existing in Poland; it recognises that the PZPR
exercises the leading role in the state ... it does
not contest the established system of international
alliances'. Kościelniak also modified another clause
in a manner which limited the right to strike very
severely (TL, 25-26 October 1980).

Solidarity's indignation, especially in the
larger factories which favoured an immediate hard
riposte, was such that on 27 October the KKP sent
Pińkowski an ultimation to meet them in the Lenin
Shipyard [25]. Jagielski's low-key discussion with
Wałęsa the following day, however,persuaded them
that these discussions should take place in Warsaw.
The repercussions were immediate. Kania and
Pińkowski were summoned after the Politburo meeting
of 29 October to meet Brezhnev and Soviet Premier
Tikhonov in the Kremlin the following day, even
though this meant leaving the British Foreign Secretary, Lord Carrington, in the lurch. The reassuring communiqué issued after their lightning visit
suggested that the Polish leaders were perhaps
licensed yet again to smooth over the crisis and
to prevent an outright conflict [26].

The 74 strong Solidarity delegation which
crowded into the Premier's office at 11 a.m. on 31
October came armed with the threat of a general
strike if their appeal against the statute amend-
ments were not accepted [27]. Pińkowski agreed to
present a meat-rationing scheme and warned of the
food shortages which would inevitably occur that
winter. He supported the Court's rejection, a few
days earlier, of the application for the registration
of a Rural Solidarity. Although he promised to
examine the complaints that local officials were
hindering Solidarity's organisation the failure to
agree a Communiqué suggested that the 14 hour long
negotiations had not made much progress, especially
over the disputed wage-increases. Wałęsa at his
press conference said that negotiations would continue and claimed a huge victory over the Government's agreement to an independent Solidarity weekly.
He considered that the decision to convene the Supreme
Court to hear Solidarity's appeal on 10 November, two
days before the threatened strike, was a hopeful

sign [28].   The KKP on 4 November decided that the
strike on the twelfth should be a selective and
rotating one starting with certain designated factories in Gdańsk and Warsaw.   Mazowsze in particular prepared for the occasion with much gusto.
Kania himself, having gained Politburo confirmation of the Moscow decisions on 4 November, helped
to unblock the situation with an important, conciliatory speech in Nowa Huta, the following day.
He admitted that the Sixth Plenum had not enabled
the PZPR to regain society's confidence.   The party
would have to examine the causes of the crisis in a
much deeper way and accept the renewal of the trade-
union movement in order to set out a credible programme and the guarantees regarding its implementation.   The PZPR was now ready to accept that
Solidarity was 'the workers' hope for the effective
defence of their rights and interests' [29].   Kania
signalled that he had gained Moscow's permission for
reaching agreement with Solidarity and for purging
the most conservative, compromised and dishonest
sections of the PZPR.   Barcikowski had already
declared that the Politburo aimed to alleviate industrial unrest by collaborating with new unions in all
the key problems at plant level (TL, 5 November 1980).
The signs of official retreat over the registration issue were signalled further by the Minister
of Justice's public polemic with a resolution of
the Department of State and Law of Warsaw University
that the Warsaw Court was <u>ultra vires</u> in amending the
substance of the Solidarity statutes.   Even
Olszowski, speaking to the Gdańsk <u>aktyw</u> on 5 November,
took an optimistic view of the PZPR's internal
changes and promised 'an open partner-like attitude
towards Solidarity' (TL, 6 November 1980).   He
blamed the continuing social tension largely on the
bad economic situation and the grave food and other
shortages which were discussed at a meeting of provincial Governors and the Presidents of the largest
cities called in Warsaw by Pińkowski on 8 November.
The round of meetings and the publicisation by
the official press of various reform proposals, such
as changes in the Sejm's Standing Orders and the
implementation of the 'free Saturdays' agreed at
Gdańsk, continued apace.   Great coverage was also
given to the Council of State's appeal of 7 November
for social peace and economic stabilisation (TL, 8
November 1980).
Informal Government-Solidarity negotiations in
the Sejm building produced a face-saving compromise
over registration which allowed the Politburo on
9 November to accept as dignified a climb-down as

was possible in the circumstances.   The following
day the Supreme Court registered Solidarity's statutes in their original form and annulled the Warsaw
Court's judgement [30].   As agreed, the first section of the Gdańsk Agreement,in which Solidarity had
accepted the PZPR's leading role, was relegated to
an appendix.   This was balanced by the inclusion
of Articles 87 and 98 of the International Labour
Organisation which guaranteed trade-union rights.
Lis, Solidarity's deputy Chairman, in a long official declaration which called off the 12 November
strike regarded the Court's decision as saving Poland
from 'a grave social crisis'.   Wałęsa, as usual,
went straight to the heart of the matter: 'Nobody
has lost.   It is not a victory.   It is a question
which has been settled ...   We can now pass on to
the second more difficult stage of organising the
union and its work.'   As part of the agreed compact
Trybuna Ludu (11 November 1980) published the foregoing declarations [31].

The Solidarity troops having been mobilised for
battle were dismayed by the compromise, although the
threats to hold the strike after all in various
regions did not eventuate.   The KKP itself was also
divided between compromise, like Wałęsa, and those
who doubted the party's sincerity and who voted to
humiliate it for its past sins, or who felt that the
appendices were a trap.   Political tension was also
increased by such events as the medical workers' occupation of the Gdańsk provincial Governor's Building
in protest at their insufficient wage-increases.
Wałęsa barely prevented a similar sit-in by sugar-
refiners in Pruszcz from turning into an industry-
wide sugar workers' strike.   The problem was that
the Government really had little to offer.   Such
groups as the teachers, medical workers and sugar
workers, on the other hand, had organised their own
branch unions spontaneously within Solidarity and
these represented very radical and corporatist
elements indeed, as these professions were badly
paid and overworked [32].

The problem was the key psychological one which
I have already stressed.   The Poles had not rebelled
in order to find that all their activity merely worsened the economic and food crises and produced a
political stalemate, but this is exactly what was
happening.   One cannot dissent from Guetta's judgement, that, although a confrontation had again been
avoided, the crisis was deepening as nothing had
been settled [33].   I would add, nor could it.
Rakowski in mid November likewise was unable to
discern any signs that the political and economic

crisis was abating. The main characteristic of
the Polish Autumn and the attempt to institute the
'renewal' was the fluidity of political relations
and a prevalent suspicion which prevented the
establishment of partner-like relations between the
authorities, Solidarity and all the other socio-
political forces. The result was 'growing nervous-
ness, "a short-wind" in politics. Day-to-day tactics decidedly dominates over strategy' [34].
    The situation was ambiguous as both sides, es-
pecially the Communist leadership, had to hide behind
alibis in order to cloak the basic political realities. The official line on the Supreme Court
decision, for example, that it 'was in accord with
the letter of the law, with the feeling of society
and with superior social raison d'état' was fair
enough; but the corollary that an acceptable way
had now been found, as envisaged in Grabski's speech
of 9 November, for Solidarity to accept the PZPR's
leading role and to establish with it 'a close,
sincere and everyday collaboration in the settlement
of the most fundamental problems of the nation and
state' was a forlorn . attempt to keep up appearances
(Editorial, TL, 11 November 1980). Such soft words
were also contradicted by disquietening signs, such
as the official publicity given to the Polish-Soviet
manoeuvres which started at this time and the turning
back of three Western journalists. PZPR ideological life hardened. Official political analysis
conceded that the new trades-unions might play 'an
important role in perfecting our socio-economic
system' but it condemned the Democratic Opposition
and not just the KPN, as in the past. KOR was now
placed fully in the ranks of anti-socialist forces
such as Radio Free Europe and the Paris Kultura.
Its perfidious tactical conception 'of the peaceful
liquidation of the gains of socialism in the PRL
and of stretching out over a number of stages the
scenario of creeping counter-revolution' was now
unmasked (Krasucki, TL, 11 November 1980).

The People start throwing out the Proprietors of
People's Poland
    The Politburo on 11 November considered that
Solidarity's registration marked the end of the
first gestation period during which the new union
had been formed and its place in the social structure defined. The next stage, now beginning, would
be 'Solidarity's involvement in the constructive
resolution of the country's problems' (TL, 12
November 1980). It also agreed to submit a plan
for rationing meat, butter, margarine and sugar for

public discussion.

Social peace, however, did not follow Solidarity's registration. Pent-up social hatred was now released against Communist officialdom at every level. The situation was aggravated by the food and other shortages. During October and November social conflicts engendered an escalating set of political crises. The Gdańsk medical workers' sit-in sparked off threats of sympathy strikes all over Poland among medical and other workers [35]. Similar demands were also raised by teachers and students. The problem of handling social discontent was aggravated, as Guetta pointed out, by the lack of Solidarity and PZPR cohesion; so effective leadership was missing in both camps [36].

The attempt to forge a régime-Solidarity partnership therefore started under most inauspicious circumstances. Solidarity faced two major dilemmas. Firstly, it was torn between the need to support all the particularist demands and grievances which were now erupting and by the desire of its more responsible leaders to alleviate the economic catastrophe. Solidarity's problem was that leadership calls for moderation would only be listened to by its constituent groups in the context of a socioeconomic framework which the PZPR would not freely concede. A very real strategic divergence emerged. Would a head-on political confrontation and national strike to round off the work begun at Gdańsk be more effective than an evolutionary policy of coexistence punctuated by recurring sub-nuclear confrontations? Secondly, Solidarity's umbrella character meant that it would eventually face hard and divisive choices between the differing, and often rival, groups which composed it. The prevalent egalitarian mood, for example, ran counter to many of its reform demands, such as enterprise autonomy.

The PZPR also faced an equally difficult set of internal divisions and policy conundrums. The post-Gierek leadership lacked the full support of the largely unchanged CC and the Politburo itself was split into, at least, 3 tendencies: residual Gierekite conservatives, Kania centrists and Olszowski strong hand reformers. Kania was therefore not in full control of the CPA and unable to steer it in a clear direction until well into 1981. The absence of cohesion among the central leadership naturally allowed the emergence of differing policies among the PZPR provincial caucuses as well as among the supporting apparats, such as the police and the procuracy, while only the Army sealed itself off from contagion. The most dramatic

example of such KW independence occurred in
Częstochowa.   Its Governor, Mirosław Wierzbicki,
backed by KW First Secretary Grygiel, on 10
November attempted to jump the gun on national
events, as he saw it, by organising a local state
of emergency to prevent Solidarity's registration.
Was the move a centrally inspired provocation designed to sabotage registration, or had the local
officials merely pre-empted precautionary moves by
the CPA for a hardline fallback alternative?

The open struggle between political tendencies
was shown in the diametrically opposed happenings
in Gdańsk the same day.   Fiszbach told his KW
plenum that the priority was 'to overcome conservative slowness in order to keep up with society's
aspirations'.   The Congress should be convened as
soon as possible, while the Sixth Plenum had barely
started to produce 'a constructive plan for renewal'
(Le Monde, 13 November 1980).   Militants had expressed similar reform demands at early provincial
plena so the centrist Kania leadership knew that it
had grassroots' support for action against the conservatives.   They decided, however, only to move
against Gierek's closest officials in order to contain and limit worker and militant demands and to
maintain the CPA's morale and internal cohesion.
Kania also wanted to allay Soviet fears, such as
the objections to Solidarity's registration expressed
by Leonid Zamiatin, Head of the CPSU CC International
Department, on Moscow TV on 15 November.

The Kania-Wałęsa talks of 14 November led to a
detailed agreement being signed in Gdańsk, two days
later, between a Government delegation led by deputy
Premier Andrzej Jedynak and the medical workers
headed by the Lenin Shipyard nurse, Alicja Pieńkowska.
This, and a whole ruck of detailed agreements covering every aspect of wages, conditions of work, hospital equipment and medical supplies, was hammered
out in arduous and emotional discussions over the
next month.   Reading the 80 page brochure setting
out these social contracts, one can, according to
taste, be either highly impressed or struck by their
absurdity given Poland's conditions.   The workers
demanded what they thought was necessary while the
Ministers promised everything without much conviction [37].   The Solidarity leaders appealed to
their supporters to hold back on their demands until
they received a reply from Premier Pińkowski to their
complaints and offer of a national compromise over
wages on the basis of immediate concessions to the
most economically disfavoured.   Such Solidarity
initiatives led to some temporary appeasement and

the steel and postal workers called off their actions.
The Częstochowa problem was partly advanced by
negotiations between Minister of Light Industry, WŁ.
Jabłoński and local Solidarity leaders who threatened
a regional strike if Grygiel and Wierzbicki were not
dismissed.   Guetta painted a graphic picture of how
social crises were resolved in post-Gdańsk Poland
[38].   Józef Kępa, the Minister of Public Administration, arrived in Częstochowa on 18 November, with
full powers to negotiate a settlement.   At a meeting
at the local bus station, which was relayed to a
crowd of 5,000 outside, the city officials faced
public accusations that they had never really accepted the Gdańsk Agreement.   The City President
was blamed for a million złoty deficit on a pig farm
and of having refused to renovate a centre for the
handicapped run by nuns while he had built a luxurious
new party HQ costing 200 million złoties.   The
deputy Governors were accused of building villas for
local notables and of assuring preferential supplies
to shops catering for officials.   Częstochowa with
a quarter of a million population because of their
neglect had only two cinemas, a wholly inadequate
library system, poorly heated schools and an insani-
tary hospital system.   The authentic voice of the
Workers' Upsurge was heard suddenly from a young
worker who called for the dismissal of all the
officials who 'had not respected Article 2 of the
constitution which declares that power belongs to
the people'.   What sort of socialism was it, he
asked, which forced parents to go hungry in order
to feed their children?   'When a nation is poor
does one have to build palaces for the party while
the people have nowhere to live?'
Kępa tried to preserve the authority of the
state by insisting on the maintenance of legal forms
and procedures.   Eventually, in the early hours of
the morning, he presided over an agreement with
Częstochowa Solidarity which involved the resignation of the humiliated officials.   Trybuna Ludu,
however, did not announce officially that Pińkowski
had accepted Wierzbicki's resignation until 12
December and he was not replaced by Grzegorz Lipowski,
a local textile factory manager, until 2 January
1981.   Grygiel's resignation was announced much
sooner but even he was not replaced by Władysław
Jonkisz, the popular Rector of the local Polytechnic,
until early December.   Apart from Walaszek in
Szczecin in December 1970, this was the first case
in People's Poland of social pressure forcing the
dismissal of unpopular officials.   Częstochowa
set a precedent for similar public denunciations of

party and state officials elsewhere in the New Year.
Faced with such a difficult social situation,
the PZPR made concessions to the Roman Catholic
Church, which,alongside the PZPR and Solidarity,
was one of the three main forces in Poland. A
Catholic deputy, Jerzy Ozdowski, was appointed as a
deputy Premier in the Ministerial reshuffle of 21
November [39]. Ozdowski was a 55 year old economics
Professor who had become a member of the Council of
State in April 1980. He belonged to the 'New Znak'
(PZKS) which under Janusz Zabłocki's leadership had
rallied to Gierek over the 1976 constitutional
changes and which had been rewarded with all 5 of
Znak's Sejm seats. Although Ozdowski was a safe,
pro-régime moderate, the nomination of an apparently
independent Catholic was an unprecedented event.
The PZPR realised that the Government needed to
enlarge its social base in order to tackle the socio-
economic crisis and that this required a more conciliatory approach to the practising Catholic majority.
The Church hierarchy did not oppose such ideas at
an open meeting in a Sejm committee room attended by
Kania and Bishop Dąbrowski, Secretary of the
Episcopal Conference.
All this indicated the search for a new political equilibrium to reflect post-Gdańsk realities.
Jagielski told the Sejm that the leadership favoured
renewal and the full application of the Social
Agreements. He intimated that the realist wing
within the PZPR had won but that its good intentions
were being hindered by 'unrealistic behaviour' and
the abuse of the strike weapon by Solidarity and by
the harmful activities of conservative party-state
officials [40]. He doubtless had in mind the likes
of Karkoszka, who had just been dismissed on 17
November as First Secretary in Warsaw and who was
reported as organising apparat resistance to Kania's
supple policy [41]. His replacement, Stanisław
Kociołek,was criticised because of his dubious activities in March 1968 and December 1970. The evidence, though, is that Kania used this still young,
aspiring technocrat, who now undoubtedly had Moscow's
support, to marshal a moderate anti-reform current
within the hardline Warsaw party.
In the last week of November Guetta, influenced
by his excellent official sources, reported the outbreak of a new wave of social, economic and political
conflicts in a most alarmist fashion (Le Monde, 25
November 1980). A rail strike was just beginning,
hard negotiations were taking place in the textile
industry and at least six open conflicts and many
more latent ones threatened to produce a general

trial of strength, even though the top leaderships
in both the PZPR and Solidarity wished to avoid it.
The former had an apparatus which was largely hostile to renewal and which found it difficult to
collaborate with a counter-power. The latter was
unable to brake the dynamics of the vast social movements towards contestation. None of the individual
crises arising from nerves, mutual distrust and
accumulated grievances should provoke a major conflict but, as conflicts multiplied, there was a
chance that the situation might run out of control.
In spite of the nation's intoxication with regaining
its liberties after 35 years and the much greater
degree of pluralism which now prevailed than in 1956,
Guetta was confident that the PZPR and Solidarity
would achieve a medium term stabilisation.

In such a charged atmosphere even trivial inci-
dents could have major consequences. The spark
came in Warsaw on 21 November. The police arrested
Jan Narożniak, who ran Mazowsze's publishing services.
A police search of his flat had discovered a 13 page
long confidential report by Procurator-General, Lucjan
Czubiński, which outlined judicial methods for combatting the opposition [42]. Narożniak's arrest,
and that of Piotr Sapieło, the minor judiciary official who had handed him the document, sparked off
a wave of warning strikes in the Warsaw region which
almost culminated in a general strike [43]. Solidarity escalated its demands from the release of
Narożniak and Sapieło into wider ones for sanctions
against the Procurator-General, the suspension of
charges against 'political prisoners' and the release of the KPN leaders. Most significantly,
Solidarity demanded that a Sejm committee be established to investigate the procuracy and the police
with a view to reducing their budgets and most
ominously from the authorities' viewpoint to seek
out those responsible for the repression of the
workers in 1970 and 1976 [44]. The crisis therefore became a very grave political one with a
frontal Solidarity attack on the Communist state's
repressive police and judicial <u>apparats</u>. At local
level dangerous flashpoints were occurring with
local officials under attack in Częstochowa-type
situations in Bielsko-Biała and Olsztyn and workers'
unrest paralysed the Bytom coalmines, the Łódź textile mills and the Wrocław-Gdańsk railways.

Once again, having whistled up the wind the
authorities collapsed in a humiliating but long
drawn out and graceless manner. In order to avoid
the threatened regional strike in Warsaw Narożniak
and Sapieło were released on 27 November through

Bratkowski's services as an intermediary. Jagielski again had to face the workers' wrath, this time at Ursus, and he had great difficulties in getting the strike at Huta Warszawa called off [45]. The Polish working class, unused to the strikes and fudged up compromises of Western Europe, showed emotional over-excitement and political immaturity by holding out for five-fold guarantees and a symbolic humiliation of the power holders.

One should note a number of basic underlying factors in the Polish situation at this point. Firstly, the party unquestionably suffered from the almost complete absence of public support in Autumn 1980. An unofficial poll of 510 Poles published by Paris Match in early November gave an accurate enough impressionistic picture, although its obvious methodological weaknesses do not give its results any academic value. Asked how they would have voted in a 'free election' to the Sejm only 3% would have supported the PZPR, as against 34% for Christian Democratic, 27% for Socialist, 19% for Liberal and 4% for Agrarian parties. Asked who best symbolised the spirit of Poland, 78% answered Wałęsa, 73% Pope John Paul II, while only 4% were hardy or committed enough to answer Kania. Disillusion with the Communist system was linked with a fair degree of pessimism as 20% thought that a Soviet invasion was likely, 40% that it was possible and only 40% were convinced that it would not take place.

Secondly, the economic situation was so bad by mid November that the noted economist, Stanisław Albinowski, called for emergency measures within the next fortnight in order to prevent its complete breakdown (TL, 18 November 1980). It also encouraged the radical economic decentralisers such as Józef Kaleta, the Rector of the Wrocław Economic Academy, to voice their case more strongly [46]. Adam Kowalik, the Minister of Home Trade and Services, also revealed that 76 out of every 100 złoties were currently being spent on food and consumption. Domestic market equilibrium was profoundly shaken as there was a surplus of 45 milliard złoties in circulation (TL, 17 November 1980). All this useless 'Hot Money' aggravated the consumer psychosis, which led to the clearing out of all goods as soon as they appeared in the shops and encouraged massive hoarding.

Thirdly, the pluralism of Polish political life was reflected in the Sejm at its lively sessions of 23 to 24 November [47]. The non-party Professor Bukowski's call for the resignation of the Ministers of Agriculture and Food Industry because of their

112

policy failures, a previously unheared of suggestion,
was greeted enthusiastically by the Sejm [48].
Moczar declared that officials who had misused their
positions would face legal and financial charges.
He cited some striking cases of notables who had
abused their positions in building private dwellings.
On the other hand, he considered that the strike
weapon was also being abused and that it was
weakening Poland's economy.   The latter theme was
echoed by General Włodzimierz Oliwa, Commander of
the Warsaw Military District, who blamed strikes
for weakening the defensive capacities of both
Poland and the Warsaw Pact.

        Lastly, CC Secretary Kurowski attempted to
clarify the party's ideological position before the
Seventh Plenum [49].   The evidence was that the
party cells (POPs) were overwhelmingly in favour of
renewal.   They accepted Solidarity as 'a permanent
element in our life'.   The party should avoid the
two extremes of ideological capitulation and of
refusing to accept the lasting character of the post-
August changes.   It would now have to accelerate
the process of cleansing its ranks.   It would also
consider the more constructive proposals to democratise the PZPR's internal life and electoral prac-
tices.   Ordinary POP members should have greater
say in electing their officers, party commissions
should be used more in future at every level and the
apparatus would have to be subordinated to the
party's elected representatives.

The Party lurches towards Reform and meets Soviet Threats

        The strikes and social conflicts of late November
provoked open Soviet political and military pressure
for the first time and a war scare of European proportions.   The Seventh Plenum took place under these
inauspicious circumstances on 1-2 December [50].
Kania's report indicated that the PZPR was now ready
to go over on to the political counter-offensive
after the shocks of August to November.   He emphasised the socialist character of the renewal process
and announced that the Ninth Congress would take
place between the first and second quarters of 1981.
Kania hoped to arrange matters satisfactorily with
the Solidarity leadership, but the problem was that
its local branches were resorting too readily to
strikes;   they refused to accept that the country's
economic situation made it impossible to fulfil
most of their aggressive demands.   Wage-rises, for
instance, merely worsened inflation and the chaos in

the shops.   Even worse, 'a dangerous tendency'
within Solidarity had gone beyond its statutory
limits as a trade-union and engaged in political
activity.   The crux of Kania's analysis was that
the working class was basically sound but that it
had been infiltrated by various anti-socialist elements who wanted to use the crisis to dismantle the
socialist system.   The PZPR line of 'agreement and
renewal' reflected the wishes of most of the membership and all conservative opposition to it would be
overcome.   The far-reaching systemic consequences
would widen the base of People's Power in Poland.
This of itself might not quieten the strike wave but
the genuine aim was 'to win over for socialism in
our country stronger social support as well as creating rather more modern mechanisms for its functioning'.
        Having made his political position clear as a
realistic and pragmatic Communist determined to
salvage the party's hegemony through new methods and
concessions, Kania accentuated his stance as a
party reformer.   The party could not be a 'discussion club or a loose association of sympathisers';
the knack was to maintain democratic centralism
while introducing more democratic methods which
needed to be set out in revised statutes.   Ideas
such as defining the respective spheres of the
apparats and of elected representative committees,
the rotation of offices by limiting the number of
terms to be served, measures to make control commissions more independent, changes in electoral
regulations and the democratic election of First
Secretaries, Executives and Secretariats when this
was demanded by more than half the members were
proposals which could be considered on their merits.
Kania accepted what he defined as the positive aspects of the ferment within the party, but he warned
the Horizontal Movement against creating 'organisational structures outside the statute ... factionalism and separatism cannot be tolerated within
the party'.
        Kania's endeavour to draw the line on a number
of issues and to form a new political centre was,
however, predicated on the need for party and state
reforms in order to close the confidence gap with
society.   This would enable the PZPR to lead the
socialist renewal, thus keeping it within strictly
defined Leninist limits which would reassure the
USSR.   The balance of forces, however, within the
CC did not provide Kania with much determined support at this plenum.   Although it produced an outright condemnation of the Gierek period, it only

marked a tentative and cautious step in confirming
the Sixth Plenum line in terms of personnel. Four
individuals (Karkoszka, Kowalczyk, Kruczek and
Werblan),who were either too compromised by their
Gierekite pasts or too opposed to the post-August
line, were cleared out of the Politburo. They were
typecast as twardogłowi who had attempted to prevent
Solidarity's registration and who had patronised the
regional hardliners in Częstochowa and elsewhere.
Two hard men replaced them as full members, one of
a nationalist stripe, Moczar, and the other, Grabski,
a managerialist. Fiszbach by becoming a Politburo
candidate emerged as the party's most extreme top
level spokesman, while the politically enigmatic
Ney became a CC Secretary.

As well as deciding to call the Extraordinary
Congress the plenum appointed a 218-strong Congress
Commission to prepare it. Kania quickly relinquished
its running to Olszowski. The guarantee to the
Soviets that nothing too untoward would happen was
reinforced by the plain fact that four-fifths of its
members were incumbents of one sort or another.
Another resolution dealt with the responsibility of
Gierek and Jaroszewicz for the crisis. The CC now
dismissed Gierek from its ranks and condemned his
voluntarism in economic and social decisions, his
unwillingness to listen to advice and his faulty
leadership style which had absorbed the Politburo,
Secretariat and CC on secondary matters while his
caucus took all the important decisions. This
politically was a most convenient interpretation for
his colleagues who still remained politically active.
Gierek had sent Kania a letter in which no less than
8 doctors certified his unfitness to attend. It
was also a long unconvincing apologia that he had
long wanted to resign as First Secretary on health
grounds. He requested that he now be allowed to
resign gracefully from the CC on that basis.
Jaroszewicz, who had been dropped from the CC at
the Sixth Plenum, was now dealt with in far harsher
terms than Gierek. He was blamed for the economic
mistakes of the 1970s, the 1976 prices fiasco and
for his 'apodictic and autocratic' governing style.
Finally, the guilty Gierek seven were told summarily
to resign their Sejm seats which 'they had received
on the recommendation of the CC PZPR in elections to
the Sejm'; thus ran the resolution, revealing quite
starkly where real power lay in Poland.

The plenum heard important decisions, such as

Premier Pińkowski's outline of the emerging Economic
Reform. The speakers then took their cue from
Kania's two main themes. The full and unreserved
condemnation of the previous ruling team was counterbalanced politically by a chorus of attacks on the
negative aspects of the October-November events.
The latter featured most strongly in the speeches of
the rising General Józef Baryła, Head of the Army's
Main Political Department, Milewski, the Minister of
the Interior and Stanisław Wroński, the Editor of
Nowe Drogi, who called for a stop to further concessions. Other specialists,such as Kazimierz
Olszewski, the ambassador to the USSR, and Piątkowski,
the CC International Department Head, and hardline
KW Secretaries such as Haładaj from Tarnobrzeg and
Szablak from Warsaw,also joined in the conservative
counter attack. The writer, Jerzy Putrament, called
for renewed class struggle in contrast to Gierek's
One Nation themes; Werblan made a dignified exit
to his remaining post as Sejm Vice-Marshal with an
intellectually sophisticated apologia pro vita sua.
     The reform line was expressed by two types of
spokesmen. Firstly, a diverse group, such as
Wróbel from the Płock petrochemical works, Jerzy
Romanik from the Siemanowice coalmine in Silesia,
Zofia Grzyb from the Radom leatherworks and
Drozdowicz, a sailor from Gdynia, supported the
Workers' Upsurge. The authentic populist 'hard hat'
voice of the Polish working class was expressed by
the much misunderstood Warsaw builder, Albin Siwak.
He called for a quicker cleansing of the party, for
increased working class representation on the CC and
for collaboration between Solidarity and his branch
union to improve the housing drive. The second
strand of reformers going beyond Kania's centrist
definition were far fewer. Some, like Jarecki from
Kalisz, called for the decentralisation of party-
state decisions and criticised 'the destructive presentation of events by the mass media', but he did
so in the context of explaining that 90% of PZPR
members in his factory belonged to Solidarity in
order, as he said, to cool hotheads and correct
'unjustified activities'. Rakowski now accepted
that radical elements had taken over Solidarity but
he still considered that the best way of weakening
them was to fulfil the Social Agreements. He had
already outlined the themes that the PZPR needed to
talk openly about its political enemies and that
opposition to socialist renewal would merely prolong
the crisis [51]. Other moderate reformers, such as
KW Secretaries Opałko from Tarnów, Józef Nowak from
Wałbrzych and Miśkiewicz from Szczecin, called for

a full and rapid settling of accounts with Gierek
and his times, measures to ensure Social Justice
such as a wage-freeze, sweeping changes in the
Politburo and Secretariat and the conclusion of the
process by the Ninth Congress.   Nowak went furthest.
He argued that stabilisation could only result from
renewal and democratisation as 70% of the Wałbrzych
PZPR had joined Solidarity.   The plea for the PZPR
to support a 'statute-clean' Solidarity was backed
up by Fiszbach's call for a summit meeting between
state and TU leaders.

The plenum's highlight was a major but rambling
speech from Moczar, the grand old man of Polish
Communism, although only 67, and the only major PPR
figure left now that Jaroszewicz had gone.   He
celebrated his unexpected return to the Politburo,
after almost a decade's absence, by supporting Kania's
search for political solutions.   He presented the
rozliczenie argument that the PZPR could cleanse
itself morally and politically and gain a new legitimacy at the Ninth Congress of the political odium
for the crisis could be ascribed to the mistakes of
the Gierek period.   Politically compromised individuals would have to be replaced and corrupt officials dismissed.   Moczar used the near civil war
conditions after the Second World War, when over
20,000 Communists had perished, as a veiled threat
against the party apparatchiks if they proved too
obdurate and to the nation if it went too far.   His
warning of the dangers of a policy of confrontation
by either side was supported by a classic rendition
of the political realist's case that Poland would
remain weak as long as the party remained feeble.

In the last week of November a 50 mile stretch
of the Polish-GDR frontier was closed.   The USSR
put about 30-35 divisions encircling Poland on a
state of alert and carried out various manoeuvres.
These measures drew warnings from Western statesmen
about the effects of a Soviet invasion on détente
and East-West relations.   A major war scare
developed but there is no direct evidence that it
diverted the Polish leadership away from a more
radical reform programme.   The contrary seems indicated by the dramatic PZPR Appeal to the Polish
people issued at the end of the Seventh Plenum.   It
began:'The fate of the nation and of the country is
in the balance.   Continuing disturbances are leading our fatherland to the brink of economic and
moral destruction' (TL, 4 December 1980).   That
this declaration was intended primarily for shock
effect as a psychological weapon in Kania's drive
to seize the political initiative was soon confirmed

when tension abated after the Warsaw Pact meeting
in Warsaw on 5 December.
   The Moscow Summit was attended by Brezhnev,
First Secretaries Zhivkov of Bulgaria, Husak of
Czechoslovakia, Honecker of the GDR, Kadar of
Hungary and, most significantly, Ceausescu of
Romania, with his well known views on socialist non-
interference, as well as their Premiers. Kania's
very full delegation included Piñkowski, Barcikowski,
Olszowski, Jaruzelski, Czyrek and Milewski. The
conference communiqué stated the participants' confidence in the PZPR's ability to overcome the crisis
and to safeguard socialism in Poland. The promise
of fraternal aid and solidarity was not pitched as
strongly as the equivalent Dresden Declaration of
March (TL, 6-7 December 1980).
   All this, linked with Ceausescu's presence,
indicated that the threat of Soviet military intervention was a tactical move. It was designed to
frighten Solidarity and the Polish people and to
pressurise Kania and the Polish leadership to restore order and to maintain Poland within the
socialist orbit in an acceptable Leninist form.
Having said that, there is no doubt that the war
scare was the most serious international crisis
during the Polish affair of 1980-1981. It was perhaps the one occasion when the Soviet leaders
seriously considered the need for military intervention. As far as the Polish crisis was concerned,
it was an additional element which ensured that the
reform programme would in practice be held up for
another 4 months and it guaranteed that strong refor-
mist-minded politicians would only play isolated
and limited roles within the top PZPR leadership in
Spring 1981.
   The PZPR Politburo ratified the results of the
Moscow meeting on 6 December and confirmed, in
fulsome terms, its loyalty to the USSR, the Warsaw
Pact and Comecon (TL, 8 December 1980). This was
insufficient to prevent a sensational TASS allega-
tion of 8 December that Solidarity supporters had
rioted and occupied a factory. Radio Warsaw and
Trybuna Ludu (9 December 1980) denied this and confirmed that 'peace and quiet' reigned in the Iskra
factory in Kielce due in no small measure 'to the
creative activities of the factory's Solidarity
branch'. Soviet pressure, though, may have tilted
the authorities against a preliminary agreement which
Minister of Agriculture, Kłonica, had initialled
with representatives of Poland's private peasant
farmers about the legalisation of a Rural Solidarity,
which was reported as already having 600,000 members.

The re-opening of the Polish-GDR frontier and
a speech by Marshal Ustinov, the Soviet Defence
Minister, had brought the invasion crisis to an end
even before the NATO Council in Brussels on 12
December declared that the West would regard a
Soviet invasion of Poland 'as a fundamental altera-
tion of the international situation' (Le Monde, 15
December 1980). The prevalent view was then summed
up by André Fontaine, the French international
affairs specialist, that Soviet military intervention was unlikely unless the PZPR lost control of
the situation [52]. CPSU Secretary, Boris
Ponamarev, also assured ex-French Premier, Chaban-
Delmas, that 'the Poles are big enough to regulate
their own affairs. The USSR does not dream of
intervening in any way' (Le Monde, 19 December 1980).
The Soviet leadership, however, signalled in its
normal convoluted manner (Petrov, Pravda, 18 December
1980) that, although this particular crisis had
passed, the USSR would still intervene militarily
in Poland if, and when, it became necessary.
    A major analysis by the distinguished French
Kremlinologist, Michel Tatu, noted that the Soviet
leaders' main concerns were to press Kania into re-
establishing social order and the efficiency and
morale of the police and judicial apparats which
had been sapped by the Narożniak affair, to protect
the reliable Leninist hard-core of officials while
sacrificing the Gierek cohort and to maintain the
Polish party apparatus, which was beginning to fray
at the edges [53]. Tatu considered that the Soviets
were going to give Kania time and support to effect
these tasks. However, if he refused to do as he
was bidden,or if he were over tardy, he would eventually receive an ultimatum that if he could not
restore order the Soviets would do it themselves.
Tatu believed that the Red Army could take over
Poland fairly quickly and efficiently. He dis-
counted Western hopes that the Polish Army would
resist. Its Officer Corps was the most carefully
screened and reliable pro-Soviet group in Poland.
However, a Soviet military occupation might be
costly in terms of civilian resistance and would
threaten Soviet lines of communication with the GDR.
Naturally the West would not react militarily but
the USSR would pay a heavy price for intervention.
Tatu concluded that all these factors reinforced
Moscow's preference 'for indirect action, large
enough to restore calm in Poland, but not brutal
enough for everyone to shout that it was a casus
belli'. Tatu was right but, like everyone else,
he could not have foreseen that it would take so

long - exactly a year - to get to the State of War.
At the time of the war scare Klasa had told
Western journalists that it would be the legally
established Polish Government who would decide if,
and when, fraternal socialist assistance were necessary
in order to save socialism in Poland (Le Monde, 6
December 1980). The implication was that the USSR
could not count on Polish stooges equivalent to
Indra or Kolder in the Czechoslovak crisis, although
doubtless many potential Husaks like Kociołek may
have surfaced after an invasion. The Kremlin must
have been influenced in its final decision not only
by the obvious demographic and national differences
between the Polish and Czechoslovak cases but also
by other clear differences. Firstly, the Polish-
Soviet relationship had remained a taboo subject in
the reform debate. Secondly, the Polish party, far
from leading the reform process, was playing a cunning
game. Large sections of its central and local
apparats were doing everything possible to brake
reforms, while its divided leadership trimmed and
tacked. Kania promised the Polish nation renewal
but he made sure that real reformers like Fiszbach
were kept isolated at the top levels while authoritarian minded personalities like Olszowski, Moczar
and Grabski were allowed to make all the running
in the CPA until late March.

A Quiet Christmas and yet another False Start
Official PZPR comment on the Seventh Plenum
stressed that there could be no return to the
pre-August realities, that Poland's geopolitical
and domestic situation meant that renewal could only
come from the party and that it and the party's
democratisation would have to take a Leninist form
acceptable to Poland's allies. The need was now
to move on from expressing past grievances to producing a detailed reform programme (TL, 5 December
1980, p. 3). At the same time Kania's assurances
that the PZPR would not stand for anarchy and 'dual
power' were reflected in a spate of attacks on
Solidarity's misuse of the strike weapon as a form
of blackmail designed to force the authorities into
political concessions (Żołnierz Wolności, 8 December
1980). Both the Church and Solidarity responded
with appeals for social calm but 28 well known intellectuals set up a Committee for the Defence of
Prisoners held for Offences of Opinion [54].
The situation quietened down as the Poles prepared to celebrate a not very happy Christmas and
to contemplate a miserable New Year. The authorities had, however, stocked up with sufficient food,

and introduced temporary rationing, to enable some
of the usual festivities to take place. The most
notable event of this period was the unveiling in
Gdańsk on 16 December of a memorial to the victims
of December 1970. The three 130 foot high inter-
twined crosses had cost 20 million złoties raised
wholly by workers' contributions. Present were
a rare assortment of individuals - notably
Jabłoński, the Chairman of the Council of State,
Cardinal Macharski, Wojtyła's successor in Kraków,
other priests including Bishop Dąbrowski, Wałęsa and
various Solidarity personalities and PZPR officials.
The heavy symbolism of this event, with its mixture
of political speeches and Roman Catholic mass, attended by a crowd estimated at 300,000, showed that the
Church, after being overshadowed by Solidarity since
the Summer, was now making a political comeback.
The men of the cloth had clearly taken fright at the
early December events. This was shown in Abbot
Orszulik's criticisms of KOR and KPN when handing
over the text of the Pastoral Letter, read from all
the pulpits on 14 December to Western journalists.
Macharski also called for 'wisdom and moderation
for the good of the Fatherland' in his Gdańsk
sermon. The Church advised Wałęsa to exclude the
radical pre-August 1980 dissidents from the KKP but
Solidarity refused to do so. The Church also wanted
Solidarity to entrust the editorship of its future
journal to the noted Catholic intellectual and historian, Andrzej Micewski [55]. Another Catholic,
Wałęsa's closest adviser, the medieval historian,
Geremek, set out Solidarity's terms for dialogue
and collaboration with the PZPR. He also explained
why 'the impossible is indispensible' in Poland
(Le Monde, 17 December 1980).
    The Gdańsk commemoration had been celebrated
in terms of Kania's call for unity and social collaboration so that such events would not be repeated.
However, Rakowski warned the leadership not to
interpret any easing of strikes and social unrest
as 'allowing them to slow the tempo' of rebuilding
the structures which had caused the crisis [56].
Political life began to resume its normal rhythm
and much formal and largely spurious controlled
activity again took place; a very tame ZSL Congress on 13-15 December, a somewhat livelier SZSP
one, meetings of economic and propaganda KW Secretaries and the declaration of the Central PZPR-
ZSL-SD Collaboration Committee in support of
socialist renewal and the Soviet alliance (TL,
13-14 December 1980).
    The sorry plight of the Polish economy was

next spelt out to the nation   at the Sejm session
of 19 December which considered the plan and budget
for 1981 [57].   Finance Minister Krzak declared that
the economy had worsened more than expected in the
last quarter of 1980.   Income would only rise by
1% in 1981 but expenditure would increase by 22%
because food subsidies and the extra post-Gdańsk
social and cultural expenditure were greater than
'permitted by the actual financial and material
possibilities of the country'.   Planning Chairman
Kisiel stressed that inflation was being stoked up
as the 1981 wage-fund would be 16% up on 1980, while
state expenditure on pensions, family and sickness
allowances would rise by 30%.   It was clear from
the presentation of these dry statistics that the
Government was mainly concerned to appeal for
realism and self-sacrifice in the face of the
economic disaster and was unable to produce a reform programme which would restore confidence [58].
Clearly the Three Year Plan for rebalancing the
economy promised by Kisiel would not generate much
enthusiasm.   The piecemeal clawbacks which the
Government now envisaged over such Gdańsk Concessions as 'free Saturdays' may have been economically justified but were bound to be politically
provocative.   The Sejm session was therefore a
damp squib.   Its 2½ hour Question and Interpella-
tion period was, however, a significant step forward
in Communist parliamentarianism while an SD amend-
ment was supported by no less than 54 votes and
36 abstentions.
     The PZPR should have taken heed of the warning
signs of social unrest which multiplied in December.
The Governor's Office in Piotrków Trybunalski was
occupied by workers protesting against the failure
to meet their meat rations promised for Christmas.
Solidarity printers threatened to black the production and distribution of Trybuna Ludu, city by
city, in the movement's now favourite tactic of a
rolling strike, unless the ban on the screening of
the documentary, Workers 80, was lifted.   Kania
heard at first hand how uncertain the stabilisation
was from the Płock PZPR militants.   They complained
about the slowness and uncertainty of the renewal
process.   The POP Secretary told him straight out
that 'the crisis in the party has not passed' (TL,
19 December 1980).
     The Ninth Congress preparations began on 20
December with a meeting of the Congress Commission
in Warsaw.   It appointed a Presidium, composed of
Politburo members plus 8 others chaired by Kania, a
30-strong Secretariat headed by Olszowski and it

established 8 working parties on specific topics,
to which a ninth was soon added.   Kania stressed
that the preparation and discussion of a sound programme for the Congress was now a priority.   He
backed the Soviet line on Western interference in
Polish affairs and drew a serious lesson from Soviet
threats by promising that the renewal would serve
both socialism in Poland and the strengthening of
bonds with the socialist bloc (TL, 22 December 1980).
        The Politburo held an end-of-year assessment of
the situation on 23 December.   According to Grabski
it welcomed the lively discussion going on within
party and social organisations.   It found less
solace in the grim economic situation.   Olszowski
later disclosed that a draft project of the Economic
Reform would be revealed in early January and that
it would be a comprehensive one covering both enterprises and the centre (TL, 24-26 December 1980).
The debate of the previous weeks on the thorny questions of 'free Saturdays' and the five day week
also came to the boil with the publication of Government proposals.
        Foreign Minister Czyrek, during his visit to
Moscow on Boxing Day, reassured his hosts that the
Polish leadership was fully aware of the dangers
presented by free TUs and over-radical reforms.
Czyrek gratified Brezhnev by attacking Western interference in Polish affairs and their support of
anti-socialist elements.   He endorsed the Brezhnev
doctrine that the strength of socialism in Poland
and her alliance with the USSR were interlinked questions.   After Czyrek's lightning visit Jagielski
spent 29 December in Moscow discussing Polish-Soviet
economic relations and Poland's 1981 NPS-G with
deputy Premier Archipov and Gosplan Chairman Baibakov.
The Poles accepted the Soviet offer of a $1.1
milliard currency loan and the supply of $200 mil-
lions worth of goods, an indicator that they would
heed Brezhnev's advice to distrust Western offers
and to rely on the Soviet bloc.
        Polish public opinion, as revealed by a mid
December PAN survey, still favoured Solidarity most
markedly and distrusted the authorities [59].
57.9% supported Solidarity decidedly, 31.2% rather
supported it and only 1.2% were decidedly against.
Almost identical percentages supported the Social
Agreements.   Men were more strongly in favour than
women, the better more than the lesser educated, SD
and ZSL more than PZPR members and workers more than
professionals and peasants.   Only local officials
and managers expressed strong opposition.   Most
worryingly for the authorities, 61.6% held them

responsible for not fulfilling the Social Agreements,
while only 1.1% blamed Solidarity. The poll showed
that the Poles were more in favour of a liberal-
pluralist than a centralised-monocentric model of
politics. It also showed that PZPR members were
noticeably less in favour of social equality than
the rest of society [60].

As well as the basic underlying problems the
Poles faced a number of specific explosive issues
at the end of the year. The list was headed by
the registration of Rural Solidarity and the Supreme
Court's decision upholding the Warsaw Court's ruling
that peasants were not employees and therefore
could not qualify for TU status. Other controversies were 'free Saturdays', the loosening of censorship, the release of political prisoners and the
introduction of meat rationing. All these were
potential mines, any one of which could easily upset
the informal strike moratorium before it expired in
mid January. Kania therefore made a very quiet
end-of-year speech in the Trójmiasto on 30 December
warning of the coming economic difficulties. Very
wisely Kania left the main New Year's Message to
the Nation to the Head of State. Jabłoński declared
that 1981 would be a bad year. Worsening economic
conditions would undoubtedly aggravate social conflicts. He was confident, however, that national
unity and determination would overcome all obstacles,
a sentiment which might strike the outside observer
as a flabby absurdity but which many Poles, influenced
by the post-Gdańsk euphoria, still wanted to
believe [61].

The 'Hot January' of 1981

The Seventh Plenum had been a politically most
ambiguous event. On the one hand, Soviet pressure
and the domestic hardline reaction within the CC
set very severe limits to the moves by Kania's centrist pragmatists and the committed worker and progressive wings towards reform. On the other hand,
the Kania-Moczar-Olszowski triumvirate who ruled
Poland between the Seventh and Eighth Plena could
not admit this openly. Their political discourse
therefore became even more convoluted depending
upon whether they were addressing a domestic or
socialist bloc audience. The latter were reassured that all that was happening was a cleansing
of socialism in Poland and that a return to the
party's Leninist roots was taking place which would
strengthen its leading role. The PZPR grassroots
were, however, promised democratisation through the
work of the Congress Commission and the debate over

the party's new programme which was to precede the
holding of the Congress in the early Spring.
 The Kania leadership, however, wasted the relative social calm of December. Symbolic gestures,
such as the Gdańsk ceremony, promises of reform and
attempts to rebalance the retail front, were insufficient to calm the Polish nation even in the depths
of Winter. The problem was that, as a general
politico-economic reform and an appeal to all sections of Polish society had been vetoed by the
Kremlin and checkmated by the balance of forces
within the PZPR CC, the triumvirate seemed rather to
have joined in the psychological tactic, started by
the Soviets in late November, of attempting to overawe the Polish nation. They attempted to regain
the political initiative by opposing some of the
economically costly Gdańsk concessions. They also
claimed that the unreserved condemnation of the
Gierek leadership and the clearing out of discredited
officials who would not accept the new realities
proved the genuineness of Kania's centrist reformism.
However, the renewed PZPR offensive against political
and counter-revolutionary elements within Solidarity
and the Communist leadership's determination to
stand firm on specific issues was bound to weaken
the efforts of the Wałęsa moderates, abetted by the
Church, to control local and extremist pressures.
The result was a recrudescence of massive régime-
society confrontations over a wide range of issues
during what politically became the 'Hot January' of
1981. In the long run this pushed the PZPR leadership back into its Army and police bunker but in the
short term it also appeared, for a while, to have
moved the political centre towards an accelerated
pace of reform. The massive social crisis and the
welter of demands at every level forced the Kania
leadership to emerge from the crisis by establishing
common ground with society through yet another politically indispensable alibi; this was that the
January crisis had been caused not by the lid's
being taken off the seething cauldron of socio-
economic discontent but by the provocative activities of hardliners who would now pay for their sins
by being cleared out in the run-up to the Ninth
Congress.
 A grave national confrontation between the
authorities and Solidarity over the issue of 'free
Saturdays' was, however, mainly a symptom of the
explosion of local and sectoral grievances in almost
every area of Polish society now that the executive
power had been seen to be weakened and its agents
humiliated. The Government presented its case,

that it had not wholly wasted the previous months
in an incredibly detailed and legalistic way, explaining point by point the extent to which every
aspect of the Social Agreements had, or had not,
been fulfilled (TL, 28, 30 January and 7-8 February
1981). Such heavy and dense defences were most
ineffective in convincing public opinion, although
they helped to rally the party faithful.

The regional crises which burst out in January
were two-pronged affairs. Local issues were linked
with popular outbursts against the manner in which
Gierek's officials had milked the public purse.
The first social force to move was the peasants in
Rzeszów province, who were the most active in demanding a Rural Solidarity. On 14 December 1980
they protested to the Sejm against the luxurious
holiday and hunting centres belonging to the MSW and
the Council of Ministers and the 170 magnificent
villas belonging to Communist dignitaries in the
picturesque Bieszczady hills. The local police
retaliated with house searches and harassment of
the peasant activists. Some peasants then occupied
the Municipal Offices in Ustrzyki Dolne, only 10
miles from the Soviet frontier. This Rural
Solidarity-régime confrontation had been fermenting
for 3 months and was to continue for as long again.

Urban discontent was sparked off by the
Government announcement that the 5 day week would
have to be postponed until 1985 and that for the
moment every other Saturday should be worked [62].
In spite of very confused presentation the Government's offer boiled down to a choice between
either an 8 hour day with 2 Saturdays worked a
month or a 5 day week with the working day extended to 8½ hours, as in the rest of Eastern
Europe [63]. Most workers heeded Solidarity's
call to boycott work on Saturday, 10 January, and
did so again on the 23rd, after Wałęsa's return
from his Vatican audience with Pope John Paul II.
The warning strike was, however, postponed until 3
February after the Wałęsa-Pińkowski meetings of 19-
21 January.

This national issue was only one among many
which led workers to occupy factories and municipal
offices all over Poland, especially during the last
ten days of January. Particularly serious flashpoints occurred in Bielsko-Biała, Jelenia Góra,
Zielona Góra, Wrocław, Łódź and Nowy Sącz. For a
while Poland again lived through a period of social
contestation which left all the leaderships momentarily helpless. The Government appeal for social
peace as well as the KKP's call in Rzeszów on 29

January for the temporary suspension of strikes had little effect on the local outbursts (TL, 30 January 1981).

The situation was typified by Jelenia Góra, where Ciosek, the recently appointed Minister for TUs, had been KW First Secretary for 5 years. The workers demanded his dismissal, alleging that he had misused funds allocated for anti-flood purposes by building luxury villas for notables instead. In general such regional outbursts were settled by local agreements which involved compromises over the purely economic demands, the dismissal of unpopular provincial and municipal officials and the re-allocation of buildings, including party and police ones, for social purposes such as schools and hospitals. The Jelenia Góra strike, for instance, ended with deputy Premiers Mach and Ozdowski agreeing to Wałęsa's compromise that a holiday home for functionaries in Szklarska-Poręba be redesignated as a hospital and that a new hospital be built within the next 5 years [64]. Elsewhere Warsaw blamed local power cliques, such as the one headed by KW First Secretary Kostecki, for the train of events which started with a Solidarity occupation of Nowy Sącz town hall on 9 January, their eviction by the militia on the 11th and the declaration of a regional strike on the 16th. This was only resolved after hard negotiations in Warsaw on 19-21 January had set up a Government Commission to investigate charges of corruption against the officials [65]. In the biggest regional crisis in Bielsko-Biała, where at peak a quarter of a million workers in 400 factories went on strike, the Governor and his deputies, who had been accused of corruption and branded as common criminals by Wałęsa, were sacked after mediation by the Church.

Western press reports at this time tended to view the situation in terms of a political morality play with Olszowski allegedly attempting to rally the party hardliners by encouraging Premier Pińkowski and Minister of Labour Obodowski to sabotage Kania's compromise line by provoking the conflict over 'free Saturdays'. The aim was to provoke Solidarity into extreme reactions which could be branded as economically harmful and anti-socialist. These pseudo-Kremlinological explanations only confuse the very complicated realities of the situation. Olszowski, in formal terms, was only the CC Secretary in charge of Ideology and Propaganda and economic responsibilities since September had lain with Grabski and others. It is doubtful, therefore, if he were more than the hard end of an agreed

division of Politburo labour which left the popular
conciliatory gestures to Kania.   On 9 January
Olszowski typically described the party, on TV, as
saying 'yes to renewal but no to chaos'.   The
latter included the onslaught on local officials
and the rejection of the working week proposals (TL,
10-11 January 1981).   Kania, on the other hand,
after meeting Marshal Kulikov in Warsaw on 13
January, together with Jaruzelski and Pińkowski, was
hardly less hardline the following day at a meeting
of KZ Secretaries.   His themes for the party faithful were that Solidarity had been penetrated by
anti-socialist elements and that there was 'no room
in our state for dual power';   only the PZPR 'could
lead the country out of the crisis' (TL, 16 January
1981).   The party ideologist, Norbert Michta, presented the emerging line on the reformability of the
socialist system but in a Leninist, not a revisionist,
form in more refined theoretical terms (TL, 14
January 1981).
     The reality of the January situation was that
the Politburo attempted to use the argument of
economic rationality to contain Solidarity and to
make it jointly responsible for the aggravation of
the economic situation in the eyes of public opinion.
It was also an attempt to raise the morale of the
party functionaries and to demonstrate the post-
Seventh Plenum policy of firmness to the Kremlin.
The impish Urban characterised the 'free Saturdays'
dispute as an argument not over where power lay in
the state but over the respective jurisdictions of
Solidarity and the party state (Polityka, 31
January 1981).   To smooth this over Rakowski had
earlier suggested the establishment of a top level
Mixed Commission to exchange views and to delineate
the appropriate spheres of Government and Solidarity
activity (Polityka, 17 January 1981).
     The result of society's renewed contestation
and refusal to back down in January was twofold.
In the short term the PZPR conservatives were
pilloried and overawed.   Gradually the initiative
moved in favour of the pragmatic moderate reformers
during the early Spring;   but the régime also
started preparing an alternative strategy based on
force from this moment on.
     Moczar, whose prestige had been increased by
his appointment as FJN vice-President, confirmed
the former aspect in a major article which osten-
sibly dealt with the pre-PZPR traditions of Polish
Communism.   He argued that the only way 'to avoid
more social outbursts' was not only to dismiss the
officials responsible for the crisis but also those

who opposed 'the great revolution' of Summer 1980
and the 'new views, ideals and activities of the
great mass of the people' [66].   Moczar had always
had an ambivalent love-hate relationship with the
Polish intelligentsia [67].   In his mellower old age
he now appeared, genuinely or tactically is debatable,
more sympathetic to its values.   In this he was,
rather oddly, at one with the conclusions of the
Third DiP Report, published at this time;   this
likewise stressed the need for far-reaching political changes in order to surmount the social and
economic crisis and to limit the capacity of the
bureaucracy to brake social renewal and to force
confrontations with society [68].   DiP, though,
called for fundamental structural changes while
Moczar wanted to stabilise the political situation
through sweeping changes in leadership personnel
and through some intra-system reforms implemented
from above.
    The short term aspect seemed to be confirmed by
the Pińkowski-Wałęsa agreement, after 13 hours of
negotiations, on 30 January [69].   The Government
suffered a humiliating defeat, even though the final
compromise of three free Saturdays a month appeared
to fall between Solidarity's bid for 4 and the
authorities' offer of 2.   The Government also agreed
that Solidarity would have its own journal and access
to the mass media and it backed down on most of the
local issues in contention.   In exchange, Solidarity,
which had earlier been accused by Kania of aspiring
to become a political opposition, called off the
general strike of 3 February.   It started forging
a new relationship with the party-state.   Wałęsa
and the TU wing of Solidarity, with the support, and
often with the actual involvement, of the Church,
began to act as 'social firemen' in helping to resolve local conflicts in late January.   The decision by the PZPR to use political means to resolve
the crisis seemed to have been reconfirmed by the
January events which put the imprimatur on the acceptance of NSZZs and the pluralist democratisation
of Polish life.   In Spring 1981 these questions were
superceded by the debate over whether the PZPR itself should guarantee these changes by transforming
itself into a democratically elected and membership
controlled party and over the methods by which this
could be achieved within a Leninist framework which
would be acceptable faute de mieux to the rest of
the Communist bloc.   However, even then the Government refused to give way gracefully, risking another
trial of strength with the decree of 3 February on
strike pay.   As usual the CPA counterpoint came

from Olszowski. He condemned political strikes
'outside Solidarity's statute', decried the PZPR's
'ideological weakness' and opposed grassroots' demands which would weaken the party's central organisation (TL, 3 February 1981).

Secondly, the long term repercussions of the
'Hot January' were not what they then seemed. At
the time Jaruzelski's appointment as Premier was
hailed as a masterstroke, putting the cap on the
failure of the alleged hardline offensive to capture
the CPA and to overawe society. The false corollary
was drawn that it confirmed the victory of a more
advanced reform line of dialogue with society.
However, seen from the viewpoint of the State of War
it is obvious that it was then that the PZPR began
preparing for the alternative policy of forcible
repression to cover the eventuality of the former
policy's failing or running out of control.

'The Counter-Revolution will not pass in Poland'
    The most important decision of the Eighth
Plenum held on 9 February was to replace Piñkowski,
who had proved a most indecisive Premier, with
General Wojciech Jaruzelski [70]. No other leadership changes took place. Jaruzelski's appointment
was obviously designed to suggest to Polish society
that the brink had been reached (yet once more!)
and to the USSR that the right man was now in the
right place if force were needed. The battered
Kania leadership also hoped that Jaruzelski's prestige and strength of character would enable him to
arbitrate the paralysing disputes between the various
state bureaux and that his standing would strengthen
the Government's handling of social conflicts and
the economic crisis. The consequences of the
internal party stalemate were now so grave that
Kania and Moczar had to call in the Army in order to
push through their policy of stabilising the crisis
by purging the PZPR's directing personnel. To this
end the 'cemetery vote' was weakened further by
the dismissal of another 8 discredited ex-incumbents
from the CC.

The Plenum was dominated by Grabski's vigorous
attack, in his Politburo report, on KOR attempts to
turn the free TUs into political forces which would
dismantle the state and destabilise society and the
economy. The political divide, he declared very
significantly, was not between the PZPR and Solidarity but ran within Solidarity itself. Grabski
attacked the local branches of Solidarity which had
fallen into the hands of the PZPR's enemies, who had
resorted to non-statutory activities such as public

130

demonstrations and the distribution of anti-leaflets
and posters and who had used regional discontents
and pretexts such as free Saturdays as excuses for
'successive trials of strength with the Government'.
Grabski warned the Solidarity leaders that they had
little time left to choose between 'ever-escalating
demands maintained in a state of tension or the path
of active participation in the effort to extract the
country from its unusually grave situation'.
    In a weak and unconvincing speech, which mirrored
the Politburo's indecision, Barcikowski confirmed
that the PZPR would continue to put its house in
order by preparing the Ninth Congress, which was now
tacitly postponed again, by democratising itself and
Polish politics generally and by carrying through
fundamental reforms,especially of the economy. On
the other hand, the Politburo had decided not to
accept Rural Solidarity and to favour self-management within its 23,000 Agricultural Circles as far
back as early January (TL, 7 January 1981).
    The plenum's main theme was symbolised in the
exchange between Jan Łąbecki from the Lenin Shipyard, who defended the policy of dialogue, and
Zygmunt Wroński from Ursus who called for a strong
party counter-attack. Two significantly new ac-
cents were the plenum's welcome of the reactivisation of the PZPR grassroots and its endorsement of
Moczar's earlier call for the cleansing of the party
before the Ninth Congress. The change in party
mood was reflected by that astute political weather-
cock, Żabiński, who considered that the situation
was now diametrically different from what it had
been the previous August. The dilemma then had
been to be 'either with the working class and its
justified protest or against it'. Now the issue
was 'whether to defend People's power together with
the working class or to surrender it into the hands
of our enemies, in spite of that same working class'.
Żabiński's call for all PZPR members within Solidarity
to oppose political strikes and anti-socialist forces
as their party duty was seconded by Siwak in his
inimitable fashion. However, workers such as
Wróbel from Płock still complained about the way in
which the Congress Commission was delaying its preparation. Gajewski, a brigade leader from Huta
Warszawa, accused sections of the PZPR leadership
of obstructing reform and of attempting 'to bring
about a tragedy'. Jamroz, a Kraków builder, blamed
the CPA for the political paralysis and the conflicts with Solidarity as 'our party structures do
not allow for a clear and effective dialogue' with
the TUs.

Kania's closing speech reflected the CC's hardening tone. He denounced the almost wholly political strikes of the past weeks which had paralysed Poland's economy and communications. Solidarity was being influenced by experienced politicians who wanted to cause chaos and liquidate socialism. But, said Kania, directing his remarks at both Moscow and domestic Polish opinion, 'the counter-revolution will not pass in Poland'. His assurances that the PZPR would continue the process of socialist renewal carried much less conviction, especially as he concluded with plain Soviet type language; the need was to 'ensure the socialist character of the new TUs, to isolate politically all the enemies of socialism and to nip in the bud all counter-revolutionary tendencies'.

Leadership and Personnel Change as a Method of Crisis-Stabilisation

I have argued elsewhere that there was a close relationship between 'the official inquest on, and diagnosis of,the causes of the crisis' and the development of 'the political programme for overcoming it' [71]. One crucial aspect was that the battered PZPR leadership decided that it could not purge the unreliable party membership and slim down to its solid cadres,as Husak had done in post-invasion Czechoslovakia. The PZPR took a directly opposite course. Leadership change fuelled by grassroots and popular demands for democratisation and 'rozliczenie' with the Gierek period became a key method of crisis-stabilisation and eventually caused the replacement of almost the entire central and provincial PZPR leadership and widespread élite change in all walks of life except the Army and the police.

The process was not completed until the Ninth Congress, so at this point I will merely draw up an interim balance sheet of the changes which occured by early February. I also propose to set out some general considerations on the nature of the power-struggle in the Polish Communist system during crisis periods.

Factionalism is banned in Leninist systems. Democratic Centralism, in theory, relies on democratic discussion before a decision is taken. It is then followed by the united support of the whole membership for that decision. In particular, the right is refused to any minority to continue to express its viewpoint after the appropriate party organs have decided. This has been the basis of Leninist party rule almost from the very beginning

of Soviet power [72].   In practice, especially
under conditions of authoritarian political culture
and the absence of civic democratic traditions, this
allows the leadership to control the CP from the top
downwards.   It does so both by setting policy and
by controlling personnel,through the nomenklatura or
its equivalent, at every party level and through it
appointments in most other walks of life.   All this
is well known but there is one aspect which particularly concerns me here.   Although factionalism
is banned it is also obvious that one of the bases
of CP rule is clientèle-politics [73].   The First
Party Secretary usually rules so long (Brezhnev,
1964-1982; Zhivkov since 1954; Kadar since 1956;
Hodja since the Second World War) because once he
has gained full control of the Secretariat, and appointed his nominees at all levels, there is a
formidable pressure group in favour of political
stability.   Any change in the central leadership
would naturally also involve regional and other
level changes.
     Now the Polish Communist case is unusual to
the extent to which normal bureaucratic Communist
politics have had to contend with external societal
pressures.   These were the predominant forces in
causing leadership change in 1956, 1970 and 1980.
Throughout the Gomułka-Gierek period they faced the
PZPR with continual challenges which made it impossible for the First Secretary and his friends to
exclude potential rivals entirely who naturally had
competing political programmes and orientations.
Hence, quite apart from the traditions of ideological
dispute and internal political contention inherited
from the KPP, the PZPR was always notorious as a
factional-ridden party.   Communist power-struggles
have usually been presented in the West as being
wholly Machiavellian affairs with the participants
regarding policies as mere slogans which the absence
of such checks as an effective public opinion, a
free press or democratic elections would enable them
to abandon subsequently almost at will.   Control of
the domestic mass media and publishing then allows
the victors to rewrite history as they consider appropriate.   All this is true but what is striking
about postwar Communist politics is the extent to
which, especially after 1956, the Polish élite,
and through it a remarkably wide section of the
population, was informed about the policy stances
adopted by Communist politicians, at various times,
and this naturally had an effect on their subsequent
credibility.   Secondly, Western analysts generally
underestimate the extent to which Communists sincerely

believe in their ideas and principles.   One can,
however, cite numerous cases of genuine political
commitment being adhered to by post-1956 politicians
such as Jerzy Morawski and even those who trimmed in
order to survive rarely wholly reneged on their original stances.   Lastly, another and perhaps most
specific feature of the Polish case in the way that
factionalism came through is that groups of pro-
Sovet or national reformist orientation tended to
take up similar political positions repeatedly as
issues came and went.   This meant that political
friendships and hatreds were formed and that politicians of similar inclinations often tended to
meet together to concert their initiatives.   Now
all this informal activity is a far cry from the
next stage of coalescence, as in the case of <u>Natolin</u>
and <u>Pu/awy</u> in 1956.   Even the more normal factional
activities, however, introduced an element of
pluralist politics, very similar to the politics of
18th century England where factions rallied around
political notables and where politics was a similar
blend of principle, self-interest and power-
struggle [74].   On the other hand, the changing,
impermanent and often artificial nature of Communist
factions can easily be evidenced by the apparent co-
hesiveness of the <u>Partisans</u> in the 1960s and the
ease with which Gierek decapitated their leadership,
sacked the irreconcilables and unsuitable and won
over the bulk to his own interest in the early 1970s.
        The relationship between such political labels
as 'reformer', 'hardliner', 'conservative' or
'nationalist' and Communist political practice is a
subject worth more extended discussion than is
allowed here.   One may doubt whether such labels
in normal times are particularly useful in predict-
ing the political behaviour of individuals.   There
is also the great difficulty in closed societies in
pinning the appropriate labels on personalities.
Metamorphoses such as those of the hardline <u>Partisans</u>
into Gierek's supporters were as nothing compared to
the rapidity with which Western journalists chopped
and changed the labels on individuals during the
rapidly moving crisis of 1980-1981.   An individual
such as Stefan Olszowski, for example, might have
appeared as an unprincipled political chameleon to
outsiders.   He started off linked with Moczar and
the <u>Partisans</u> in the late 1960s, then became a representative Gierekite as Minister of Foreign Affairs
in the first half of the 1970s, while his skilled
political footwork in the late 1970s allowed him to
pose as an economic reformer.   His dismissal from
the Politburo and Secretariat at the Eighth Congress

and short temporary exile as ambassador to the GDR
then allowed him to make his stunning political comeback.   In September 1980 Olszowski presented himself as a pragmatic Communist reform candidate for
First Secretary, but this stance was soon left
behind by rapidly moving events.   Olszowski personally did not change much but by Autumn 1980 he
was considered to be the hardline spokesman of the
party apparatus.   By the following Spring he was
unjustly regarded as a pro-Soviet Targowiczan, or
the sort of Pole who was willing to sell his country
to the Russians [75].
     The social crisis and the pace of political
change, however, ensured that the pall bearers of
Gierek's régime (pogrobowcy) such as Żabiński,
Wojtaszek, Waszczuk and Pińkowski, even though they
survived for a while, found that their political
pasts in this instance robbed them of all political
credibility.   Their political survival, and soon
even that of intra-régime critics such as Moczar,
Olszowski and Grabski, naturally impelled them therefore into conservative positions against the rising
wave of politicians with cleaner or, even better,
no political pasts who were now baying reform slogans in order to get their posts.   Additionally,
large numbers of Gierek's officials lost their posts
but many remained as the 'cemetery vote' on the CC.
They complicated the situation by refusing to accept
a rapid, complete and quiet political demise and
retarded reform until Kania overwhelmed them by
calling in the PZPR grassroots from late March to
the Ninth Congress.
     In power terms, as we have seen, Kania's post-
September strategy was to blame the crisis on the
mistakes of the Gierek régime and to pander to the
traditional Polish desire for scapegoats by throwing
its more corrupt representatives to the wolves.   A
modulated policy of personnel change was also designed to convince Polish society that significant
and irreversible political changes were taking
place.   Starting at Politburo and Secretariat
level with the removal of the inner ring of Gierek's
tem and then spreading out to affect slightly less
close supporters by the Seventh Plenum 11 Politburo
members had been replaced by 8 new ones and only 7
survived (Barcikowski, Jabłoński, Jagielski,
Jaruzelski, Kania, Pińkowski and Wojtaszek).   Only
Kania remained in the Secretariat, although one of
the members, Kurowski, moved up to become a full
Secretary while the other, Zieliński, still remained.   21 members of the CC had been dismissed
and replaced by 24 new ones, an unprecedented

development between Communist congresses. Significant changes had taken place among the Heads of
CC Departments. The provincial changes were a bit
slower but by the Eighth Plenum Kania had replaced
about half of the 49 KW First Secretaries and considerable changes had taken place in the composition of most provincial, municipal and factory party
Executives. Radical calls for democratic elections
at every party level before the Ninth Congress were,
however, largely unheeded and only slow and limited
moves in this direction started from January onwards [76]. From October onwards KW First Secretaries started resigning as Chairmen of their Provincial People's Councils and the CPA quietly decentralised the choosing of their replacements to local
forces through the use of secret and contested
elections.

At the state level 33 ministerial changes (including the Government reshuffle of 12 February
1981) had occurred including the appointment of 2
new Chairmen of the Council of Ministers. The most
sweeping changes were in the Planning Commission,
the Ministry of Mining and the Committee for Radio
and TV. Most noteworthy was the reappearance of
Józef Tejchma as Minister of Culture and the appointment of Czyrek to Foreign Affairs, Milewski to the
Interior, Krzak to Finance and Kisiel as Planning
Chairman. Numerous deputy Ministers were replaced,
as were various Chairmen of state agencies. Eight
Sejm deputies had gone (the Gierek inner team plus
Szczepański) and some minor changes affected the
Council of State. Lastly, provincial Governors
and their deputies were replaced gradually from
November onwards and the process accelerated during
the Winter and Spring.

Greater changes took place among the leaderships of social organisations such as the Youth and
Co-operative movements and of associations such as
the SDP and the ZLP. University and Polytechnic
Senates were now electing their Rectors in genuine,
contested elections, while the reinvigorated life of
the People's Councils was only one step behind what
was going on in the TUs. It is significant, though,
that, unlike 1956, the subsidiary political parties,
especially the ZSL, were left behind by the political ferment which encouraged the formation or
development of a wide range of discussion clubs.

What was significant about the top level
changes was the extent to which the discredited
Gierek generation was replaced initially by its
intra-party critics and individuals who had lost
power with the ending of Gierek's early reform period.

Many had, in a traditional Communist way, been packed off to diplomatic posts like Klasa to Mexico, Tejchma to Switzerland and Kociołek to Belgium. What was usually the last post before retirement, however, on this occasion afforded a haven for many surprising comebacks. What was also striking was that in the first months after August all that happened was that officials like Wojtaszek or Waszczuk who were next in line merely moved up a step. Not surprisingly, Polish public opinion regarded such moves as cosmetic irrelevancies, while the failure to give Kania a Politburo majority at the Sixth Plenum paralysed the CPA's capacity for instituting decisive changes. At most Kania could only chip away at the provincial organisations and build up a clientèle and a consensus slowly around his person. This painfully slow process, however, lagged behind the expectations of Polish society which was not impressed by the purely statistical aspect of these changes. The prevalent view was that safe politicians were being rotated around for effect according to what was colloquially called the leadership 'carousel'. The problem was that the only individuals who had the experience and the qualifications to run the Ministries and Agencies were bound to be politically reliable individuals. However the matter may have been regarded by outsiders, one should note that insiders involved in the process felt that they were not on a quiet carousel which sooner or later would bring them back to their original starting point, but rather that they were 'riding an unsafe and heady roller-coaster without a definite stopping-off point' [77]. As individuals Kania, Barcikowski, Jagielski and Olszowski were just as much identified with the Gierek period as Karkoszka, Kowalczyk or Kruczek; but the former were forgiven to some extent because of their espousal of the reform line which allowed them to squeeze the latter out who were consequently forced into the negative actions and attitudes which allowed them to be typecast as twardogłowi. Hardly surprisingly, the young, under 35, generation in particular felt alienated from such a realpolitik form of élitist Communist power politics. What was peculiar was that some of them should risk so much in 1980 in trying to change it, although even here the mixture of idealism and ambition was not as clear as one might suppose from the rhetoric of moral renewal. Commentators such as Kazimierz Koźniewski took a pessimstic view of those elements of Polish political culture which worked against genuine pluralism and individualism. He condemned the Poles as 'a society of conformists' who went along with the

prevailing fashion irrespective of whether it was
a reform or a conservative one [78].

Notes

1. On the interconnection between the PZPR's leading role
and the Soviet alliance as perceived by a prominent CPA
spokesman, the Editor of the PZPR's theoretical monthly,
see Stanisław Wroński, 'Socjalizm i sojusz polsko-
radziecki - gwarancja i bezpieczeństwo PRL', Nowe Drogi
(January-February 1981). For the emigré opposition
viewpoint, Obserwatorium, 'Niepodległość i Rosja',
Kultura (Paris, July-August 1981), pp. 18-24.
2. Guetta, 'Le PC polonais désemparé', Le Monde, 7.10.80.
See also Szeliga's account, Polityka, 11.10.80.
3. English text in Contemporary Poland (September-October
1980), pp. 22-60.
4. A lively discussion took place at this time on how to
abolish crises from the Polish political scene. Cf.
M. Gułżyński, 'Zrozumieć kryzys', Literatura, 16.10.80.
5. VI Plenum, KC PZPR, 5-6 września, 4-6 października 1980r
(Warsaw, KiW, 1980). Edited versions were as usual
published in TL, 6 & 7.10.80. All the speeches and proceedings of this and subsequent plena were reproduced in
full in Nowe Drogi. I have therefore adopted the con-
vention of citing the page references to the latter, in
this instance to a special double issue of Nowe Drogi
(October-November 1980): Kania, pp. 9-32 and 39-42;
Olszowski, pp. 132-136; Moczar, pp. 78-82; Tejchma,
pp. 165-172; Łukasiewicz, pp. 86-90; Grudzień, pp. 90-
96; Wrzaszczyk, pp. 96-108; Jankowski, pp. 186-190;
Kruczek, pp. 242-246; Bielecki, pp. 296-300; Kowalczyk,
pp. 261-264; Werblan, pp. 251-254; Fiszbach, pp. 68-72;
Jagielski, pp. 177-181; Barcikowski, pp. 199-203;
Jaruzelski, pp. 146-149; Proceedings and Decisions,
pp. 5-8; 'Report on Strike Situation', pp. 43-58.
6. These ideas were later set out in two significant
articles: 'W tyglu polskich przemian', Życie Warszawy,
10.10.80, and 'Dawne kryzysy i dzisiejsze problemy',
Życie Warszawy, 13.1.81. The latter was a key analysis
of the crises of 1948, 1956 and 1970 in which Werblan
showed why reformist tendencies in Poland tended to be
weaker than revisionist ones. His mature synthesis of
the reasons for the cyclical pattern of post-1948 developments was 'Spór o granice władzy', Polityka, 21.3.81.
7. The Warsaw KW Plenum of 18 November, for example, wanted
to combat 'ever more active anti-socialist forces',
Życie Warszawy, 20 & 21.10.80.
8. SSS, VIIIth Sejm, 6th sitting of 8.10.80. Pińkowski and
Ministerial Changes, cols. 142-159; Kisiel, cols. 49-58;
Krzak, cols. 58-71; NIK debate, cols. 6-48, 6 abstentions
against Moczar.

138

Power-struggle and social conflicts

9. Ludwik Krasucki, 'W kręgu negacji', TL, 18-19.11.80.
10. Cf. W. Giełżyński, 'Eskalatorzy i zamazywacze', Polityka, 20.10.80.
11. Dziennik Zachodni, Katowice, 6.11.80.
12. See Żabiński's interview, Polityka, 31.1.81.
13. 'Rzecz naprawdę pospolita', Polityka, 20.10.80.
14. Życie Warszawy, 30.10.80. Bratkowski settled in as Editor of its weekly supplement, 'Życie i Nowoczesność'.
15. On Piasecki, see L. Blit, The Eastern Pretender (London, Hutchinson, 1965).
16. See the statement by Dr. Andrzej Drawicz, its programme director, Dziennik Polski, 15.10.80, and ICPA News Bulletin, 81/2, for the TKN Declaration of 6.1.81.
17. Adam Krzemiński, 'Między fasadę a tyłami', Polityka, 4.10.80.
18. Cf. R. Matuszewski, Polityka, 18.10.80; Miłosz's interview, ibid., 6.6.81.
19. The Captive Mind (London, Secker & Warburg, 1953).
20. Le Monde, 1.10.80.
21. 'Nożyce', Polityka, 25.10.80.
22. Cited in Le Monde, 5.10.80.
23. The Kraków party consulted its members in novel ways by instituting a Resolutions Committee on 13 October, headed by the UJ sociology Professor, Hieronim Kubiak. These motions were discussed by 500 delegates in a lively session on 20 December which generated a whole range of proposals for the democratisation of the PZPR; TL, 22.12.80.
24. Stanisław Paweł, President of the Warsaw Provincial Court, detailed the official objections to Solidarity's draft statutes in TL, 20.10.80. As usual, the Warsaw wags produced an appropriate quip - Question: Why cannot Brezhnev join Solidarity? Answer: Because he does not accept the leading role of the PZPR!
25. See ICPA News Bulletin, 18.11.80, for the KKP protest of 24 October, the telegram to Pińkowski, the Jagielski discussions and the KKP resolutions of 27-28 October.
26. TL, 31.10.80.
27. The most prominent Solidarity spokesmen - Wałęsa, Gwiazda, Borusiewicz, Lis and Pieńkowska - set their views out in a round table discussion in Polityka,1.11.80.
28. N. Carroll, 'Wałęsa claims biggest victory', Sunday Times, 2.11.80.
29. TL, 7.11.80; English text, Contemporary Poland (November 1980), pp. 24-32.
30. Taking the number of registered NSZZs to 28, Życie Warszawy, 12.11.80.
31. For Solidarity's reaction to registration, ICPA News Bulletin, 18.11.80.

139

32. Wałęsa's letter to the sugar workers in ibid.; on teachers, see M. Bajer, 'Czego chcę nauczyciele?', Polityka, 6.12.80.
33. Le Monde, 12.11.80.
34. 'W kręgu sprzeczności i nadziei', Polityka, 15.11.80.
35. See KKP communiqué of 9 November, ICPA News Bulletin, 18.11.80.
36. Le Monde, 18.11.80.
37. Protokóły porozumień rząd-służba zdrowia(Warsaw, IW, ZZ, 1981). On the problems of the health service and its near collapse from the late 1970s onwards, see L.F. Millard, 'The health of the Polish health services', Critique, No. 15 (1981), pp. 57-67, and the May 1979 KOR report on hospitals, pp. 68-91. For official views, see Marcisz, TL, 12.12.80, and Professor Stefan Malawski, Polityka, 18.7.81.
38. 'Les dirigeants sur la sellette à Częstochowa', Le Monde, 20.11.80.
39. The reshuffle also introduced Stanisław Ciosek as Minister without Portfolio to deal with the TUs. The PAX leader, Ryszard Reiff, opposed this inadequate administrative response: SSS, VIIIth Sejm, 7th sitting of 20-21 November 1980, cols. 210-211.
40. TL, 21.11.80.
41. Koperski, another hardline Gierek throwback, was replaced as Łódź KW First Secretary, at the same time, by Tadeusz Czechowicz, a KW Secretary who had previously been a textile union official.
42. The document was reproduced in The Times, 27.11.80, and ICPA News Bulletin, 27.11.80.
43. The two Mazowsze declarations of 21 and 25 November; Kultura (Paris, January-February 1981), pp. 207-208.
44. The ICPA News Bulletins for late November 1980 for the Solidarity viewpoint.
45. See Ascherson, Polish August, pp. 204-208.
46. 'Ominąć stare błędy', Polityka, 8.11.80.
47. Proposals for a bicameral parliament with an Upper Chamber of Producers representing workers and an elected Lower House were also raised in the context of the general debate about how to dismantle Bureaucratic Socialism in Poland. Cf. A. Albrecht, Życie Warszawy, 24.11.80, and Z. Szeliga, 'Sejm. Sięganie po władzę', Polityka, 3.1.81. On this question, G. Sanford, 'The Functions of the Polish Sejm. Crisis periods and the conditions for its revitalisation', Paper presented to the PSA Workshop on Legislative Behaviour, Manchester University, November 1981.
48. SSS, VIIIth Sejm, 7th sitting of 20-21 November 1980. Bukowski, cols. 46-48; Moczar, cols. 145-155; Oliwa, cols. 170-174; Kłonica, cols. 6-19; Załęski, cols. 19-25; Wojtecki, cols. 26-31.
49. 'Partia umacnia się w działaniu', TL, 29-30.11.80.

50. VII Plenum KC PZPR, 1-2 grudnia 1980r (Warsaw, KiW, 1980).
    All references to Nowe Drogi (December 1980): Kania,
    pp. 3-24 (English text, Contemporary Poland [December
    1980]); Pińkowski, pp. 25-35; Gierek's letter, 65-68;
    resolutions and decisions, pp. 36-60. The following
    speeches are in the January-February 1981 issue: Baryła,
    pp. 47-50; Milewski, pp. 67-70; Wroński, pp. 75-78;
    Olszowski, pp. 133-138; Piątkowski, pp. 122-125;
    Putrament, pp. 59-62; Werblan, p. 155; Wróbel,
    pp. 7-9; Romanik, pp. 15-17; Drozdowicz, pp. 56-59;
    Siwak, pp. 70-75; Jarecki, pp. 98-101; Moczar, pp. 83-
    89; Fiszbach, pp. 139-143; Nowak, pp. 80-83; Rakowski,
    pp. 19-24, also Polityka, 6.12.80.
51. 'Porozmawiamy o partii', Polityka, 29.11.80.
52. 'Un Rubicon plus large qu'en 1968', Le Monde, 11.12.80.
53. 'L'économie d'une guerre', Le Monde, 19.12.80.
54. For their letter of 20 December to Jabłoński, Kultura
    (Paris, March 1981), pp. 152-154.
55. The post eventually went to another Catholic intellectual,
    Mazowiecki.
56. 'Nigdy więcej', Polityka, Życie Warszawy, 16.12.80.
57. SSS, VIIIth Sejm, 8th sitting of 19.12.80. See DzU
    No. 27 of 29.12.80 for the budget law which authorised
    expenditure of 363 milliard złoties,as against an income
    of 290 milliard złoties for the first quarter of 1981.
58. Régime spokesmen such as Wiatr attempted to popularise
    the argument that a heavy economic price would have to
    be paid for 'the deepest and longest wave of strikes in
    postwar Europe', Życie Warszawy, 10.12.80, p. 3. How
    this could be squared with party led reform and demo-
    cratisation was unclear, but see the sophisticated argu-
    ment by Jan Szczepański in Polityka, 3.1.81.
59. Władysław Adamski, 'Solidarność w oczach opinii publicznej',
    Kultura, 22.3.81.
60. Lena Kolarska and Andrzej Rychard, 'Polacy 80 - wizje
    ładu społecznego', Aneks, No. 27 (1982), pp. 101-121.
    One of their key conclusions was that 'above all PZPR
    members are characterised by a non-egalitarian orienta-
    tion in relation to the rest of society', pp. 103 & 107.
61. TL, 2.1.81; English text, Contemporary Poland (January
    1981). On the other hand, the 59% of Poles who in mid
    September had thought that things would get better had
    now dwindled to 38%; J. Maziarski, Kultura, 25.1.81.
62. On the course of the dispute, ICPA News Bulletin, 1981/2,
    pp. 7-15. The draft of 'The Basic Provisions of Econo-
    mic Reform' published at this time did little to offer
    the public any way out of the economic impasse, while
    the experts soon fell to quarrelling over the proposals:
    Komisja do Spraw Reformy Gospodarczej,Podstawowe
    Założenia Reformy Gospodarczej(projekt) (Warsaw, Nakł.),
    TL, January 1981.

63. The Szydlak Commission had prepared the trial introduction of the Bulgarian model in selected factories in Radom, Płock and Opole in the mid 1970s but the plan was never implemented. See Rajkiewicz interview in Polityka, 29.10.81, and Helena Otto, 'Czas pracy i czas odpoczynku', ibid., 24.1.81.
64. For the official version of Jelenia Góra events, TL, 11.2.81. For the Solidarity MKS demands, AS 25/1-2/2/1981, pp. 1-2.
65. M. Szulc, 'Lekcja Sądecka', Polityka, 31.1.81.
66. 'Historyczne tradycje PPR a współczesność', TL, 21.1.81.
67. Cf. his Eighth Plenum speech in October 1956; Nowe Drogi (October 1956), pp. 218-223.
68. Konswerwatorium DiP, 'Raport Trzeci. Społeczeństwo Polskie po sierpniu 1981r', Kultura (Paris, September 1981), pp. 115-175.
69. TL, 2.2.81. Le Monde, 2.2.81. KKP communiqué on meeting in ICPA News Bulletin, 1981/2, pp. 11-15; also AS 25/1-2/2/1981, pp. 10-15.
70. VIII Plenum KC PZPR, 9 lutego 1981r (Warsaw, KiW, 1981). All refs. to Nowe Drogi (March 1981): Grabski, pp. 7-25 (English text, Contemporary Poland [March 1981]); Barcikowski, pp. 26-35; Łębecki, pp. 83-86; Wroński, pp. 71-73; Żabiński, pp. 78-83; Siwak, pp. 90-95; Gajewski, pp. 100-102; Jamroz, pp. 49-51; Adamek, pp. 62-64; Kania, pp. 41-48 (English text, Contemporary Poland [March 1981]); Resolution, pp. 36-40.
71. Sanford, 'Response of the Polish Communist Leadership ..', p. 33.
72. M. Waller, Democratic Centralism: an historical commentary (Manchester UP, 1981).
73. For a useful bibliographic guide to recent discussion on leadership maintenance, recruitment and succession and the new behavioural approaches to Communist studies, see V. Bunce and J. Echols, 'From Soviet Studies to Comparative Politics', Soviet Studies, XXXI, No. 1 (January 1979), pp. 43-55.
74. On this see G. Ionescu and I. de Madariaga, Opposition (Harmondsworth, Penguin, 1972).
75. For his official biography, TL, 20.7.81.
76. Witkowski, Polityka, 7.2.81.
77. Sanford, 'Response of the Polish Communist Leadership ..', p. 44.
78. K. Koźniewski, 'Pluralizm', Polityka, 7.2.81. Like the French the Poles are a nation of individualists who all demand the right to be able to choose to do the same thing. A small indicator of this is the phenomenally high percentage of Poles who within a short time flock to see a popular film like the latest Wajda or Zanussi and the dominance of a single controversy or theme among the intelligentsia at various times.

Chapter Five

NOT YET TIME TO REVERSE THE COURSE OF EVENTS
(FEBRUARY TO MAY 1981)

In the months since the Gdańsk Agreement political and intellectual life and public discussion
had flourished.   The periodic confrontations
between the régime and Solidarity had produced a
formidable radicalisation of the working class,
whose wide-ranging demands now presented formidable
problems of political and social control.   But the
balance sheet of institutional changes, apart from
Solidarity's registration, was a remarkably thin
one.   The Laws on Censorship and the TUs had stuck,
as had the Economic Reform.   The CP and other
apparats had changed their leading personnel around
but had prevented the influx of non-party and
Catholic individuals into responsible positions,
although they now had some influence in certain
social, local and educational bodies [1].   Solidarity,
as yet, did not have its journal or regular access
to the mass media, while the questions of Rural
Solidarity and of 'political prisoners' remained
highly contentious.
The CPA, although divided by personal and
policy disagreements, had remained fairly solid to
the outside world but the PZPR's provincial, municipal and factory apparats were highly demoralised.
The odd exceptions were where a local chieftain,
like Fiszbach in Gdańsk, Dąbrowa in Kraków, Opałko
in Tarnów or Porębski in Wrocław, had succeeded in
riding the reform tide.   The local functionaries
now knew from the Częstochowa experience that the
CPA could not be relied on to support their hardline initiatives.   Their morale and standing were
sapped by the accusations of personal corruption
and political incompetence which accompanied the
rozliczenie process.   The actual alignment of forces
in the Politburo seems to have been dominated by
the following conflict in political orientation.

Olszowski's determined Leninism had probably gained
him Soviet support and the backing of those KWs which
had not, as yet, been renewed.   It is likely, although one cannot be certain about these things,
that he was supported in the Politburo by Grabski,
Pińkowski and the Gierek pogrobowcy, Żabiński,
Waszczuk and Wojtaszek.   Kania's more pragmatic
policy of using concessions to prevent major social
conflicts from getting out of hand was supported by
Moczar, by Jaruzelski who replaced Olszowski in the
dominant triumvirate, and by Barcikowski, Jagielski,
Fiszbach and probably by Kruk and Ney.   In the
Secretariat, however, Kania only had Barcikowski,
while Olszowski, Grabski, Waszczuk and Wojtaszek
could sabotage Kania's and Jaruzelski's conciliatory
policies.   Above all, the conservative stranglehold
on the Secretariat of the Congress Commission enabled
them to delay the Congress, which would undoubtedly
have decimated their hardline clientèle.
     The PZPR membership had on the whole supported
Solidarity in the January strikes and confrontations.
The more politically active grassroots were also
beginning to support both the Horizontal Movement
within the party and the general radicalisation of
political life which stemmed from the Congress preparations and debate.   The latter generated demands for new and democratic elections at every party
level, which enabled radicals in such places as
Poznań to gain control of their Congress Preparatory
Commission (WKP).   The grassroots appeared to be an
important potential ally to Kania in his campaign
against Olszowski's camouflaged domination of the
CPA but they were a dangerous two-edged sword which
would have to be handled with extreme care, as Kania
wanted to inherit, not to disable, the party machine.
     The Polish domestic situation was therefore
highly unstable.   Local and particularist forces
and discontents pushed both the régime and Solidarity
leaderships towards confrontations.   These, for the
moment, could be resolved on an ad hoc basis with
the mediation of the Church, but they contained the
danger that all these specific outbursts would be
aggregated into one vast and final showdown between
Polish society and the Communist system.   Under
these circumstances it was hardly surprising that
moderate elements in both society and the CP should
look to the Army, which was the only body to have
been unaffected by the ferment of the previous five
months.   Because of its conscript base and historical
traditions, stemming from the struggle for national
independence, it was regarded with much popular af-
fection.   It was, however, the great unknown in

the Polish equation as Jaruzelski had, until now,
prevented its direct involvement in the Polish political arena.   Jaruzelski had admittedly been reproached for the Army's role in December 1970 so
the very convenient theory was publicised that he
had, in some mysterious way, been isolated at that
time from the levers of power, and that it was all
the fault of General Korczyński, who was packed off
as ambassador to Algeria, where he died soon afterwards.   There was much speculation during 1980-1981
about whether the Polish Army would resist a Soviet
invasion or agree to repress the population in the
event of an uprising.   We now know that its disciplined, well paid, highly selected and scrutinised
and ideologically schooled Officers' Corps, whose
High Command had independent lines of communication
to the Red Army hierarchy and the Warsaw Pact, proved,
at the end of the day, to be the most reliable force
in support of the Communist system in Poland [2].
The conscripts accepted military discipline and
special police units kept an eye on them.   A conscript rebellion could only have succeeded during
a Hungarian type of insurrection, not during the
establishment of a state of Martial Law, which
largely involved picking off isolated pockets of
factory resistance.

Jaruzelski's Government and the Fate of his 'Ninety Days'

Jaruzelski's appointment as Premier, however,
signified not the immediate intention of using force
but that a firm and determined line would now be
kept.   His first move was to call, in the Sejm on
12 February, for a 90 day moratorium on strikes,
and implicitly on the socio-economic demands which
generated them [3].   This would enable the current
social conflicts to be resolved, the economy to be
stabilised and the economic reform to be prepared
and implemented.   Jaruzelski promised that he would
press on with the socialist renewal, that he would
work closely with the Church and that he would do
his utmost to establish a dialogue with all social
groups, although he did not mention the problem of
Rural Solidarity.   He announced the setting up of
a new Committee of the Council of Ministers on the
Economy and presented a ten point economic recovery
programme.   Rumours that Jaruzelski had been kicked
upstairs to Premier in order to put control of the
Army into safer hardline, pro-Soviet hands were
scotched when he retained the portfolio of Minister
of Defence.
Jaruzelski's most significant appointment was

that of Mieczysław F. Rakowski as deputy Premier
heading a new Committee of the Council of Ministers
for relations with Solidarity and the TUs.   Rakowski
(born 1926) had started in the early 1950s as a CC
Press Bureau official.   From 1958 he had been Editor
of Polityka and had made that weekly one of the
highest quality journals in Europe and the spokesman of the decent, progressive Communist intelligentsia.   The sense of political realities of
Rakowski and his immediate team of collaborators
(Jan Bijak, Zygmunt Szeliga, the incredibly sharp
columnist Daniel Passent, the satirist Michał
Radgowski, Jerzy Waldorf and Zygmunt Kałużyński
the doyen of Polish film critics) kept the journal
going through thick and thin, although their enemies
reproached them for some coat-turning towards both
Gomułka and Gierek [4].   Although Rakowski was
incredibly well informed he had little direct political experience.   Over two decades as a journalist
inevitably also made him somewhat volatile.   His
gifts as an articulate communicator and his youth-
ful good looks (a Western journalist described him
as 'a Polish Steve McQueen') made him an inspired
choice for his new job, which he defined as fulfilling the Social Agreements and working for 'a
policy of understanding, agreement and dialogue with
society' (Le Monde, 15-16.2.81).   Rakowski had
always stressed that the Government should resolve
its problems in collaboration, not in conflict,
with Solidarity and he was very critical of the way
the 'free Saturdays' issue had been handled.   He
was therefore a credible exponent of the line that
the leadership should always listen, and then respond, to societal demands.   He was a liberal Communist realist who could now be useful to the CPA
in practising the pluralist Communist politics which
were such uncharted territory for it [5].
     Rakowski had a conversation with Wałęsa on 14
February and enjoined him to give a clear answer to
Jaruzelski's appeal.   The Solidarity leader replied
that his movement could not accept the strike moratorium until the new Government's policies and intentions became clearer.   Solidarity's press spokesman, Karol Modzelewski, soon afterwards declared
that Solidarity wanted to be a recognised and respected social partner and was willing to respond
positively to Jaruzelski's offer of a social
dialogue [6].
     Rakowski had a busy time in the third week of
February establishing contacts with union representatives.   He mediated an extremely detailed agreement with the Łódź students signed by Janusz Górski,

the Minister of Education, which ended their near
month-long sit-in and the widespread student unrest
[7]. The agreement conceded autonomy to University
and Faculty Boards, especially on curriculum matters,
and agreed to student representation of a third on
these bodies. An independent students' association
(NZS) was also registered on 17 February. The
authorities agreed to new regulations on military
service and on compulsory physical labour for students and the ending of compulsory Russian, while
the police were banned from all Higher Education
campuses. In return, the students agreed to write
into their statute that they would work within the
constitution and they accepted an obligatory course
element of Marxism-Leninism.

At the same time an agreement was signed with
another difficult social group, the peasants, by a
Government Commission in Rzeszów (Słowo Powszechne,
10.3.81). Assured that the private ownership of
land constituted 'a permanent and equal component
of the national economy' and that detailed measures
would be taken within set time limits to favour its
development, the peasants ended their sit-in in
Rzeszów and, after an annexe had been signed in
Ustrzyki Dolne on 20 February, terminated their
agitation in South-Eastern Poland as a whole [8].
The question of Rural Solidarity was left out,
though. It had taken a turn for the worse with the
Supreme Court's confirmation of the Warsaw Provincial
Court's ruling that it was not a TU as peasants were
not employees and the Ministry of Justice's declaration that all attempts to organise a Rural Solidarity
were illegal (TL, 11.2.81).

The foregoing developments made Poland strike
free in late March for the first time in 1981 and
the auguries seemed fair for Jaruzelski's 90 days.
Some progress was even made on Solidarity's access
to the mass media. Rakowski, threatened with a
newspaper strike by Solidarity printers, hastened
to assure the SDP Executive that the Law on Censorship would be dealt with rapidly. The draft bill
on TUs was also submitted for public consultation
in early March (TL, 5.3.81).

The easing of the domestic situation allowed
Kania to spend more time on reassuring his neighbouring socialist allies. On 15 February he met
Husak in Prague. According to a typically banal
communiqué there was an 'agreement of views of
both sides on all fundamental questions' (TL,16.2.81).
We do not know whether this was a blatant lie or
whether Kania really sat down to a congenial chin-
wag with 'Iron Gustav' about the best strategy for

taking the sting out and then strangling the Polish
reform upsurge.   Two days later Kania probably had
a tougher time with Honecker.   The communiqué was
much more reserved and directed mainly to international problems (TL, 18.2.81).   Kania's crucial
voyage, though, was to Moscow to address the 26th
CPSU Congress on 24 February.   His message was that
the PZPR would be able to resolve its problems on
its own by using political means and that it could
cope with its domestic counter-revolutionary enemies
[9].   The congress heard warnings from Castro,
Husak, Honecker and even Kadar that the West was
attempting to destabilise Poland, which had now
become socialism's weakest and most exposed link.
The Communist Head Vicar himself then read the Poles
the following sermon.   Brezhnev declared that the
onslaught by Western Imperialism and the PZPR's own
mistakes had enabled the enemies of socialism to
cause anarchy in Poland.   Their counter-revolutionary attempts to turn back the course of history
now threatened the bases of the socialist state.
However, the Polish comrades were working hard to
overcome the crisis by increasing the party's com-
bativeness, by strengthening its links with the
working class and by tackling Poland's economic ills.
The Poles, concluded Brezhnev, with grim benevolence,
could depend 'absolutely' on their socialist allies
(TL, 24.2.81).
     The Polish delegation (Kania, Jaruzelski,
Żabiński and Wojtaszek) was hauled over the coals
and upbraided for its weakness and concessions at
the end of the Congress on 4 March by a high level
CPSU delegation composed of Brezhnev, Suslov,
security chief Andropov, Defence Minister Ustinov,
deputy Premier Tikhonov and CC Secretary Rusakov.
The communiqué of their meeting, in a very double-
edged phrase, expressed the hope that 'the Polish
Communists have the possibilities and the strength
to reverse the course of events to liquidate the
dangers hanging over the socialist achievements of
the Polish nation' [10].   In other words, the PZPR
could keep control of the situation as long as it
normalised politics in Poland according to Soviet
wishes.   Failure to do so would activate the communiqué's second proposition.   This repeated the
Brezhnev doctrine of 1968 that the defence of the
socialist order in any particular country was the
concern of the whole bloc.   What the French historian, Madaule, expressively called the 'nomenklatura international' would guarantee all the fraternal assistance that was needed to maintain it.
The Soviet leadership thus served notice that it

was not satisfied with Jaruzelski's conciliatory
measures.   The Polish delegation therefore promised
more firmly in the communiqué that it would provide
a 'firm and energetic riposte' against 'the intrigues
of Imperialism and the domestic reaction'.   Poland's
36 million population, PZPR weakness and Solidarity's
strength and the country's anti-Russian traditions
ensured that the Polish leadership, although coming
under constant and firm Soviet pressure, would remain
under 'guarded liberty' (Vernet, Le Monde, 6.3.81).
However, it had far more time granted to it than
anyone could have expected after reading the cold
and economically phrased threats of the Moscow communiqué.   One can presume that events worked out in
this way as Kania and the Kremlin were at one over
their strategic aim - the maintenance of the Soviet
form of Leninist rule in Poland.   But the former
was able to convince the Soviet leadership that only
a policy of reform and democratisation from above,
couched in the language of making Leninist democratic
centralism work, could hold out any alternative to
the total and obvious discrediting and possible collapse of Communist rule in Poland which would render
Soviet military intervention inevitable.   For the
present the PZPR Politburo on 5 March thanked the
CPSU leadership cordially for its proffered support
but emphasised that the key part of the Moscow communiqué was the Soviet party's belief that the
Polish party had the means and the strength to
liquidate the dangers on its own.   The Soviet call
to reverse the course of events was most pointedly
ignored (TL, 6.3.81).
    The Kania leadership was ground between two mill-
stones in early 1981.   On the one hand, it faced a
Soviet veto on substantive changes in the political
structures and methods of ruling Communist Poland.
This was backed up by the threat of eventual Soviet
intervention if they did not pacify Polish society
and suppress the anti-socialist elements in Solidarity
and in the country as defined by Moscow.   On the
other hand, it faced a society whose nationalism
demanded that it stand up to the Kremlin and provide just those very same reforms that had been
blackballed.   Ehrlich, for instance, considered
that the leadership faced a crucial choice between
continuing with the bureaucratic party politics of
the past or of identifying itself with society and
its real interests [11].   Kania himself popped back
to Warsaw during the CPSU Congress and the Żerań
workers on 26 March let him know in no uncertain
terms that the Polish working class could be as
obdurate in defence of its rights as the USSR.   The

Kania leadership therefore had no political alternative but to carry on with the renewal and to work
for a genuinely democratic centralist CP.   Only
such a startling innovation would enable it to
maintain its leading role in Polish society, to
guarantee the implementation of the socio-economic
reforms and to preserve the rule of a renewed and
politically, morally and ideologically cleansed PZPR.
    We must therefore follow two apparently dia-
metrically opposed themes though which in practice
were linked almost dialectically.   Jaruzelski's
and Rakowski's conciliatory policy was counterbalanced by CPA moves, usually attributed to
Olszowski, Grabski and their friends, to reassert
party rule in order to overawe Polish society and
to assuage Moscow.   Party ultras such as Kociołek
(TL, 18.2.81) were, however, more than balanced by
the pressures for the democratisation of the PZPR
emanating from its worker and intellectual membership.   Kuźnica (the Forge), the Kraków Club of
Party Intellectuals and Activists, for example,
kept up the pressure for new electoral rules which
would allow the direct, secret and democratic election of PZPR officials at every level [12].
    In the short term both East and West seemed to
have an interest in making the Polish experiment
succeed.   The USSR agreed to a moratorium on all
debts contracted by Poland during 1976-1980 until
1985 including the repayment of the $1,100,000 loan
of October 1980.   The trade agreement signed in
Moscow on 19 February envisaged that Polish-Soviet
trade in 1981 would remain at the level of about a
third of all Poland's foreign trade.   Poland's
fifteen most important Western creditors agreed in
principle in Paris in late February to postpone
payments on Poland's debts to them until a further
meeting in early April.   At home, the Jaruzelski
Government set to work with increased vigour.   It
set up yet another Committee of the Council of
Ministers on 20 February headed by deputy Premier
Malinowski to put some order into food and agricultural production, it increased alchohol prices
and it worked out a plan for rationing meat and
fats as of 1 April.
    The growth of a wide range of discussion clubs
reflecting the diverse political currents within the
PZPR was a striking feature of this period.   They
paralleled the post-1957 development of Catholic
Intelligentsia Clubs (KIKs) which until 1976 had
been associated with Znak [13].   At one extreme the
Klub Karola Marksa was animated by Wojciech
Lamentowicz for the radical Warsaw party intelligentsia,

while Kuźnica catered for similar tastes in Kraków.
At the other extreme, the officially sponsored
'Warsaw 80' Club of Creative Party Intellectuals
headed by ZBoWiD and hardline elements stressed
that renewal was most threatened by the economic
disaster and the absence of social peace (TL,27.1.81).
Other party initiated forums, such as the Trybuna
Ludu Discussion Club in Toruń and the Central Co-
ordination Committee for the Academic Community in
Warsaw, aired the whole range of proposals for democratising the party (TL, 4.3.81). The debate on
the latter point between the radical Poznań WKP proposals and the apparat's suggested revision of the
party's electoral rules to allow half the nominations
to come from the floor instead of the previous 15%,
thus allowing '35% more democracy', as a Poznań
academic aptly termed it, was summarised by Moszyński
[14]. He argued that in the long term such elections would strengthen, not weaken, the party, that
too little had been done so far to implement those
reform proposals and that there would be a major row,
which could still be easily avoided, if this were
not done quickly. The Poznań radicals wanted the
banning of the recommendation of officials by higher
levels to lower levels ('appointments in a briefcase, w Teczce') as the Poles colloquially put it,
and secret voting on the admission of members and
candidates to the PZPR [15].
     Olszowski, who was in charge of the Congress
Commission's work, therefore had to explain away the
failure to hold the Congress in late March-early
April as originally planned. He promised that the
draft bases of a programme (Założeń programowych ...)
would be submitted soon and he claimed that the CPA
was sympathetic to reform proposals including those
for democratic elections. What he opposed were
the suggestions which would 'wash away the party
ideologically', weaken its organisation and transform it into 'a discussion club'. The 'Założeń'
would, however, need to be supplemented by important
modifications to the party statutes which thus became the main political issue contested by the PZPR
democratisers (TL, 27.2.81). This line was publicised by CC Organisation Secretary Kurowski, who
ridiculed the conception of a party leading the
building of socialism in Poland but deprived of the
elementary instruments of rule and influence on
state organisations, the mass media and cadres policy
(TL, 3.2.81). Kania himself also put the CPA case
that nobody organised the delays in holding the
Congress which resulted from 'the tempo of work in
the Commissions' (Gazeta Robotnicza, 4.2.81).

The Third Congress Commission session met on 12
March to discuss an amended and enlarged version of
the draft programme. Kania defined it as being
concerned with Poland's socialist democratisation,
with strengthening the party's leading role and with
stabilising the socio-economic situation. He repeated his new theme that the PZPR would only be
able to function effectively as a Marxist-Leninist
party when it had 'inner party democracy linked with
centralism'. He announced that the next plenum
would settle the matter of party elections, while
the one after that would examine the proposed programme. The discussions then split between the
reformers such as Mitak, Kurz, Rajkiewicz and
Bratkowski [16], who considered that the reforms
needed to be spelt out in greater and sharper detail,
and the conservatives, such as Krasucki, Duraczyński
and Urbański, who thought that the document was
complete as it stood (TL, 13.3.81).
      Although the authorities arrested Kuroń and
Michnik in early March they were soon released. It
became clear from the dilatory procedures adopted
by the procuracy in investigating KOR's alleged
anti-constitutional activities and in the trial of
the KPN leaders that the PZPR leadership was only
going through the motions of satisfying one of the
main Soviet demands. They were more concerned not
to arouse Solidarity's anger. Nevertheless the
sensitivity of the domestic situation was shown by
the immediate and strong public reaction, which
involved an hour long local warning strike,to even
minor matters such as the sacking of 5 workers, 4
of them Solidarity activists, from an MSW hospital
in Łódź [17]. The anniversary of the 1968 repression of the Warsaw University students on 8 March
was marked by the unveiling of a bronze commemora-
tive plaque which used unprecedentedly plain
language about police repression in a socialist
state [18]. At the same time a meeting took place
in the old Stalinist Secret Police offices in
Mokotów which now belonged to the MSW. Here the
Grunwald Patriotic League was set up, about which
more later. The Army and police apparats thus
mounted their own type of political counter-attack.
      After having a preliminary conversation with
Rakowski on 9 March Wałęsa met Jaruzelski the following day [19]. The Premier intimated that proceedings against KOR would be dropped but no progress was made over Rural Solidarity, which at its
first National Congress in Poznań the previous
weekend had elected the 23 year old Rzeszów peasant
organiser, Jan Kulaj, as its President [20].

Wałęsa effected a compromise over the Łódź hospital dispute and the imminent regional strike was called off. The more explosive issue of a threatened regional strike and the 20 demands presented by the Radom workers, including the dismissal and trial of the party, state, judicial and police functionaries, whom they held responsible for the 1976 repressions, was also settled by 16 March thanks to Wałęsa's intervention, supported by Kuroń (Le Monde, 18.3.81). Prokopiak, the KW Secretary since 1975, the provincial Governor, the President of Radom City and the local police commander, all resigned, although the CPA defended them against accusations of corruption.

Local problems also aroused potential strike situations in Suwałki, Nowy Sącz and Bielsko-Biała and even minor issues occasionally assumed national importance. Whole industries, such as forestry, also threatened a one hour warning strike for 23 March to be followed up by an indefinite one two days later if the Minister of Forestry and Wood Industry did not agree to fulfil an agreement negotiated the previous December. What was the effect of all this regional, sectional and national ferment, now well into its third month, on the CPA and its supporting police and judicial apparats? All had come under attack but none had been more than stung so far. Did their patience finally snap at this point and the wish for a final showdown to resolve the situation one way or another prevail?

On 6 March the Sejm set up a 16-strong Extraordinary Commission to check on the fulfilment of the Gdańsk, Szczecin and Jastrzębie Agreements chaired by Jan Szczepański, the world famous sociologist. It also considered the draft bill on Agricultural Self-Management which embodied the Rzeszów Agreement's guarantee of private land ownership and the pledges for its development, but, as pointed out by Zabłocki (PZKS), it did not make it possible to register Rural Solidarity alongside the Agricultural Circles [21]. The right of peasants to associate together in professional unions which served their interests, like all other workers, was supported by the Episcopal Conference on 12 March. They repeated the themes enunciated by Pope John Paul II in his Vatican audience with Wałęsa and what Wyszyński had said to Kania on 7 February (Le Monde, 15-16.3.81). The Bishops thus continued with their open and firm support for their most important social base. The CPA view was stated a few days later by CC Secretary Kurowski, who reiterated the argument that Polish agriculture was a

single whole and that the resurgent Agricultural
Circles should be given a fair chance.   He made it
plain that the PZPR refused to accept its political
expulsion from the countryside by Rural Solidarity
(TL, 10.3.81).
    The SD Twelfth Congress in Warsaw on 14-18 March
was a much livelier affair than the ZSL's.   The SD
with its 115,000 members naturally could not challenge
the PZPR's leading role but it was much more strongly
committed to the democratisation of the system than
the ZSL and it demanded a greater say in the country's
government.   This applied in particular to its two
main social bases, the private handicrafts sector,
whose 227,000 workshops employed half a million
people, and the intelligentsia, to whom the SD now
made a strong PZPR licensed bid for support [22].
    The Warsaw Pact was holding its 'Alliance 81'
manoeuvres at this time and its Commander, Marshal
Kulikov, arrived in Warsaw on 17 March to meet Kania
and Jaruzelski and a bevy of the most senior Polish
Generals - Siwicki, Urbanowicz, Molczyk and Baryła.
One does not know what transpired, but the Polish
hosts made their guest comfortable with a spate of
articles dissecting KOR's strategy for dismantling
the socialist state [23].

Bydgoszcz
    Poland's biggest political crisis between
Gdańsk in August 1980 and December 1981 started off
with the occupation on 16 March of the ZSL provincial offices in Bydgoszcz by a group of peasant
farmers demanding the registration of their provincial union.   This sit-in sparked off a train
of events which within a few days took Poland to
the brink of the abyss.   It might be significant
that Kania was abroad in Budapest on 19 March seeking advice from the wiliest and most successful of
all moderate reform Communists within the Soviet
bloc on how to balance between domestic and Soviet
pressures during a period of political crisis.
Apart from a friendly communiqué, though marked by
the absence of any criticism, Kania received little
else apart from friendly advice, drawn from the post-
1956 Hungarian experience, about the tactics of his
difficult task (TL, 20.3.81).   Was Kania's Budapest
trip a diplomatic absence from Poland to shield his
prestige from direct involvement in a flashpoint,
or did his enemies take advantage of such a favourable moment to mount a hardline initiative?   One
should also note that Jagielski was in Moscow carrying on economic negotiations, Jaruzelski was occupied with the Warsaw Pact manoeuvres, while Moczar

was immobilised by a serious heart illness during
this period.
    To answer the question in the preceding para-
graph one needs to examine the sequence of events
in Bydgoszcz which started with the occupation of
the ZSL office, the constitution by those peasants
on 17 March of the All-Poland Strike Committee of
Rural Solidarity and the full-scale regional crisis
which then developed with local industrial Solidarity
support [24].   The peasants planned to put their
case to the Provincial People's Council which met to
discuss the province's budget in the Council Chamber
of the Governor's Building on 19 March.   Large
crowds gathered around the building and this led to
the calling of police reinforcements.   Heated and
tense negotiations took place before the session and,
although it was unclear how many Solidarity representatives would be allowed in and how many were to
speak, it was certainly agreed that they should raise
their desiderata under Any Other Business.   The
session was adjourned most abruptly, though.   Bitter
exchanges then took place between officials, the
Solidarity representatives and some sympathetic
councillors who effected a compromise agreement that
a further session should be called within a week at
which Solidarity would be invited to put its case.
These heated and nerve-wearying exchanges had
started at 1.45 p.m. and continued until early
evening.   The authorites' case was that deputy
Governor R. Bąk   then called in the police to clear
the chamber as the Solidarity people refused to go
after the agreement had been reached and he feared
that a full-scale occupation was being planned.
Although some force had to be used to remove the
more determined Solidarity activists it was neither
the legality nor even the, admittedly resented,
fact of their forcible eviction which caused the
subsequent furore.
    The central issue was who, and on whose orders,
took three Solidarity activists (Jan Rulewski, a KKP
member and prominent Solidarity leader in Bydgoszcz,
M. Labentowicz and M. Bartoszczak) into a quiet yard
outside the Governor's Building and beat them up to
such an extent that they needed major hospital
treatment?   Such injuries could not have been self-
inflicted and emotion-raising photographs of the
damaged men were flashed all over Poland.   The
authorities, however, through thick and thin, in
spite of incredibly heavy pressure, refused to
reveal who the culprits were.   The Procurator-
General admitted in May 1981 that because of the
confused nature of these events 'it will probably

not be possible to establish the specific individuals responsible for the beating up' [25]. The question was 'frozen' by the procuracy in September 1981 (TL, 22.9.81) [26].

Although local and spontaneous factors were important it is difficult to imagine that a few over-enthusiastic policemen on their own initiative beat up three troublemakers who had earlier provoked and baited them. The Politburo's desire to prevent the demoralisation of the police by supporting it so demonstrably against all attacks would not have held out for so long in such an event; nor should one believe the rumours that the perpetrators were Soviet plain clothesmen. The evidence suggests that the Bydgoszcz police acted on the orders of the party apparat in Warsaw which were transmitted to them by Stanisław Mach, the deputy Premier, on the spot. The only question is whether these orders came from the whole leadership or only from a section which wanted to provoke a confrontation? My personal hypothesis is that the explanation in terms of a power-struggle between hard and soft-liners within the CPA may be overdone in this episode. Perhaps the leadership was in general agreement to call a halt to the sit-in movement and wanted to gauge society's reaction to the use of force? Different emphases and hopes then certainly followed amongst the politicians. All that one can say in retrospect is that the hardliners were incredibly inept in their tactics, unless they were banking on provoking such a social outburst that only force, Polish or Soviet, would suffice to suppress it. The Bydgoszcz events, however, brought the early 1981 situation to the boil and clarified it in such a way that the cui bono argument suggests rather that the confrontation helped the moderate centrists and re-formers to precipitate matters and to push through the PZPR's democratisation at the Ninth and Tenth Plena. The theory that Bydgoszcz was a calculated hardline provocation not only against Solidarity but also against Jaruzelski's Government and the bulk of Polish society was expressed immediately afterwards by political, academic and literary circles but it still remains non-proven (TL, 23.3.81).

On 20 March the KKP called for the punishment of the perpetrators of the Bydgoszcz events which it described as 'an obvious provocation directed against the Jaruzelski Government' and started preparing for a general strike. Wałęsa, who called off his visit to France, declared that Solidarity would be finished if it backed down now. As a preliminary a two hour protest strike involving half a million workers took place in the Bydgoszcz region.

On the 22nd the Politburo reacted by calling for moderation but it justified the decision to maintain law and order in Bydgoszcz. Jaruzelski sent a high level Government Commission headed by the Minister of Justice, Bafia, to Bydgoszcz to report on the affair. Important preliminary contacts then took place between Solidarity and Government working groups in Bydgoszcz and Wałęsa, in spite of his threats to cut off all contacts with the Government, met Rakowski in Warsaw for 4 hours on 22 March.

The wave of national anger which swept through Poland after Bydgoszcz was followed by a period of nail-biting tension during which the Warsaw Pact manoeuvres were prolonged. It seemed that the Government and Solidarity were heading towards the most dangerous of their confrontations in the form of an indefinite national strike. Solidarity considered that the Bydgoszcz incident had been prepared well in advance but offered a way out by accepting that it had been directed against Jaruzelski's conciliating policies. Many of their leaders considered that the opportunity should be seized to force the PZPR to clear itself of its hardliners and to bring it to accept a more institutionalised and permanent modus vivendi with Solidarity. Wałęsa, aided by Wyszyński's calm but clear condemnation of the irresponsible actions of public functionaries, had managed to contain the explosive situation in Bydgoszcz. He now began 9 days of difficult and protracted negotiations with Rakowski from 22 March onwards. Initially he met with a very firm and uncompromising official stance on all the issues from police violence to Rural Solidarity. The KKP meeting in Bydgoszcz on the night of 23-24 March quarrelled over the form but not that there should be a strong Solidarity reaction. Finally, the KKP agreed unanimously that a state of emergency should automatically meet with a general strike and by 33 votes to 8 it set the following calendar. A 4 hour warning strike was scheduled for Friday, 27 March, while if negotiations had not succeeded by then an unlimited general strike would start on 31 March [27]. A National Strike Committee headed by Wałęsa was elected to direct operations from the Lenin Shipyard, while all over Poland Solidarity Committees started preparations and installed themselves in their factory strongholds. Solidarity presented a five-fold set of demands and fixed a six-day period for a compromise to be effected, but

most observers considered that little room for
manoeuvre existed over the issues of Bydgoszcz,
Rural Solidarity and political prisoners.

Support for Kania and Jaruzelski's policies and
for compromise solutions came from the PZPR grassroots and the radical Communist intelligentsia in
the form of an Open Letter entitled 'Our Choice'
by Stefan Bratkowski circulated on 23 March.
Bratkowski's Letter was a fearsome blast against the
hardliners who had brought Poland to the brink of
civil war. This was 'the last chance crisis for
those who wanted to drive our party from the path of
social agreement and in this manner to guide our
state on to the road of an unavoidable catastrophe'
[28]. He accused a group of hardliners at the
highest party levels, supported by the Warsaw party,
of trying to postpone the Congress, of not wanting
agreement even with the mass of their own party, of
provoking conflicts between the police and society
and of seeking Soviet support as they were ideologically bankrupt. Bratkowski called for their removal from office. He saw no alternative to Kania,
Barcikowski and Jaruzelski. Only they could win
over the nation to 'the politics of social understanding' as in his view 'all other roads must lead
to the political cemetery'. Bratkowski's argument
was supported sotto modo by various local party organisations, most notably the KZs in the Gdańsk and
Szczecin shipyards, the Cegielski Works in Poznań,
by the PAN Presidium, by the Bydgoszcz ZLP and WRN
and by numerous other bodies who called for a full
explanation of Bydgoszcz or defended Jaruzelski's
policy of social dialogue. It was also a propi-
tious moment for the noted sociologist, Władysław
Markiewicz, to argue that Poland's deepest crisis
could only be realised by fundamental changes in
the PZPR's nomenklatura and directive style of
ruling [29].

Kania's view was that strikes were 'a call to
self-destruction' now that the economic and food
situation was so bad. He wondered who had 'the
temerity to make out of a local incident a matter
which threatened to cause a national catastrophe'
(TL, 25.3.81). Kania thus confirmed the party's
hardline in its negotiations with Solidarity and he
echoed Rakowski's harangue to Wałęsa about the economy's being on the verge of breakdown. But within
the party a different stand now came into play with
the news that the Ninth Plenum would be held on 29
March. The official press denounced the hardliners
for sabotaging the party's consolidation on the
basis of socialist renewal. Fearing that democratic

elections would sweep them away they banked everything on making political settlements impossible so
that 'the use of force would bring back the status
quo ante' (Siedlecki, TL, 25.3.81).
    Was an October 1956 scenario thus being pre-
pared with the PZPR grassroots supporting an apparently reform-minded First Secretary and General-
Premier against their hardline opposition while the
country lived through a ferment of political debate
and was inundated with wall posters and leaflets?
But the outcome depended upon whether Rakowski and
Wałęsa could clinch a deal before the 30th. Their
first 70 minute long meeting on the evening of 25
March was most inauspicious. Rakowski attacked
the forces in Solidarity who wanted confrontation
and blamed 11 local conflicts on Solidarity. He
doubted whether Bydgoszcz was more than a pretext
and was firm that the authorities were right to safeguard public buildings which might be under threat
of occupation. Rakowski's conclusion was that a
strike would confirm that independent and self-
managing unions could not co-exist with socialism as
they caused political and social chaos. Rakowski's
obvious playing for time before his receipt of the
Bafia Report naturally ruled out any serious response from the Solidarity delegation. That his
declaration was read out solely for effect was confirmed by its publication in full (TL, 26.3.81).
Wałęsa's conciliatory reply that Solidarity was
neither a threat to the Government, the party nor
socialism, that it had no ambitions to become a
political party and that it only wanted to guarantee
that the 1980 renewal would not go the way of those
of 1956 and 1970 was, however, read out on radio and
TV and reproduced in the press (TL, 27.3.81).
    The 4 hour warning strike passed off without
major incident on 27 March. It was supported very
widely in all key branches of the national economy
in all regions of the country. Some hopeful signs
then indicated that the situation was slowly and
painfully unblocking itself. Kania met Wyszyński
on 26 March. The same day Edward Berger, the
Chairman of the Bydgoszcz WRN, whose adjournment of
the session had sparked off the subsequent events,
resigned. He was replaced, and this was a significant first swallow, by General Franciszek
Kamiński, the deputy Commander of the Pomeranian
Military District, who in another important development, a secret election, gained 114 votes out of a
possible 152.
    The content of the Rakowski-Wałęsa Agreement of
30 March is more significant than the tedious, and

often interrupted, negotiations in the previous 3 or
4 days which led up to its signing.   The Bafia
Report, published on 27 March, although it maintained
a pudic silence as to who was responsible for the
Bydgoszcz outrages, accepted, in as many words, that
the fault lay with the police [30].   This opened up
the way to agreement on the most contentions point
and Wałęsa was encouraged by Wyszyński on the 28th
to negotiate an agreement to prevent the strike.
On the other side, Klasa revealed after it was all
over that the Government had received full powers
from the CC to prevent the strike at all costs
(TL, 2.4.81).   The communiqué setting out the
Agreement, which in practice called off the strike,
started with the Government's admission that the
adjournment of the WRN session and the decision to
use force to clear the Council Chamber was a mistake
but the fate of the provincial officials was left
open (TL, 31.3.81).   The Government expressed regret
for the beating up of Rulewski and his friends and
promised full and rapid investigations by the procuracy to determine who was responsible.   The
promise contained in the first point of the Warsaw
Agreement was disregarded shamefully by the Government.   To this day the matter of the guilty policemen has been wreathed in silence.   The second point
agreed that work on the TU Bill would be accelerated
and that the Sejm would consider it before the end
of April.   No formal agreement was reached over
Rural Solidarity but the matter was referred to the
Szczepański Sejm Commission and a mixed Government-
Solidarity working party would discuss the results
of its work.   The question of political prisoners
was ignored except for vague assurances that the
Government would try to negotiate procedures with
Solidarity to prevent local issues being blown up
into national confrontations in future.
     Wałęsa felt that he had gained 70 per cent of
what he wanted.   He was rather more enthusiastic
about this 'great agreement' than Rakowski, who
merely expressed the hope that in future Solidarity
would become a real trades-union and rather less a
social movement [31].   Wałęsa was reproached by
the KKP on 31 March for the high-handed and undemocratic manner of his negotiations and for having
conceded too much but he gained a large majority
for calling off the strike.   The PZPR members of
Solidarity also condemned the pusillanimity of
Wałęsa's advisers.   Some of the radicals thought
that Solidarity's soft position had prevented the
PZPR grassroots from sweeping the hardliners away
as the leadership would not have risked losing the

support of party organisations at cell and factory
level during such a crisis.   From that point of view
they were right.   Rakowski had succeeded in 'making
a horse' out of Wałęsa, as the expressive Polish
colloquialism has it, to describe someone who had
been made a fool of.   If Solidarity were to survive
it had to force the Communist state to accept it as
a permanent institution.   To do so it could either
transform itself into a locally based workers' TU,
as the régime wanted, or alternatively it would have
had to help the reform elements within the PZPR to
dispose of their mutual enemies.   Wałęsa's policy
of evolutionary growth into the system was an even
longer shot than the other two alternatives.

The Victory of Reform but not of the Reformers
The Ninth Plenum met on 29-30 March at a moment
of high tension.   It was a most confused meeting
politically whose significance was unclear and underestimated at the time [32].   While it confirmed
that the leadership and CC stalemate would continue
until the congress, it also determined that the policy
victory would go to the centrist reformers who would
be allowed to renew and democratise the party and
to rewrite its programme and statutes in their own
fashion.
    The problem of leadership and factional con-
flict was not resolved at this plenum.   Olszowski
and Grabski offered their resignations but it is
unlikely that this was an appeal to their CC supporters to overthrow Kania.   The rumours during the
plenum (that they banked on the CC's rejecting their
resignations but accepting those of the rest of the
Politburo) seem a far-fetched explanation.   More
likely they were just testing out their political
positions or had been ordered to behave in this way
by the Politburo majority.   The hitherto politically
ambiguous Roman Ney, on the other hand, now showed
his colours as a radical by calling for the political mobilisation of the membership in order to
carry through the renewal in full.   He offered his
resignation because he wanted the old Politburo to
be dismissed and a new one elected 'which would base
itself fully on the new methods of work' and be 'the
actual leading force in the socialist renewal'.
After much corridor intrigue a motion proposed, on
Kania's initiative, by Edward Szymański, the First
Party Secretary in Włocławek, that the CC express
its confidence in all the members of the Politburo
and Secretariat and that the resignations be with-
drawn was accepted with only one vote against.
The crucial policy decisions were then taken to hold

the Extraordinary Congress by 20 July and that the
party should be renewed by the grassroots in the
report and election campaign. This would elect the
Congress delegates according to new rules of secret
and democratic election, which were now confirmed.
At the same time the policy line of 'agreement and
dialogue' was confirmed even more firmly in the
plenum's final resolution. Finally, the Gierek
functionaries were undercut further by the clearest
statement yet of the 'clearing of accounts' trend.
    Barcikowski, in his report, opened the door to
agreement over Bydgoszcz by stating that this
'impermissible incident' should be clarified in
full. However, he condemned the political activities of Solidarity extremists and KOR counter-
revolutionaries and what he considered a blatant
campaign to discredit the police. He assumed a
centrist position on the grassroots' movement in
the party but condemned Bratkowski's Letter for
drawing such a sharp dividing line between the
leadership and the membership. The matter was referred to the CKKP. Barcikowski then set out eight
crucial guides to the aims of the Kania leadership
in preparing the Ninth Congress. Broad discussion
of key policy issues and consultation about them
should be guaranteed. The minority should naturally,
as in all Leninist parties, accept and implement the
majority view loyally but individuals should be
allowed to voice different, but honestly held,
opinions while criticism and self-criticism should
be encouraged. Party officials should be elected
democratically at all levels, the practice of holding numerous posts simultaneously should be dis-
couraged, while the number of terms of office should
be limited to encourage rotation. The party apparatus should be 'reduced in size so that it would not
usurp the functions of the elected authorities'.
This democratised party of a new type would take
shape during the electoral and report campaign to
the Congress which Barcikowski implied would elect
a leadership which was more at one with the membership.
    This pragmatic strategy was therefore designed
to renew the party and to overcome the opposition of
the PZPR ultras and Soviet machinations without the
process getting out of hand. Kania and Barcikowski,
however, had to tread more radical paths than they
had originally envisaged. There was no alternative short of declaring a state of emergency and
facing Polish society in late March under much less
favourable circumstances than turned out to be
present later in December.

Not yet time to reverse

        The CC had come under unprecedented pressure
in the last week of April, partly from the Horizontalists but mainly from the pent-up and frustrated
radicalism of factory, cell and middle-level organisations who telexed over 350 resolutions to the
plenum.   Of the 44 speakers who participated in
this plenum's debate the vast bulk were reformers.
A formidable workers' offensive was unleashed with
Kania's tacit encouragement and this was supported
by some of the younger and recently appointed KW
Secretaries.   Their main themes were the need to
avoid being provoked into a final confrontation with
Solidarity and to fulfil the Social Agreements in
order to retain society's confidence.   The pressing
need to close the gap between the leadership and
the grassroots would have to be effected by changes
in Politburo personnel and methods, by speeding up
the holding of the congress, by adopting democratic
inner-party procedures, especially 'free elections'
with multiple candidates (only 12 per cent of party
organisations had been renewed in this way by then)
and by improving the poor, delayed and incomplete
information for which Olszowski was responsible.
I consider that well over two-thirds of the speeches
by 21 worker members of the CC reflected the above
current in a very decided manner.   Unprecedentedly
strong and open language was used.   Jadwiga Nowakowska
from Łódź said plainly that the leadership's stance
was contrary to what the membership wanted.   She
called for the punishment of officials guilty of
'unnecessary social confrontations'.   She was supported by Pustelnik (Gryfia dry-dock, Szczecin),
Jarząbek (Bierut steelworks, Częstochowa), Drabik
(Skarżysko-Kamienna Metalworks), Gromada (Mielec) and
Janina Kostrzewa (Wrocław), who diagnosed the causes
of the crisis as lack of membership confidence in
the leadership, the efforts of local officials to
manipulate workers which had impelled them towards
Solidarity and strike activity and the slowness in
instituting democratic elections to renew the party,
as well as the 'bureaucratic' nature of the Congress
preparations.
        Most notable among the reform contributions
from the political functionaries was Ryszard Bryk's
(Siedlce KW, First Secretary), who was to change
his tune dramatically by the Eleventh Plenum.   He
made it plain that a working class party could not
fight the working class.   Solidarity was now a
very differentiated force and the PZPR had to work
sincerely with it, and not use force, as in
Bydgoszcz, if a national tragedy were to be avoided.
Dąbrowa (Kraków KW, First Secretary) called for a

negotiated settlement with Solidarity and a more
open leadership style. He welcomed the end of 'the
compromising and nonsensical quarrel over the electoral regulations'. Ney considered that this might
be 'a last chance plenum'. He was highly critical
of the way in which reforms, such as intra-party
elections, had to be extracted by the membership
from the leadership, whose responses were always
half-hearted. Now Ney had been a CC Secretary
since December so perhaps, as a junior and expend-
able member, he had been delegated to present the
Politburo's Samokrytyka in order to confuse the
Olszowski-Grabski issue. Ney was supported by
Rakowski at his most mercurial. He considered
that Bydgoszcz had developed into such an extreme
political crisis because 'the party base as well as
important sections of society nourish rather significant doubts as to the credibility of our works
and actions' [33]. The policy of drift was something which poor Rakowski could no longer bear, so
he was ready to discard the present Politburo which
just could not cope with the problems facing the
party and the nation.
     The hardliners or CC backwoodsmen were under-
standably overawed by the workers' and reformers'
onslaught and by the social and political crisis
and the grassroots' ferment. So they left the
running to a small number of their usual standard-
bearers, such as Kiociołek, Milewski and Baryła.
Kisiel also provided them with extra ammunition by
declaring that Poland stood on the brink of an
economic catastrophe. Henryk Bednarski (Bydgoszcz
KW, First Secretary since October 1980) pointed out
that the Bydgoszcz events had not caused the present
social tension: 'In reality we have had to face a
continual many months' long systematic political
struggle leading to the weakening of People's power.'
Prokopiak, a prominent representative of the 'cemetery vote', criticised Barcikowski's report. He
put up a smoke-screen of apparent reform proposals
to mask the real purpose of his call for the re-
structuring of the Politburo and Secretariat, which
we can surmise would have benefited individuals
like himself.
     The highlight of the plenum came from the ebul-
lient and ever-aggressive Grabski. As at the Eighth
Plenum, Grabski considered that the counter-revolutionary forces were stepping up their offensive and
that the real line of division was not between alleged hard and soft-liners but between socialism
and its enemies. The policy of renewal had not
gone beyond platitudes; 'dual power has become a

fact' and the 'absurd escalation of strikes which
has nothing in common with the defence of the economic and social rights of the working people' had
brought the country to the brink of economic bankruptcy, insolvency, unemployment and hunger.
Grabski was, however, most unclear how his policy
and leadership alternative would produce a more
united leadership and a better quality of renewal
than Kania's, which is why he failed to persuade the
CC to brace itself to accept major leadership changes.
This effect was strengthened by a most unconvincing
performance from Olszowski. He lost his nerve at
the crucial moment as the firm Soviet support on
which he had counted had suddenly evaporated.
Being realistic enough to realise that his time
(again!) had not yet come, he clinched a face-saving
deal with Kania, who had cunningly forced him into
the defensive by choreographing attacks on Olszowski's
running of the mass media and the Congress Commission Secretariat.

The result of this plenum was the victory of
the reform line which was elaborated at the next
(Tenth) Plenum a month later. The old CC was, however, given a stay of execution until the Ninth
Congress to guarantee to the Kremlin that the democratisation process would remain under control.

The compromise nature of the Ninth Plenum and
the guarantees that the PZPR grassroots would not
be allowed to overwhelm and capture the CPA then had
to be explained to the rest of the Soviet bloc.
Fortuitously three East European CPs held their congresses in April and these provided suitable occasions for the Polish leadership to reassure its
hosts. Grabski at the Twelfth Congress of the
Bulgarian CP listened with undoubted glee to Zhivkov's
assurance that the Polish Communists could rely upon
Bulgaria's fraternal support. Olszowski had a
more difficult task in Prague. At the Sixteenth
Congress of the Czechoslovak CP he found himself
facing Brezhnev, attending his first fraternal Congress for over a decade. The Soviet leader left
it to Husak to suggest that the PZPR had not done
enough since the Eighth Plenum to overcome the
counter-revolutionary forces which were causing
political and economic anarchy and threatening 'the
foundations of socialism' (Rude Pravo, 7.4.81).
On 7 April Brezhnev, as was his wont, took a softer
line, although he established the parallels between
the 1968 Czechoslovak situation and the current
Polish one: 'The Polish Communists, with the support of all real Polish patriots, will be able, we
may suppose, to administer the necessary rebuff

against the aims of the enemies of the socialist
order' (TL, 5.4.81). The atmosphere of temporary
détente in the Polish crisis was also aided by the
abrupt ending, the same day, of the 'Alliance 81'
manoeuvres which had kept up the pressure on
Poland since 17 March.

All these domestic and international developments suggested that the Kremlin did not judge the
moment right as yet for a full-scale showdown with
Solidarity and the Polish reform upsurge. It therefore helped to quieten the situation after the post-
Bydgoszcz brink. The PZPR Politburo also continued
with the agreed division of political labour in
which the domestic hardliners reassured their socialist allies, while the others went ahead with the
domestic reforms. One can therefore believe Kania's
statement that 'none of the disagreements of view
within the Politburo goes beyond party norms, beyond
what is an acceptable relationship to socialist
renewal' (TL, 3.4.81).

The key to the matter, as Barcikowski told the
Tenth SED Congress on 12 April, was that the PZPR
'was and would remain the leading force in the Polish
nation and state' (TL, 13.4.81). This would ensure
that Poland would remain loyal to all her socialist
alliances, especially in the case of the GDR, where
a mutual interest existed in combating West German
revanchism. My hypothesis is that the Kania leadership, after Bydgoszcz, managed to convince the
Kremlin that its strategy of socialist renewal and
the peaceful resolution of social conflicts would
now be best served by the controlled mobilisation
of the PZPR's grassroots and that the congress, the
election of a completely fresh and uncompromised CC
and the presentation of a new programme could no
longer be delayed. Kania's promise that he would
square all the possible circles and produce a democratic Leninist CP and a less politicised Solidarity
and assure the survival of Communism in Poland at
the cheapest possible cost may have been received
with some scepticism by his hard-boiled Soviet patrons; but their patience and tactical sense of
timing is not to be underestimated. However, Kania
could not really come clean as to how sweeping the
renewal process would have to be in order to be
credible. The Soviet leaders therefore reacted
with constant demands for guarantees that the process was not going too far or getting out of hand
and this caused Kania many domestic difficulties.
There is little evidence that the democratisation
process carried out between the Ninth Plenum and the
Ninth Congress was effected in outright defiance of

Soviet wishes.   In spite of the Moscow Letter of
early June I do not believe that the Kremlin ever
attempted to pre-empt the renewal; either by using
the residual hardline and 'cemetery vote' in the CC
to replace Kania in order to annul the democratisation measures and cancel the congress, or by mooting
military intervention.   Much of the speculation at
this time about the alleged intrinsic conflict between the Soviets, the Polish leaders and the PZPR
reformers and grassroots was highly fallacious; it
was stoked up even more by such events as the Moscow
Letter and the political choreography which had to
be put on at the Eleventh Plenum to respond to it.
A good indicator supporting my argument is that
Kania seems to have passed the test with Suslov, the
guardian of the purity of the Leninist ideological
grail, during his visit to Warsaw on 23 April.
Their communiqué, which had a decidedly Polish gloss,
ignored the earlier Soviet demands for reversing the
course of events (TL, 24.4.81).   Although the Soviet
leaders remained highly concerned by the challenges
to traditional Leninism in Poland, and by the
inability or unwillingness of the Polish leadership
to repel the offensive presented in turn by workers,
intellectuals, peasants and now grassroots PZPR
members, they decided to accord the Kania-Jaruzelski
leadership the same period of grace which Solidarity
had done (cf. Vernet, Le Monde, 23.4.81).   Their
leaders, such as Chernenko, merely attacked Western
interference in Polish affairs and attempts to destabilise the socialist system while passing the
domestic situation over largely in silence except
for ritual attacks on KOR and its influence on
Solidarity's extremists (Nowe Drogi, May-June 1981,
pp. 257-269).
     The second aspect of the leadership's inter-
national activity in April was a drive to obtain
economic concessions wherever possible.   In particular, it wanted the West to freeze the massive
repayments due on its foreign debt, which by April
were reported as mounting towards $23,000 million.
Jagielski saw President Giscard d'Éstaing and his
Foreign and Economic Ministers in Paris on 31 March
to this end.   Giscard promised that French assistance to Poland, which had totalled 4 milliard
francs ($364 million) in 1980, would continue and
that food aid would be expedited.   Jagielski's top-
level talks on 2 April in Washington were less fruit-
ful, although he was promised a rapid and positive
US response to a Polish request for $200 million aid
in foodstuffs.   Poland's official debts were considered in Paris on 9-10 April by the 15 main creditor

nations [34].   The agreement reached on 27 April
covered just over half of Poland's total hard currency debt and postponed interest repayments of
$2,500 million due in 1981 until 1986-1989.   Nine-
teen commercial banks, from 11 Western countries,
also started negotiating in London on 16 April with
the Polish Commercial Bank over the $1,900,000 1981
interest repayments due to them (out of a total of
$3,100,000 due in 1981 to all commercial banks).

Unchastened by radical criticisms against him,
Wałęsa considered that the time for exhausting confrontations had passed.   The need now was to ensure
that existing agreements were implemented, not by
brinkmanship but through 'a policy of small steps'
(Słowo Powszechne, 7-8.4.81).   Wałęsa felt that the
radical leaders thrown up by the strike confrontations would not survive the elections which Solidarity
would soon start.   Mazowiecki, one of the criticised
experts, also took over as Editor of Tygodnik
Solidarność.   Its first 16-page number, appearing,
with a circulation of about half a million, on 3
April after months of conflict and delay, proved to
be fairly stodgy and remarkably unsubversive.

A series of meetings, arranged through the good
offices of Halina Skibniewska, a noted architect
and Sejm Vice-Marshal, started from 6 April onwards
between Barcikowski, the ZSL Chairman Gucwa and Rural
Solidarity's Chairman, Kulaj, which led to rapid
progress on the vexed question of Rural Solidarity's
registration.   The Sejm Szczepański Commission then
tackled the legal problem of how it could best be
registered.   A week later, Szczepański gave an
assurance that a new TU Bill would allow the functioning of Agricultural Unions.   Negotiations, pressurised by another farmers' strike in Inowrocław,
were then resumed in Bydgoszcz between Ciosek and
the peasants who had occupied the ZSL office there
since mid March.   The Government in the Agreement
of 17 April accepted that a 'legal basis for the
functioning of the union' would be written into the
bill on Agricultural Self-Management and Self-Governing Agricultural Organisations (TL, 18.4.81) [35].
These bills were passed by the Sejm on 6 May [36]
and the Warsaw Provincial Court ratified Rural
Solidarity on 12 May.   The issue had poisoned
political life since September 1980, when the first
attempt at registration had been made [37].   It
represented a great victory for the Church's quiet
behind-the-scenes' diplomacy, as Wyszyński had
delegated Dr. Romuald Kukułowicz to advise the
peasants.   It was also a great defeat for the
hardline Communist forces [38].   In passing it also

led in early May to the replacement of Gucwa, the
long-time ZSL Chairman, by the more progressively
minded Stefan Ignar, who had already presided over
one peasant renewal, which came to nothing, in 1956-
1962 [39].   The Council of Ministers also appeased
the agricultural sector by raising the prices paid
to farmers by between 30 and 55% and it implemented
various other concessions.   A minor example of
Poland's lunatic price structure and the madcap relationship between state purchasing and retailing
prices was that a litre of milk at this time cost
4 zloties in the shops but the farmer was paid 14
zloties [40].   Hardly surprisingly, the Government announced, through PAP, that it wanted to
diminish this burden, which had risen from 240-260
milliard zloties the previous year to 340-360 milliard zloties now, by raising food prices.

Developments within the PZPR after the Ninth
Plenum were marked by a political debate and differing standpoints at the top, by the implementation
of the reform measures agreed at the plenum, and by
an unprecedented outburst of activity by the grassroots.   The Horizontalists now grew into a national
force.   Even official editorials admitted that the
organisational links and the mutual confidence between organisations at different levels of the PZPR
had collapsed (TL, 2.4.81).   The leaders therefore
scattered all over Poland to drum up support in the
main factories and to rally the party after the Ninth
Plenum.   On 2 April Kania heard the discontent of
the Warsaw workers' aktyw at the unsatisfactory and
incomplete character of the Ninth Plenum.   He now
gave the POPs the green light for a more resolute
offensive 'breaking down the bureaucratic barriers
of factory administrations and the petrified forms
of party apparat work at all levels'.   He rejected
the calls for slimming down the PZPR to its most reliable cadres but emphasised the need for a cohesive
and disciplined party (TL, 3.4.81).   At the same
time Barcikowski promised the Rzeszów aktyw in
Mielec that the democratisation of the party and
the legal bases of socialist renewal in the form of
bills on censorship and workers', farmers', Co-
operatives' and People's Councils' Self-Management
would be completed by late June.   Olszowski told
the Huta Warszawa workers that the Politburo stood
united on the basis of socialist renewal.   Rumours
regarding its alleged divisions had been thought up
by the likes of Bratkowski, who held unacceptable
views on democratic centralism and party pluralism.
This view was contradicted by Fiszbach in Gdańsk
(TL, 4.4.81), but two days later the CKKP warned

Bratkowski as to his future conduct.

On 9 April Kania attended a 5 hour long session listening to the party aktyw's grievances in the Lenin Shipyard - a difficult mission 'designed to regain the confidence of the party's base'. The KZ First Secretary, Jan Łąbecki, promised 'a ruthless struggle' against the groups interested in provoking social conflicts who were responsible for Bydgoszcz. The participants criticised the delays in holding the Congress, demanded that a firm date be set for it, and that delegates should be elected solely by revised democratic electoral rules. The congress should also give a clear answer as to how the present crisis had arisen, while the PZPR should settle accounts with the individuals and mechanisms responsible for it. The healthy aspects of horizontal contacts between party organisations were stressed. It was argued that they were less of a threat than 'conservatism, opportunism and non-ideologically committed passivity'. Kania noted the atmosphere of optimism but warned that it was out of tune with Poland's economic difficulties. He promised that the leadership would take note of the criticisms expressed, that it would break down all the barriers to renewal and that those responsible for the crisis would be punished (TL, 10.4.81).

The pluralism of politics at this time can be gauged by contrasting the above workers' meeting and the politically radical tone of a Kraków KW plenum with the conservative views of the ZBoWiD Executive - all of whom were held simultaneously. Another sign of pluralism was an interesting defence of the full-time apparat workers against the popular charges that they were responsible for the deformations in the party's inner life, that they had dominated the elected officers and state officials and that they were to blame for de-ideologising the party, for stifling grassroots' initiative and for selecting information as desired by their bosses [42]. The party's elected committees should have a greater say over the appointments of functionaries, whose service role should be written into the party statutes and who should return to their original jobs after a spell of party work [43]. The Chairman of the Gdańsk WKP,on the other hand, stressed that the PZPR's main internal problems, inherited from the Gierek era, were how to select the right functionaries and how to change the party's leading role from administration to policy inspiration. This would depend on limiting the number of nomenklatura appointments, on delimiting the powers of individual offices and in assuring inner party democracy [44].

The CPA was also preoccupied with internal party matters. On 7 April the Politburo decided to hold its May Day celebrations after all and considered the draft party statutes (TL, 8.4.81). Barcikowski then issued his new instructions to KWs on how to carry out the electoral report congress preparations, a process which had advanced furthest in Higher Education, where 40% of party groups had already done so (Ney, TL, 9.4.81). At the Twelfth Plenum Barcikowski revealed that only 10% of cells had renewed themselves between the Sixth and Ninth Plena (TL, 11-12.7.81).

The Sejm session on 10 April was dominated by Jaruzelski's call for a bill suspending strikes for two months and a wage-freeze till the end of the year [45]. He criticised the excessive reaction to Bydgoszcz. Jaruzelski painted a grim picture of the state of the Polish economy, which was worse than most people thought. Kisiel also had little constructive to offer and therefore spent his time cataloguing Gierek's many economic sins. Rakowski hoped that Solidarity would now evolve away from political programmes and concentrate on economic and social problems. The Sejm's nine point resolution confirmed Jaruzelski's policy of the previous two months of seeking social appeasement in collaboration with Solidarity. It left the banning of strikes hanging as a threat in reserve, although it appealed for a voluntary suspension of strikes for two months [46].

Poland after the Warsaw Agreement thus entered on its third period of relative social calm since August (October and December 1980 being the only other fairly tranquil months). Had a turning-point been reached with the CP and Government at long last accepting the consequences of Summer 1980? Had the domestic forces in favour of reversing the course of events been defeated politically? Had Bydgoszcz broken the political deadlock and accelerated the process of socialist renewal? On the other hand, the Ninth Plenum compromise of no personnel change in the CC and leadership linked with full powers for Jaruzelski and Rakowski to resolve the Bydgoszcz crisis and for the party to accelerate its democratisation was a highly unstable one. The question now became whether the Kania leadership could keep control of the democratisation movement, as it had promised its Soviet allies, and whether if it succeeded the reforms would appear credible to the PZPR grassroots and Polish society. On the other hand, the fundamental problem of Solidarity's existence

was shelved for the moment.   The Jaruzelski Government now took a very practical attitude in negotiating with it and in working for the proposed social
contract and period of strike-free appeasement.
Numerous Solidarity-Ministerial meetings took place
to resolve contentious issues such as those between
Barecki and Onyszkiewicz over Solidarity's access to
the mass media.   A bewildering series of meetings
between Government and Solidarity working parties
then continued on a regular basis throughout the
Spring and early Summer, such as the Bafia-Bujak
exchanges on Law and Order [47].
        The Congress Commission met on 15 April to dis-
cuss the texts of the party programme and statutes.
Although the latter incorporated most of the democratic   proposals, including the strengthening
of Central Commissions, the weakening of the party
apparat, secret voting on multiple candidates and
rotation of cadres, there was much criticism of
their unspecific character and the omission of such
suggestions as the ban on nominations for office
without the prior consent of the POP involved (TL,
16.4.81).   At about the same time the electoral and
report campaign started in earnest with the election
of 28 delegates, by 15 April, in the largest factory
and Universities granted the privilege of directly
electing one delegate per 850 party members.
        The Polish August at first produced a wave of
demoralisation and resignations amongst the PZPR
grassroots membership.   Unlike 1955-1957, though,
most dissatisfied members decided to stay on and
fight or to survive to protect their personal positions.   They did the former by becoming 'bigamous'
and joining Solidarity or,from the October Sixth
Plenum onwards, by agitating within their party
organisation or eventually in novel discussion clubs
or horizontal forms of party organisation.   The
Ninth Congress report stated that only 197,300
members and candidates (6.3% of the total) left the
PZPR, mainly by handing in their party cards between
1 August 1980 and 15 May 1981 [48].   About 72% of
these were workers and 8% peasants, with the greatest
efflux taking place in Katowice, Łódź, Gdańsk and
Rzeszów.   They were counterbalanced by the admission of just under 57,000 new members.   Official
figures put PZPR membership at 2.87 million in mid
July 1981, whereas it had been 3.08 million on 1
January 1980.   Western analysts consider that these
are misleading figures which underestimate the loss
of membership,but not to a dramatic extent.   The
best, although internally inconsistent, Ninth
Congress figure is that only 300,100 members had

been deleted in the year prior to it. The PZPR
therefore went through its period of greatest crisis
with the staggeringly small loss, between 1 July
1980 and 31 May 1981, of no more than 10% of its
membership, about two-thirds of whom were workers
[49].   Does this suggest that the PZPR was more
firmly anchored in Polish society than might appear
from the crises which have periodically buffeted it,
as I have argued elsewhere? [50]   Moreover, were
the bonds of mutual self-interest and self-preservation stronger among the PZPR professionals than
among the workers?
     The basis for the success of the workers' move-
ment in late August 1980 had been that the strike
committees in individual factories had grouped themselves in larger horizontally based organisations,
the MKSs.   These had prevented the authorities from
isolating or buying off factory outbursts in the
Baltic region one by one.   The ordinary party
members, after wavering between demoralisation and
entryism into Solidarity, from the October Sixth
Plenum onwards started groping towards similar independent horizontal links between party cells in
order to reinforce their demands.   They also wanted
to offset what Kolankiewicz terms vertical 'bureaucratic centralism' [51].   This had allowed the CPA
and its regional apparats to manipulate the grassroots by breaking them up organisationally into
powerless, isolated units whose voice was not allowed to go up the line but who were expected to obey
and support decisions coming down from the top
leadership.   The post-Gdańsk ferment of ideas, proposals and criticisms were, on the other hand, partly
catered for the intelligentsia by the emergence of
discussion clubs, ranging from genuine radical intelligentsia forces like the Karol Marks Club in
Warsaw with 350 members, Kuźnica in Kraków, Odnowa
in Wrocław and the Szczecin Discussion Forum to
such tame clubs as the Forum of Party Thought organised and controlled by the Białystok KW.
     The main impetus for horizontal links and as-
sociations within the party originally came, from
early October onwards, from such bodies as the
Gdańsk and Kraków WKPs, which were encouraged by
their reform-minded provincial chieftains to collate
and aggregate the specifics of the reform debate.
The PZPR cell in the Social Sciences Institute of
Toruń University took the initiative in associating
itself with 8 of the city's largest KZs in what became the first and model horizontal 'Consultation
and Agreement Commission' (Komisja Konsultacyjno-
Porozumiewawcza POP) [52].   The example was

followed in neighbouring provinces, especially
Poznań, where the University set up similar links
with the radical Cegielski Works.   The problem became a national issue with the <u>cas célèbre</u> of the
Iwanow Affair,which marked a determined counter-
attack by the CPA to stem the movement and to define
the limits within which such autonomous grassroots'
organisational activity could be permitted.
Zbigniew Iwanow, in his own words a 32 year old
believing and practising Roman Catholic Solidarity
supporter, who declared that he was a Social Demo-
crat not a Communist, was elected KZ First Secretary
in a free election in early September by his very
radical work mates in the TOWIMOR marine engineering
works.   The whole KZ, half of whom were party members, went straight into Solidarity.   The party
reacted to the 'Toruń disease' by sending down, in
early October, the very tough Zygmunt Najdowski 'in
a briefcase' to oversee the situation as KW First
Secretary.   Following Józef Tejchma as Minister
of Culture, he had undone much of his conciliatory
policy towards the intellectuals.   The Toruń academics organising the new horizontal organisation,
however,wanted to reduce the KW to an inspirational
and co-ordinating role.   The free election of party
officials was one of their main demands.   Their
spokesmen considered that the primary need was to
renew and to cleanse the party by forcing the PZPR
establishment to settle its accounts with the membership and to fulfil their demands in future.
This would render the old manipulatory-directive
style impossible and convince the <u>apparat</u> that the
new forms would not inevitably lead to factionalism,
indiscipline and the breakdown of all loyalty to
agreed policies [53].   The <u>apparat</u> was not persuaded
by such arguments.   It responded by having Iwanow
expelled from the PZPR by the provincial Party Control Commission in late November.   The decision was
not accepted by TOWIMOR, who renominated him as
their KM delegate, but was confirmed demonstratively
by the CKKP and in increasingly strong attacks on
him by official spokesmen [54].
     Kania was only partly successful in drawing a
line between permissible and impermissible forms of
grassroots' activity within the PZPR and this debate
over organisation was quickly subsumed in the main
policy debate within the PZPR from November onwards.
The hardliners, supported by most of the incumbent
functionaries, wanted the congress to be delayed
until such time as it had been carefully 'prepared',
as in the past.   The radicals wanted immediate elections to clear out the old guard.   They wanted the

congress to be convened as soon as possible and for
it to have a working character which would allow
issues and policies to be resolved by it [55].
The leadership's nuanced position on the Horizontal
Movement was perhaps best expressed by Barcikowski,
who appreciated the movement's liberalism and intellectual values but who feared its potential for
factionalism and party disunity (TL, 28.4.81).   In
the event Horizontalism could not survive being
taken in hand by the party apparatus once the latter
had been renewed.   Horizontalism faded away as a
significant force in the run-up to the congress as
it was only of secondary interest to the PZPR worker
members within Solidarity.   As early as the Tenth
Plenum, Jan Łabecki declared that a Second Horizontal
Party Forum would only be held in Gdańsk under the
aegis of the Politburo, CC and KW and would in no
case be held against their wishes (Nowe Drogi, May-
June 1981, p. 116).
     Horizontalism was not confined to the party.
It was adopted in various forms by the Universities
and by professional and occupational groups.   The
significance of the Toruń case was only partly that
it pioneered horizontal organisational forms.   It
was also that an entire municipal party organisation
had its orthodox apparat overwhelmed by radical intellectuals and professionals who cemented an alliance
with equally radical workers.   In mid December the
radicals, with the support of over 30 lower party
organisations, drummed up the statutory one-third
support required for convening an election conference
to the Toruń KM, thus anticipating the Ninth and
Tenth Plenum decisions.   The democratically elected
KM was then in a strong position to attack but not
overthrow Najdowski's provincial caucus.   What would
have happened if Kania had patronised similar developments all over Poland in December-January rather
than May-June?   Would the congress have been an
altogether more credible affair, and could this have
prevented the subsequent five month long slide towards the State of War?   As it was, Kania's desire
to manage the CPA and the existing CC and not to
defy the Kremlin openly at any point, as well as the
massive socio-economic confrontations from
Częstochowa to Bydgoszcz, all took their toll and
decided against such a Dubcek-like course.   One can
only speculate now whether the Toruń alliance of
radical intellectuals and Solidarity working class
could have produced the political programme which
might have led to an October 1956 type of political
alliance and unity.   But the Gdańsk alternative of
free TUs had more steam behind it, if only because

of the economic crisis.   The Communist intelligentsia also proved too weak to take over the CPA.   The
result, as we now know, was that the Leninist <u>apparat</u>
renewed itself by promoting similar types of officials from a few rungs down.   At the end of the day
it preferred to save the system's authority and
values by calling in the Army.
    Contrary to Kolankiewicz, I therefore feel that
the Horizontalists had certainly missed the boat by
the time they held their Party Consultative Forum in
Toruń on 15 April.   It was a fascinating event for
the 62 Western journalists who attended it and gave
it massive international publicity as well as for
political scientists interested in the comparative
evolution of Communist systems.   By then, however,
the Horizontalists were merely playing an additional,
if somewhat discordant, note in Kania's centrist
controlled choreography of the PZPR's renewal leading up to the delayed Congress.   The Toruń Conference assembled about 500 delegates from 13 provinces where the Horizontalists were strongest,
including Toruń, Gdańsk, Szczecin, Łódź and Poznań.
It was semi-officially sanctioned by the party as
CC Organisation Secretary Kurowski was originally
scheduled to attend, although in the end he sent
his deputy,Ryszard Łukasiewicz, as an observer.
Other prominent attenders were Najdowski, Werblan,
(now attempting a political comeback by backing the
radical tide),and Wojciech Lamentowicz from the much
radicalised Higher Party School of Social Sciences
(WSNS), whose articles on the revised forms of democratic centralism appropriate to a developed Leninist
party had caused enormous controversy [56].   The
lively Forum debate was dominated by the usual demands for the democratisation of the party, by
attacks on the hardliners and by warnings against
what Iwanow called 'the danger of new manipulation'.
The strength of radical feeling was such that
Lamentowicz, representing the most radical intellectual wing of the Communist establishment, had to
plead for the re-election of about 15-20% of the old
leadership and CC in order to maintain continuity
and to reassure the socialist bloc.   In practical
terms, the Horizontalists wanted to influence the
Tenth Plenum by having their delegates admitted to
its proceedings, which should be broadcast, but both
demands were refused.   They also called for the
replacement of the CC 'cemetery vote' by worker representatives.   The Forum's declaration demanded
the legalisation of the Horizontal Movement in the
new party statutes and it criticised the dilatory
proceedings of the Congress Commission which had

lost the militants' confidence. Its main call was
for the rapid and free election of all Congress delegates on the basis of unhindered multiple candidacies
[57]. This unprecedented happening remained a once
and for all affair in Communist politics. The CPA
blocked the possibility of a second one and the Horizontal Movement was submerged in the general preparations for the Ninth Congress, which followed the
Tenth Plenum [58].

The Tenth Plenum: the too belated victory of controlled democratisation

The Tenth Plenum, held on 29-30 April, confirmed
the victory of the party reformers and that the PZPR
would go into its Congress in a democratised form.
The Plenum resolved that the Congress would be held
between 14 and 18 July and ratified the preparations
sketched out for it at the Ninth Plenum. One delegate would be elected per 1,700 members at party
electoral conferences, according to the provisional
electoral rules accepted in late March. Drafts of
the party programme and statutes were also submitted
to it at long last by the Congress Commission and
these would be discussed in full during the election
report campaign [59]. A 15-strong Commission,
chaired by Grabski, was set up 'to appraise the work
done up till now on the question of responsibility
and to accelerate its labour'. The optimistic aim
was to complete the process by the end of June 1981.
Grabski's view, stated a little after the plenum,
was that the party would not be able to function
constructively until it had cleared its ranks of
all those who were guilty of political mistakes or
personal corruption in the Gierek era. The bulk
of innocent party workers would thus be freed from
'the present psychosis of the witchhunt' which kept
them on the defensive. The Commission's work would
also serve the socialist renewal by helping to explain the causes of the crisis and by establishing
the responsibility of individuals for specific mistakes and the deformations of social, political and
economic life (TL, 11.5.81, Grabski interview).
True to the spirit of the political compromise
struck at the Ninth Plenum to postpone substantial
leadership changes until the congress, only minor
changes now occurred. The resignation of the
pogrobowcy Piñkowski and Wojtaszek from the Politburo and Wojtaszek, Zieliński and Wojtecki from the
Secretariat probably strengthened Kania's position,
though. The two new members of the enlarged Politburo, voted on by the CC for the first time since
1956, were not genuine representatives of the

177

Workers' Upsurge.   Zygmunt Wroński, although described as a foundry worker from the Ursus tractor
plant, had been assimilated into the party officialdom there.   He was representative of that peculiar
brand of hard-hat workers' populism which was most
unashamedly and colourfully expressed by Siwak.
Gerard Gabryś,on the other hand, was a simple-minded,
'tame' Silesian miner, if the sentiments which he
expressed at the Ninth Plenum are any reliable guide.
He may have had connections with the Stalinist
Katowice Forum, as it claimed him as its Chairman,
although he denied this and the truth was never
established.   Józef Masny, the Opole KW First Secretary, became a Politburo candidate, while another KW
First Secretary, Kazimierz Cypryniak, from Szczecin,
entered the restricted Secretariat, which now became
dominated by Kania for the first time.   Both of the
latter were politically colourless organisation men.
Such a blatant example of political cosmetics neither
deceived nor satisfied anyone.
     Kania laced the announcement of the important
decisions on the congress,its programme and its statutes with a restatement of what were now becoming
his stock themes.   The PZPR must exercise and renew
its leading role through the democratisation and
reform processes which must be based on a return to
the fount of pure Marxist-Leninist principles.   The
gap between the leadership and the grassroots would
be healed by the debate, which would be reported
reliably by the mass media, on the congress reports,
agenda and programme and the new statutes.   It would
culminate in democratically elected delegates democratically electing their own new CC.   The dangers
to the Polish state, such as the anarchy caused by
the over-readiness to resort to strikes and the open
activities of counter-revolutionaries, were, however,
causing grave concern to Poland's allies.   Unity
and discipline were as important as discussion.
The reactivisation of the grassroots, although a
largely positive factor, and the spread of horizontal structures, would have to be appraised in the
light of a century's experience of the Leninist
workers' movement.   This nègre blanche formulation
had the merit of appeasing both the reformers and
the Soviet leadership.
     The debate at this plenum, in contrast to its
predecessor, was a fairly quiet although very long
one.   The overwhelming bulk of the 41 speakers ap-
proved of the decisions taken, but if anything found
them insufficient, and demanded that the party really
set about punishing the incapable and corrupt officials responsible for the crisis.   Kania's centrism

was supported by the major speakers, such as Rakowski, who after two months in office sang a different tune. He was more concerned now with the methods by which the situation could be stabilised and the 600-odd social and economic agreements which had piled up in his locker be fulfilled. He also warned in dramatic language about the dangers to Poland's international position and criticised the domestic opposition strategies which menaced the country with 'self-destruction'. Moczar showed skilled political footwork by reminding his party reform enemies that they had often been prominent 'decydentów' (an expressive ungrammatical term which achieved popular currency at this time, describing individuals who had had complete decision-making power) in Gierek's time. Most pointedly he took Dąbrowa to task for the way in which he, as a CC Department Head, had manipulated the Eighth Congress. As this plenum was dominated by the reformers and pro-Solidarity workers, who pressurised the leadership for a full, rapid and more extensive democratisation of the party, the real interest lay in the isolated criticisms by conservatives such as Kąkol, the ex-Minister for Religious Affairs, and branch unionists such as Siwak that too much had been conceded. In his last major plenum speech before he very sensibly took a political back seat in the run-up to the congress, Olszowski considered that Poland's anarchic domestic situation and the devaluation of her international standing had become the greatest dangers and that both were caused by the economic collapse. He contrasted the PZPR's democratic draft programme and statutes with the clear intention in Solidarity's 'Directions of the Union's Activity ...' of transforming the organisation 'from a trade-union into a socio-political movement' [60].

As CC plena became less choreographed personal matters and current problems tended to make unscheduled appearances. Albin Szyszka, the Chairman of the Official Branch Unions, raised the question of the bitter and protracted inter-union dispute between the drivers in the Ostrów Świętokrzyski bus-depot in Kielce province. Two of his members, supported by a third, had allegedly driven over two Solidarity pickets from the same depot who wished to prevent their taking their buses out to work during the Solidarity warning strike. They had been suspended because of the enormous pressures generated by Solidarity in Kielce. Szyszka pointed out that 140 of his members in the depot demanded their re-instatement and that the right not to be forced to participate in strikes was guaranteed by

Article 34 of the proposed draft bill on TUs [61].
This socialist mini-Grunwick showed that the break-
up of the CRZZ could lead to genuine conflicts between rival workers' unions in a socialist system,
as in a capitalist one.

Although the régime-Solidarity conflict now
abated the domestic situation remained highly charged.
Social discipline did break down to some extent.
Criminal offences increased by 26% over the year,
the figure for burglary increasing by a massive 39%.
Police interventions increasingly met with social
contestation and one such incident in early May
escalated into the burning down of Otwock police
station near Warsaw [62].   The beating up by the
police of a crippled foundry worker in Białystok
in early May also almost caused another regional
outburst [63].   On 20 May the Politburo felt it
necessary to call for a strengthening of social
discipline and public order.   Their reminder that
'democracy does not mean anarchy' (TL, 21.5.81) did
not prevent an outbreak of looting in Zamość.

Two other events threw yet more cold water on
the extravagant and unrealistic hopes and expectations of the previous Summer.   Cardinal Stefan
Wyszyński, the Primate of Poland since 1948, died
on 28 May 1981 after a long illness.   He had been
a great force for moderation during the Polish crisis
and had accumulated considerable authority as the
moral spokesman for Polish society as a result of
over three decades of conflict and mutual accom-
modation with the Communist state.   The great
sadness surrounding his death came only a fortnight
after the emotion, fear and bitterness aroused by
a Turkish terrorist's attempt to assassinate Pope
John Paul II in St. Peter's Square.   Wojtyła's
election as Pope had been a great psychological
boost for the more pugnacious forces in Polish
society, so the opposite was now true.

The party reformers, Solidarity worker members
and the grassroots did not quite sweep the field
after the Tenth Plenum.   The hardliners made determined efforts to organise themselves with the benevolent support of the police, ZBoWiD and Army and
the more covert assistance, if not inspiration, of
the Olszowski-Grabski wing of the CPA.   The registration of the Grunwald Patriotic League in March
had already aroused much suspicion, especially of
its anti-semiticism, as evidenced by the letter of
124 intellectuals to Życie Warszawy (20.3.81).
Grunwald produced leaflets and broadsheets attacking the party's 'Liberal Mafia', notably Rakowski
and Klasa, in violent terms.   Many of Grunwald's

leaders, like its Chairman, Bohdan Poręba, the film
director, who had personal and professional as well
as political reasons for attacking Wajda's 'monopoly' over the film world, and the actor, Ryszard
Filipski, had played unsavoury, although minor, roles
in 1967-1968. Grunwald claimed 100,000 members and
organisation committees in most major cities as well
as Initiative Groups in some factories, but in reality it had a shadowy existence. Grunwald's members had extreme radical right wing views and pre-
judices and many of their organisers were quarrelsome
and disreputable individuals. In a convoluted
way they stated a minor part of the truth, which was
that many of their AK and other members had been
persecuted by Stalinists of Jewish origins who had
played disproportionately prominent roles in the
1948-1956 period. But,as a censored, unpub-
lished letter from 86 AK soldiers to Kurier Polski
stated, the causes of Stalinism were the responsibility of the whole of the then leadership and
police irrespective of racial origins. The real
danger, however, lay not so much in Grunwald itself,
however dubious its motives and methods, as in its
camouflaged political patrons. Many liberals feared
that the latter were attempting to blend Natolin
values with Partisan tactics in order to form a
widely based hardline national-Communist alliance.
       A real pluralist, ideological debate now de-
veloped. The liberal reform press, such as Polityka
and the much rejuvenated Kultura and Życie Warszawy,
as well as the party dailies in reform strongholds,
such as Gdańsk, Kraków, Wrocław and Szczecin, ex-
changed polemics with their hardline opponents, such
as Prawo i Życie, the Kraków Życie Literackie and
the Army papers Żołnierz Polski and Żołnierz Wolności.
The ideological divide widened with the publication
of Solidarność and the launching of its polar equivalent, a new weekly, Rzeczywistość (Reality), with
a 150,000 production run. It was dominated by the
only writers on whom the apparat could rely unequi-
vocally - a mixture of residual Partisans, PAXers
discontented with Reiff's new found liberalism and
strident fourth-raters who would never have had such
a chance under normal circumstances. Rzeczywistość
attacked socio-liberal and anarcho-syndical elements
in Solidarity and philosophical and political radicalism within the PZPR with much primitive gusto.
These straw men were knocked down repeatedly by their
more sophisticated and intelligent betters on the
quality papers. The really significant straw in the
wind,though,was the formation of the Katowice Forum
at the end of May, which will be dealt with in the
next chapter.

Notes

1. Cf. Sołtysiński on non-party individuals, Polityka, 28.2.81.
2. 'The Polish party leadership appears to have been success-ful in instilling party values, at least within the officers' corps, in that officers accepted the legitimacy of the system even though they may have disagreed with certain policies', D. Herspring, 'Technology and the changing political officer in the armed forces; the Polish and East German cases', Studies in Comparative Communism, X, No. 4 (Winter 1977), pp. 370-392, 392.
3. SSS, VIIIth Sejm, 9th sitting of 11 & 12.2.81. Jaruzelski cols. 29-44, English text in Contemporary Poland (March 1981); Gertych cols. 16-25; Bryl, cols. 26-27; Barcikowski, cols. 50-55; Moczar cols. 67-79; Rakowski cols. 143-146.
4. See the account of Polityka's life by Radgowski in the 6.12.80 issue in which he revealed that CC Secretary Artur Starewicz had actually sacked Rakowski in 1960. However, Gomułka changed his mind, a rare case of an appeal being carried against a firm CPA appointment decision.
5. Rakowski was also extremely useful as an intelligent and credible régime publicist in the Western mass media; especially notable was his interview with Oriana Fallaci, Times, 22 & 23.2.82.
6. The KKP resolution of 12 February described Solidarity as 'the main guarantor that a solution based on the August-September Agreements can be found'. ICPA New Bulletin, March 1981, p. 1.
7. Complete text in Sztandar Młodych, 19.2.81; English text in Contemporary Poland (April 1981) and ICPA News Bulletin, March 1981, pp. 7-12.
8. See the PAN early December poll for the state of peasant opinion, Polityka, 7.3.81.
9. TL, 25.2.81; Contemporary Poland (March 1981).
10. TL, 5.3.81; full French text, Le Monde, 6.3.81.
11. S. Ehrlich, 'Koniec kultu potulności', Życie Warszawy, 23.2.81.
12. For a description of Kuźnica, Contemporary Poland (March 1981), pp. 16-17. The 'Open Letter' is reproduced par-tially in Dziennik Polski, 3.3.81. See also their pub-lication, Zdanie, notably Zeszyt Specjalny (Kraków, KAW 1981).
13. By April 1981 7 KIKs had been registered and another 30 were awaiting registration. Their membership totalled 8,000, of which over 2,000 was in Warsaw. Contemporary Poland (April 1981), p. 15.
14. 'Sprawa wyborów', Polityka, 7.3.81; Moszyński covered earlier Poznań demands in ibid., 24.1.81.

15. Nowe Drogi (April 1981), pp. 185-192; cf. Kultura,5.4.81.
16. The radical Communist intelligentsia's argument that
     socialism had been appropriated by the party bureaucrats
     but that reform was possible on the basis of a 9-point
     socio-economic egalitarian programme was presented by
     Bratkowski in Życie Warszawy, 11.3.81.
17. ICPA News Bulletin, April 1981, pp. 1-3.
18. Kania revised the official view of 1968 to the extent of
     conceding that it had signalled a crisis of social con-
     fidence. He denied that the PZPR ever had, or ever
     would, resort to anti-semitism. He also confirmed that
     the 1968 revisionists remained beyond the PZPR's ideo-
     logical pale. TL, 13.3.81.
19. Solidarity communiqué, ICPA News Bulletin, April 1981,
     p. 5; TL, 11.3.81.
20. ICPA News Bulletin, April 1981, pp. 1-3.
21. SSS, VIIIth Sejm, 10th sitting of 6.3.81. Zabłocki
     cols. 16-21; voting on the Extraordinary Commission -
     6 against, 27 abstentions - col. 71.
22. Edward Kowalczyk, a Warsaw Polytechnic electronics Pro-
     fessor, who had been Minister of Communications from
     1969 to 1980, was elected as SD Chairman in place of the
     extremely personable Tadeusz Młyńczak. See his article
     in TL, 1.4.81. A good study of the SD is P. Winczorek,
     Miejsce i rola SD w strukturze politycznej PRL (Warsaw,
     Epoka, 1975).
23. E. Modzelewski, 'Teoria i praktyka działania KSS-KOR'.
     Ideologia i Polityka (March 1981). See the TL commentary
     of 18.3.81 under the same title.
24. See the detailed chronology of Bydgoszcz events, TL,
     23.3.81, and the more objective communiqué drawn up jointly
     by Bydgoszcz WRN councillors and Solidarity on 19 March
     and published as one of the conditions of the Warsaw
     Agreement, TL, 2.4.81. A pro-Solidarity account is
     K. Czabiński in Kultura, 5 & 12.4.81.
25. Procurator-General's communiqué, TL, 15.5.81.
26. Rakowski told Rulewski on 6.6.81 that the Soviet Letter,
     which had just arrived, had changed the political situa-
     tion. The Government therefore wanted Solidarity to
     regard the Bydgoszcz Question as closed, AS 81/9, p. 001.
27. The preceding and subsequent account, concerning Solidarity,
     is based on AS and ICPA material for the period.
28. ICPA News Bulletin, May 1981, pp. 11-12; Le Monde, 25.3.81.
29. Życie Warszawy, 21-22.3.81. See also the material on
     nomenklatura reproduced in Aneks, No. 26 (1981), pp. 38-58.
     Cf. the challenging analysis by T. Lowit, 'Le parti poly-
     morphe en l'Europe de l'Est', Revue Française de Science
     Politique, XXIX, No. 4-5 (August-October 1979), pp. 812-846.
30. 'Raport Komisji Rządowej o przebiegu wydarzeń w Bydgoszczy',
     TL, 30.3.81. Full English text, ICPA News Bulletin,
     81/5, pp. 1-6.

31.   Lech Będkowski argued in Polityka, 7.3.81 and 16.5.81,
       that many of Solidarity's failings would fade away as
       the situation became normal and as it became an orthodox
       TU.   The contrary case for a political Solidarity was
       put by Ryszard Bugaj, one of its expert advisers,
       Polityka, 21.3.81.
32.   IX Plenum PZPR, 29-30 marca 1981r (Warsaw, KiW, 1981).
       References to Nowe Drogi (April 1981);   Barcikowski, pp.
       9-22;   Nowakowska, pp. 41-42;   Pustelnik, pp. 43-45;
       Jarzębek, pp. 45-46;   Drabik, pp. 53-56;   Gromada, pp. 105-106;
       Jarecki, pp. 65-68;   Kostrzewa, pp. 85-86;   Ney, pp. 106-
       107;   Dębrowa, pp. 86-89;   Bryk, pp. 82-85;   Rakowski, pp.
       137-139;   Kociołek, pp. 97-99;   Baryła, pp. 112-115;
       Milewski, pp. 124-126;   Kisiel, pp. 78-82;   Bednarski,
       pp. 50-53;   Prokopiak, pp. 68-71;   Grabski, pp. 102-104;
       Olszowski, pp. 109-112;   Kania, pp. 28-33;   resolution,
       pp. 23-26;   proceedings and decisions, pp. 5-8.
33.   'Wiarygodność' (credibility) was a key-phrase of the whole
       reform period.   Rakowski had used it as far back as
       Polityka, 6.9.80.
34.   See A. Paszyński, Polityka, 9.5.81.
35.   Text of Agreement in Więź, XIV, No. 6 (June 1981), pp. 79-
       93;   Contemporary Poland (May 1981).
36.   SSS, VIIIth Sejm, 12th sitting of 6.5.81, cols. 6-14.
37.   Kulaj's views and those of other RI Solidarity activists,
       Polityka, 16.5.81.
38.   The arguments such as those of Kozłowski's, Kultura,
       1.3.81, in favour of private peasant farming therefore
       prevailed.
39.   Ignar's biography, Contemporary Poland (June 1981), p. 11.
40.   On the 'absurd, anachronistic' price-structure, see
       M. Nasiłkowski, Polityka, 11.4.81.
41.   See Moszyński's account, Polityka, 11.4.81.
42.   Janusz Łaziński (Departmental Director, Warsaw KW),
       'Działacz i urzędnik',TL, 6.4.81.
43.   On the problem of what to do with redundant apparatchiks,
       Moszyński, Polityka, 30.5.81, and the réplique by A. Adamus,
       ibid., 27.6.81.
44.   Z. Kowalski, TL, 8.4.81.   For the full range of Gdańsk
       demands, Nowe Drogi (March 1981), pp. 173-180;   for the
       debate on the party's 'identity', ibid. (May-June 1981).

45.   SSS, VIIIth Sejm, 11th sitting of 10.4.81.   Jaruzelski
       cols. 6-21 (Contemporary Poland, May 1981);   Rakowski
       cols. 70-77;   Holoubek cols. 94-97;   Kisiel cols. 24-34;
       Szczepański cols. 48-56.
46.   On the legal position of strikes in a socialist state,
       see the forum 'Prawo o strajk', Polityka, 14.2.81, and
       T. Zieliński, 'Strajk (Aspekty polityczno-prawne)',
       Państwo i Prawo, XVI, No. 4 (April 1981), pp. 3-16.

47.   'Stanowisko rządowe do rozmów z Solidarnością', TL.
      18-19.4.81; ICPA News Bulletin, 81/7, pp. 3-8.
      AS 81/17, pp. 001-006.
48.   Nowe Drogi (August 1981), p. 58.
49.   Ibid., pp. 90 & 95.   By the end of 1982 PZPR membership
      had fallen to 2.37 million.   779,000 members had left
      between August 1980 and December 1982; Polityka, 22.1.83.
50.   G. Sanford, 'Polish People's Republic' in B. Szajkowski
      (ed.), Marxist Governments, op. cit., pp. 564-580.
51.   G. Kolankiewicz, 'Bureaucratised political participation
      and its consequences in Poland', Politics, I, No. 1
      (April 1981), pp. 35-40.
52.   See G. Kolankiewicz in Woodall, op. cit., pp. 64-65.
53.   W. Pawłowski, 'Weryfikacja', Polityka, 8.11.80.
54.   J. Czula, 'Sprawa Iwanowa, czyli równia pochyła', Kultura,
      10.5.81.
55.   Cf. Zygmunt Simbierowicz, 'W pionie i w poziomie',
      Kultura, 10.5.81.
56.   Lamentowicz's Yugoslav and Eurocommunist conceptions of
      the leading role of the party were outlined in a series
      of stimulating articles in Życie Warszawy, 25-26 October,
      14, 28 and 30 November 1980.   Also Płomień, 14.12.80.
57.   See TL and Życie Warszawy, 16.4.81.   M. Wesołowska and
      P. Moszyński, 'Żyć własnym zyciem', Polityka, 25.4.81.
      Guetta's graphic account in Le Monde, 17.4.81.   ICPA
      News Bulletin, 81/6, p. 1.
58.   The equivalent of Horizontalism also developed within
      Solidarity with Sieć (the Network) from late April onwards.
      Cf. Robotnik, No. 76, 12.6.81.
59.   Both documents were reproduced in the unusually compre-
      hensive 299 page long X Plenum KC PZPR, 29-30 kwietnia 1981r
      (Warsaw, KiW, 1981).   References to Nowe Drogi (May-
      June 1981); resolutions re congress, pp. 29-30; re
      Grabski Commission, pp. 33-34; Kania, pp. 1-28 and
      35-37; Putrament, pp. 38-39; Romanik, pp. 39-40;
      Grzyb, pp. 43-47; Moczar, pp. 49-54; Kękol, pp. 69-73;
      Siwak, pp. 81-86; Rakowski, pp. 86-90; Olszowski,
      pp. 104-109; Łębecki, pp. 115-118; Szyszka, pp. 132-134;
      Jaruzelski, pp. 141-144; Prokopiak, pp. 151-154;
      Fiszbach, pp. 167-169.
60.   'Kierunki działania związku w obecnej sytuacji kraju.
      Tezy do dyskusji', supplement in Tygodnik Solidarność,
      17.4.81.   The above document received a barrage of
      official criticism backed up by the Soviet press, notably
      a half page denunciation in Pravda, 15.5.81.
61.   'Co wydarzyło się w Ostrowcu', TL, 4.5.81.
62.   Jan Walc, Tygodnik Solidarność, 15.5.81; ICPA News
      Bulletin, July 1981, pp. 3 and 16.
63.   For a fascinating study of the rise and activities of
      Solidarity at regional level, see Bohdan Skoradzyński,
      'Odnowa w białostockim', Więź, XIV, No. 7-8 (July-
      August 1981), pp. 5-35.

Chapter Six

THE HOLLOW TRIUMPH OF COMMUNIST REFORMISM FROM
ABOVE (MAY TO JULY 1981)

The election of delegates to the Ninth Congress
took place in two stages. Firstly, factory and
municipal party organisations met, mainly in May, to
elect delegates to the forthcoming electoral report
provincial conferences and to renew their own Executives. The latter process had started earlier
but had proceeded very slowly and with only about
10% of all basic level party organisations doing so
between the Sixth and Ninth Plena. The early results
were a foretaste of things to come with over three-
quarters of the First Secretaries and half of the
party committees being new. Roughly a quarter,
however, were manual workers, while three-quarters
were white collar of one sort or another. The low
percentage of workers elected gave rise to much
leadership concern. A lively debate on the subject was sparked off by Sufin's early analysis that
the workers preferred to elect others to party functions rather than be elected themselves, but that
this did not matter now because the democratic procedures ensured that only honest and competent individuals would be elected irrespective of sociological origins [1]. Some of the University and
larger factory organisations were also allowed to
elect their Congress delegates directly; even here
the striking feature was the high percentage of
managers, foremen, engineers and the like, being
elected rather than manual workers.

The pre-Congress Campaign democratises the PZPR
The second stage was a round of electoral report conferences in all 49 provinces, starting with
Olsztyn and Szczecin in late May and finishing with
Warsaw at the end of June [2]. In just under a
month, in one of the most sweeping and unprecedented
developments in world Communism, the PZPR used democratic procedures of election and discussion to renew

all its vitally important provincial committees and to produce the 1,964 delegates for the Ninth Congress. These events worried the Kremlin to such an extent that it sent one of the sternest warnings ever directed at a fraternal CP. It also provoked the final, and unavailing, attempt by the CC hardliners to replace Kania. On the other hand, both the committed reformers and the hardliners lost out in the Congress Campaign which elected completely fresh delegates,who in turn produced an almost totally new set of leaders at the Politburo and CC level.

Taking the elections to the KW Executives first, an unprecedented turnover of officials and committee members took place. Firstly, 22 out of 49 new KW First Secretaries were elected. In just under half the cases the incumbent was re-elected unchallenged by receiving a straight majority of the delegates' votes from the floor, like Porębski in Wrocław with 288 out of 340 votes and Jonkisz in Częstochowa (306 out of 320). What was totally novel was that multiple candidacies were proposed in 27 cases, the numbers running as high as 8 in Sieradz, 6 in Zamość, 4 in 5 other cases, 3 in 10 cases and 2 in the remaining contests. What was most striking was that the incumbent only won in 5 of these contests. Kania had to throw all his influence behind the incumbent in order to persuade the delegates to re-elect Kociołek in Warsaw (who beat his one opponent, a Warsaw University political scientist, by 247 to 132) and Żabiński in Katowice, who managed rather better with 332 out of 492 votes against his two competitors. Others, such as the popular Dąbrowa in Kraków, managed under their own steam (won by 280 to 109). With the exceptions of Fiszbach in Gdańsk, Kruk in Lublin and Dąbrowa, all the re-elected incumbents were new in their posts since September 1980 and had not suffered from the same degree of political backlash as the residual third or so survivors from the Gierek era. The post-September men, with a few exceptions, therefore maintained themselves, either decisively, as with Szablak in Ostrołęka, or comfortably, as with Bednarski in Bydgoszcz (301/372) and Zawodziński in Białystok (170/286). A very odd case was that of Alfred Wałek, Płock KW First Secretary since October 1980. Although he failed even to get elected as a conference delegate, with Kania who belonged to the Płock organisation personally backing him on the spot, he managed to persuade 240 out of the 358 delegates that he should be allowed to stand and then 200 to vote him back into office. On the other hand, the Poznań party refused to renominate

Kusiak, their outgoing KW First Secretary, who had
failed to get himself mandated to the conference.
They replaced him with Skrzypczak, a Horizontalist
supporter from Cegielski.

The KW committees emerged three-quarters to
nine-tenths new.   The results were sometimes dramatic, with a complete sweep of the 86-strong Executive in Gorzów,and only Golis, the KW First Secretary since February 1981, was re-elected out of
101 members in Jelenia Góra.   Splits between urban
and rural parties also occurred, most dramatically
in Toruń.   There the City organisation, dominated
by radical intellectuals and Horizontalists, suffered
from a rural backlash judiciously managed along by
Najdowski's KW apparatus.   Toruń City ended up with
a mere 4 seats on the new KW Executive instead of the
40 to which its numbers entitled it as well as a
mere smattering of congress delegates.   The Toruń
Municipal Conference, held on 28 May, had distinguished
itself by confirming Iwanow's mandate to it by 363
to 354 votes, even though he had been expelled from
the party.   The minority then walked out in protest
(TL, 4.6.81).   The issue naturally raised fundamental questions of principle as to how to resolve
disputes between the top and the bottom of the party
once the orthodox Soviet definition of democratic
centralism had weakened, as with the TOWIMOR defiance.

As a result of elections at the lowest party
level about 600,000 members of basic cell Executives
were produced.   About half were new, 39% were working class, 10% peasants and 46% white collar.   60%
of the 45,000 strong factory Executives were new and
of these 42% were workers and 54% white collar [3].

The future CC and leadership, however, depended
upon the outcome of the elections for congress delegates.   Many of the electoral report conferences
had bitter wrangles over whether only conference
delegates could be elected as congress delegates or
whether to heed Kania's call to make an exception
for members of the old leadership team.   Only a
handful of provinces, perhaps half a dozen, agreed
to hold such 'open' elections (notably Warsaw and
Lublin) but the overwhelming majority were 'closed'.
Only 71 (some sources claim 74) out of the 236 members of the outgoing CC became congress delegates
with a chance of re-election to office, so two-
thirds were eliminated at the outset.   Many of the
Politburo and Secretariat members faced considerable
difficulties in getting elected.   Only Kania's personal intervention allowed such hardliners as
Olszowski and Grabski to scrape in.   On the whole
moderate party reformers had it much easier.   They

188

very often won the most votes,as in Kania's case in
Kraków (365/392) where Rakowski, Klasa, Ney and
Kubiak were also elected, or in the cases of Fiszbach
and Łabecki in Gdańsk. A number of 'backwoods'
apparat-dominated provinces provided safe enough
havens for notables such as Jagielski in Elbląg,
Jabłoński in Tarnów and Kurowski in Ciechanów. In
comparison with lists of provincial delegates in
the past, which were crammed full with national incumbents and dignitaries, what was particularly
striking was the extent to which notables of all
sorts and the most prominent activists, radical as
well as conservative, were rejected. The individuals who were now favoured had almost no office-
holding past to blot their copybook. On the whole
they had medium length terms as party members, sufficient to have established them as loyal, decent,
safe and reliable but not particularly outstanding
individuals. Five of the smaller rural provincial
parties took this fastidiousness to the extent of
refusing even to elect their First Secretaries as
delegates. Even an industrial party like Katowice,
after rejecting central candidates like Planning
Chairman Madej, Mining-Minister Glanowski and Kąkol
managed to elect 233 delegates with only Żabiński's
name, and possibly that of a General, ringing any
bells with anyone outside Silesia. The big city
delegations were usually more mixed and politically
plural and supported a wider range of individuals.
These ranged from reform-minded academics such as
Afeltowicz, Kaleta and Orzechowski in Wrocław to
ex-Partisans like Tadeusz Walichnowski (Rector, MSW
Academy), hardline academics such as Duraczyński,
populist workers (Siwak) and progressive Editors such
as Horodyński (Kultura) and Główczyk (Życie Gospodarcze)
in Warsaw. In the end only 3 of the most compromised members of the Politburo and Secretariat,
notably Waszczuk,who was rejected humiliatingly in
Chełm and more quietly elsewhere, failed to get
elected as delegates. But in some cases, such as
Olszowski's in Warsaw (246/426), this depended upon
Kania's express appeal. The Poznań party, in spite
of heavy pressure, refused categorically and repeatedly to elect Grabski. He had to crawl away to
his old fief in Konin where opinion was sufficiently
favourable for him to be acceptable because of his
anti-Gierek criticisms. Candidates recommended by
the Politburo had mixed fates. Szyszka was accepted in Leszno and Ciosek and a General in Bydgoszcz
but two others were also refused there.
     The debates at these electoral report con-
ferences were normally very long, stretching over

2-3 days in some cases.   They were also extremely
lively with delegates making the most of the previously unheard of luxury of uncontrolled discussion
with non-manipulated and unchoreographed proceeding
and results.   Above all the voting habit encouraged
much procedural wrangling.   Decisions as to whether
elections for KW committees and congress delegates
should be 'open' or 'closed' and whether exceptions
should be made for worthy individuals did, however,
have important consequences.   The main themes of
this discussion can only be sketched in here.   They
concerned the party programme and statutes, the
'settlement of accounts' with previous office-holders,
interventions on either side of the political struggle
within the party, the methods and structures which
might assure intra-party democracy and a whole host
of specific and local demands as well as suggestions
for resolving Poland's economic and social problems.
The later conferences also faced firmer leadership
responses after the Soviet Letter.
    Of the electoral report conferences, the one in
Gdańsk on 5-7 June was interesting as it provided an
opportunity for Fiszbach to rally the reformers.
It laid out a full critique of the Gierek period and
of the insufficiencies of the current reform programme
(TL, 6-7.6.81).   Fiszbach declared that the changes
of the previous 9 months 'were less than expected'
and that both 'the coherent vision' and the capacity
to implement reforms in order to overcome the crisis
were missing.   He demanded that all the politicians
responsible for the crisis should answer for their
corruption, arrogance and mistakes, that responsibility for the December 1970 tragedy should be
clarified and that the congress should be presented
with a document setting out the causes of Poland's
crises.
    The Poznań conference, which had to be ad-
journed twice, and which stretched over most of June,
was dominated by the issue and personality of Grabski.
He attacked the Horizontalists as a 'form of party
dual power'.   In spite of a hostile reception he
repeated his Eighth Plenum remarks.   As at Gdańsk,
the memory of an uprising, that of 1956 and why it
had taken a quarter of a century for the demands
of the Poznań workers to be taken seriously, played
a potent role.   275 out of the 486 delegates voted
for a 'closed' election which as well as Grabski
eliminated the outgoing KW First Secretary, plus
other outsiders such as Wiatr and Tokarski.   The
decision was reaffirmed in an open vote in spite of
a passionate appeal by Grabski and a message from
Kania himself over the telephone.   Only after

intense pressure was the Solomonic decision taken
to place Grabski on the candidates' list for delegates but then not to vote for him.   The humiliation left Grabski muttering about the 'amok wyborczy'
(electoral murderous frenzy) which he had experienced.
     The Radom conference was also dominated by a
workers' memory, that of 1976, and a bitter condemnation of Prokopiak's caucus.   Intelligent analyses
of the causes of the crisis were presented both by
a largely workers' conference in Łódź and an 85%
white collar dominated one in Wrocław.   The final
conference in Warsaw on 28-29 June rehabilitated
Kociołek's December 1970 conduct in full.   In his
long and detailed whitewash of Kociołek Kania was
motivated by the need to demonstrate the wisdom of
the political resolution of conflicts.   He waxed
lyrical about how the Poles were now not only learning democracy but bathing in it (TL, 29.6.81).
     The report of the Congress Mandates' Commission
revealed the following statistical breakdown about
the 1,964 delegates elected, of whom 1,962 were
confirmed: 1,599 had been produced by the provincial conferences and 349 directly,by the largest
factories, which together grouped 482,000 PZPR
members, and another 16 by University party groups
(TL, 15.7.81).   438 (22.3%) were manual workers,
180 were peasant farmers and another 15 members of
agricultural co-operatives (9.9%) but the remaining
1,344 (66.7%) were white collar (136 enterprise
managers, 63 engineers and technicians, 104 teachers,
44 academics, 50 doctors and pharmacists and 17
journalists) [4].   This included 125 military representatives, 42 elected by provincial and 83 by
military district conferences, as well as 19 pen-
sioners.   Ninety-one per cent were congress delegates for the first time, but much light is thrown
on their behaviour at the congress by the crucial
fact that 84% had been party members for over a
decade, 38% for over two decades, while a mere 88
delegates had membership terms of under 5 years.
The delegates were overwhelmingly male (94.5%) and
mature in age, as 1,328 were over 40 compared with
only 38 under 30.   Although 16 out of the 19 full
members of the outgoing Politburo and Secretariat
became delegates only 43 out of 142 full members
and 28 out of 94 candidates managed it as well, as
did 44 out of the 49 KW First Secretaries.   A most
influential pressure group was now constituted by
the 321 KZ First Secretaries and 247 POP Secretaries
while the bulk of the 394 full-time functionaries
were communal and factory officials (299).   The
central and provincial representatives totalled a

mere 95 [5].
    The three main features concerning the compo-
sition of these congress delegates were, firstly,
the underrepresentation of workers which stemmed
from the abolition of the CPA klucz or key (literally
cypher). This had ensured an artifically fair representation of all social groups in the past. One
can also surmise that successful professional men
who had gone through a highly competitive form of
Higher Education were likely to benefit from something akin to a 'deference vote' from a not fully
mature working class. Secondly, the more prominent
radicals and Horizontalists had been outmanoeuvred
by the local and central party apparats even in
radical strongholds such as Toruń, Gdańsk and Kraków.
In the big cities they lost for the same sort of
reasons why there is a moderate backlash against
Bennery in the British Labour Party. In the
countryside they were overwhelmed by the conservatism
and self-interest of the rural and small town petty
officialdom, the party secondary élite, who stepped
into the shoes of the discredited central notables
with much gusto. Lastly, the PZPR survived by
decentralising very substantially indeed from
central and provincial to factory and basic cell
level.

Did the Kremlin take fright? Political Charades
at the Eleventh Plenum
    External appearances indicated that the Soviet
leaders had agreed to the Ninth and Tenth Plena decisions to democratise the PZPR. Did they take
fright, though, when the intensive round of factory
and municipal conferences started in real earnest in
May? Were they really worried by the sweeping extent of the renewal of party committees, the unknown
character of the delegates elected and the low percentages of manual workers represented on the new
slates, as was indicated by their sharper press comment from late May onwards? Or was their pressure
largely tactical in order to brake the democratisation process and to prevent the Kania-Jaruzelski
leadership from achieving too sweeping a success
which would have increased their independence?
    The Soviet, Czechoslovak and GDR press had
never ceased attacking Solidarity as a counter-revolutionary force, far removed from being a TU, which
contained elements which were attempting to destabilise Poland and to dismantle the party state in
the interests of Western Imperialism. What was
new was that, as the Kremlin digested the municipal
and factory results, it perceived a dangerous alliance,

endangering the healthy socialist renewal, between
the anti-socialist forces within Solidarity and a
section of the PZPR which had succumbed to what
Pravda on 22 May called Solidarity's 'demagogic
verbiage'.

    The electoral report conferences, as well as
producing the results discussed above, had also
offered a public forum for one of the most open
political debates and struggles ever held in any
Communist state. On the one hand were the moderate
hardliners such as Olszowski, Grabski, Siwak and
their friends, flanked by more extreme and exotic
outriders such as Grunwald and the Katowice and
other Stalinist Forums; on the other were the Kania-
Jaruzelski centrist pragmatists, the Fiszbach-
Dąbrowa-Rakowski party reformers and the more radical and pro-Solidarity elements agitating in their
own right.

    To their credit Olszowski and Grabski did not
lose their heads and throw themselves into more extreme courses. Olszowski, for example, ventured
into the lion's den of Toruń radicalism in the Elan
factory on 1 May to explain why he had described
Toruń, on TV, as a city of raging anarchy and to
defend pugnaciously his unpopular themes. He wondered how long Poland's allies would be willing to
supply her without any reciprocal fulfilment of
obligations as Poland has not sent them a ton of
coal, oil or sulphur since January. Olszowski, although a conservative in matters of party organisation, information policy and attitudes towards
Solidarity, was, however, an economic radical and
he promised that the directive centralist structures
of management would be dismantled (TL, 20.5.81).

    The counter-attack by the orthodox party
apparatchiks surfaced in a different fashion with
the formation, in the shadow of Żabiński's Katowice
party organisation, of a Forum of about 140 Silesian
neo-Stalinists. Their leaders were obscure individuals - notably Stefan Owczarz and Wsiewolod
Wolczew from the Silesian Scientific Institute and
two enterprise officials, Krzystof Wilczek and
Grzegorz Kmita. They had attempted to form a
Bierut Discussion Club the previous Winter. Their
ambition now was to raise the voice of real Communism as the PZPR had 'ceased to be a Leninist
party' and had split into 'diverse, political
trends' (Sztandar Młodych, 29-30,5.81). Their Ideological Declaration was published by the official
press, as the Forum benefited from Olszowski's covert protection, but without overmuch comment.
Its significance was that it was the first open

ideological attack upon the current leadership;
linked with its Silesian origins the tone of its
language immediately suggested the long arm of the
Soviet Embassy in Warsaw.   The Declaration considered
that the 1980 crisis had been caused by the party's
'ideological disarmament';   the loss of direction
during the 1970s had been caused by the strength of
'bourgeois liberals' and 'right-wing opportunists'
within the PZPR itself [6].   They now wanted to
turn the rozliczenie process against these elements.
Their aim was to rally all the real supporters of
Scientific Marxism-Leninism in an 'ideological and
political offensive' to ensure the correct ideological shape for the PZPR at its Ninth Congress.
     The Soviet gloss on these proceedings was that
the Forum had stated that more damage had been done
to the PZPR in the previous 10 months than in the
previous 10 years as the leadership had split into
factions and had no clear strategy for overcoming
the crisis.   The main ideological charge which
Suslov and his minions now hurled against the PZPR
was that real Bolsheviks could, and should, act
against the subjective wishes of the working class
if need be.   It was not enough to serve the proletariat, as the new PZPR programme stated;   what
was paramount was to shape its consciousness and to
act as its vanguard.   If this were not done the
workers would succumb to bourgeois ideology, the
implication being that this was what had occurred
with the Polish workers' flight into Solidarity
(Pravda, 2.6.81).
     The Katowice Forum met with strong and imme-
diate condemnation which forced sympathisers to
distance themselves from it.   The PZPR Trybuna Ludu
cell called it an 'ideological political anti-party
platform' which lay outside the framework of the
Ninth Congress debate (TL, 30-31.5.81).   The Forum
was also condemned by other factory and basic cells
all over Poland.   On 2 June the Politburo rebuked
it as not serving party unity, although it considered that the matter had been blown up out of all
proportion (TL, 3.6.81).   Olszowski was forced to
cover his tracks and, as often happens to losers in
a Politburo argument, to present the majority line
that their views were 'unsubstantiated and dogmatic'.
     On 28 May the 230 congress delegates elected so
far assembled in Warsaw to allow Kania to sound out
opinion.   Very significantly, 90 out of the 97
Katowice delegates signed a round-robin motion opposing the Katowice Forum as being organised by 'the
forces opposed to renewal' (TL, 29 & 30-31.5.81).
On 4 June Kania, flanked by Barcikowski, Grabski,

Olszowski and Klasa, held a similar national conference for radio, press and TV journalists.   The
meeting stressed that the Poles could cope on their
own with their problems (TL, 5.6.81).   Kania also
directed the mass media to deal very carefully with
the sensitive question of the daubing of Soviet War
and Friendship memorials.   The latest incident in
Przemyśl had elicited a Government communiqué and a
strong protest by ambassador Aristov.   Secondly,
Kania faced another worry with police demands for a
NSZZ and the setting up of a Foundation Committee
on 1 June to negotiate its recognition by the MSW.
The committee was discreet in public and most concerned with bread and butter problems, but the police
had not been entirely insulated by their functions
and their privileges from the ferment of renewal [7].
On the other side of the fence this period saw much
agitation, including hunger strikes, against the
Draconian conditions in Poland's prisons [8].
     The PZPR leadership was blasted by TASS for
another 'concession to the counter-revolution' when
it decided to head off a Solidarity warning strike
in 4 cities, scheduled for 11 June, by agreeing to
the provisional release of the 4 KPN leaders.   As
this was happening the CC CPSU sent the CC PZPR a
strongly worded letter which most unexpectedly necessitated the holding of the Eleventh Plenum on
9-10 July.   The letter claimed that 'a critical
point' had been reached because the PZPR had given
way, step by step, to the demands of the anti-
socialist forces in Poland who were using Solidarity's
extreme wing for their counter-revolutionary purposes which threatened Poland's frontiers and her
independence [9].   The Soviets charged that the
enemy had gained control of the mass media, that
the authority of the Army and police was not being
maintained, that experienced and loyal Communists
were being replaced in the congress election campaign by opportunists and revisionists marshalled
by the Horizontal Movement ('an instrument for breaking up the party') and that a wave of nationalism and
anti-Sovietism was sweeping Poland.   Most seriously
it blamed Kania and Jaruzelski for not fulfilling
their promises to correct their policy of compromise
and surrender to the counter-revolution.   Had the
Kremlin's patience with Kania's inability or unwillingness to restore order and to assert the leading
role of the PZPR finally snapped?   Was the letter
designed to encourage and rally the hardliners in
the run-up to the congress and to brake the radical
momentum?   Or did the Soviets want to use the unre-
constructed CC to replace Kania and his friends with

stronger and more reliable hardliners as a firmer
guarantee that the renewal process would not get out
of hand?   Was it perhaps a final political warning
that not only domestic solutions were possible?
Soviet ambassadors, like Ponamarenko in Poland in
1956 and Chervenenko in Prague in 1968, have been
known to mislead their masters.   Aristov, in this
instance, is unlikely to have sent over-optimistic
reports concerning the likely support for the Katowice
Forum and the residual hardline forces.   On balance
the evidence favours the interpretation that the
letter was largely a form of pressure designed to
brake the extent of the democratisation movement.
This seems borne out by the ease with which Kania
brushed off the Eleventh Plenum onslaught against
him and by the fact that the only reformer to be
thrown to the wolves was Klasa, who was replaced by
Lesław Tokarski as Head of the CC Press, Radio and
TV Department.

     One should perhaps pause at this point to re-
flect on the complicated duplicity of Communist politics and the difficulties involved in deciphering it.
The CC Secretary in charge of the mass media,
Olszowski, was reviled by the grassroots for his neo-
Stalinist running of this sector, which in point of
fact he undoubtedly controlled.   His deputy, Klasa,
on the other hand, became the scapegoat for allowing
the mass media in the words of the Soviet letter to
be taken over by the class enemy and to become 'an
instrument of anti-Soviet activity' [10].   Now
Olszowski was depicted by the PZPR radicals as a
Soviet stooge willing to sell himself to the Russians
in order to gain Kania's job.   What, then, were the
Soviets doing weakening him politically at the very
moment when they had mounted an apparent offensive
against Kania?   The implication must be, as I have
argued repeatedly, that the Politburo was more cohesive than is generally assumed and that Kania and
Olszowski continued with their mutually agreed division of labour while their differences with the
Kremlin concerned timing and tactics, not the basic
strategy.

     By the Eleventh Plenum it was absolutely certain
that, short of Soviet intervention and the postpone-
ment of the Congress, the vast majority of the CC
would not be re-elected.   Kania attempted to hold
the fort at the beginning of the plenum by making it
plain that the Congress elections were an irreversible fact and that it would take place as scheduled
[11].   The 493 delegates already elected, of which
admittedly only a low figure of 22% was workers,
were ideologically sound and not opportunists chosen

by chance, as the Soviet letter had claimed. However, the 'mechanism of eliminating' candidates with
long periods of party work or activism behind them
was 'a very dangerous tendency'. Kania appealed
for moderation in this regard. Kania's keynote was
that the socialist renewal would continue. The
party need not apologise overmuch about the general
soundness of the mass media and the congress preparations but it would retreat no longer.

The Eleventh Plenum was the hardliners' and
incumbents' swansong. It saw an open and uninhibited
onslaught on the Kania leadership as even the centrists and reformers wished to appease the Soviets
verbally. The Eleventh Plenum was later completely
overshadowed by the Ninth Congress and forgotten as
a result; but the new hardline themes mooted there
were a major intimation of the PZPR's subsequent drift
towards the State of War. Najdowski proposed that
the party maxim of overcoming the crisis peacefully
should be replaced by the new formula of 'overcoming
the crisis at all costs through our own resources',
meaning not necessarily peacefully but without Soviet
intervention. A new hardline Politburo should be
elected to combat Social Democratic tendencies
within the party and to situate Solidarity within
'Poland's political landscape' by ending its activity
as a political opposition. Ryszard Żabus (Gorzów
KW First Secretary, but only for another fortnight)
wanted all strikes banned and the mandates of all
Congress delegates who had been elected by conferences which had not applied the Tenth Plenum rules to
be invalidated. Support for the Soviet letter and
Politburo changes came from General Sawczuk,
Putrament and Kazimierz Olszewski. Żabiński claimed
that KOR and its 'commandoes' had sabotaged the
Silesian Solidarity's positive response to his policy
of collaboration. This showed that there 'was no
chance of agreement with a decided enemy ... of the
socialist order'. These themes were summarised in
a massive and personalised attack on Kania and
Rakowski and their policy of concessions by
Prokopiak. He moved that the CC should have a
secret vote on all individual members of the Politburo and Secretariat. Only a handful of the 18
speakers opposed the anti-leadership tide on the
first day but they were sufficient to prevent a
vote being taken there and then. The Łódź textile worker, Nowakowska, opposed Prokopiak's 'unreal
suggestions'. The party needed to raise, not to
undermine, the credibility of the congress delegates. These in her Łódź experience, although 70%
new, were a good bunch ideologically with a fair

degree of Youth Movement and lower level party experience. Jarząbek, from the Częstochowa steelworks, considered that the need was not to change the
leadership but to get it to implement its stated
policies in a credible way, which would be helped by
the dismissal from the CC of ex-KW Secretaries of
the ilk of Prokopiak, who had lost their posts in
'an atmosphere of social indignation'.
    The following day Kania outmanoeuvred and in-
flicted a resounding defeat on the hardliners.
Rakowski led the counter-attack by reminding the
hardliners that their policies of force had not only
failed but had been responsible for the Poznań and
Baltic tragedies. They would lead to a third and
more extensive one if they were given their head.
Undismayed by the boos and desk-banging of his opponents, he asked them why they had proved incapable
of combatting the anarchy which they denounced at
their own provincial and factory levels. The
pensioning off and disgrace of the élite which had
run Poland since 1956, if not earlier, was undoubtedly a painful experience. The reality was, however, that 'a nationwide rebellion' had taken place.
There was no alternative to the policy of renewal
and political compromise. Delaying the Congress
would only lead to the party's disintegration, so
it was better to avoid confrontation and to plough
on with the policy of social agreement. Warm support for this line came from Fiszbach, Barcikowski,
Ney and the genuine worker representatives such as
Pustelnik, Romanik and Józef Nowak. Jaruzelski
let it be known that he controlled the Army and that
the military supported his Premiership and Kania's
continuation in office. The plenum discussion ebbed
to and fro with further hardline interventions from
Andrzej Wasilewski (Director, PIW Publishing House),
whose maxim was that 'whatever was anti-Soviet was
anti-Polish in its consequences', Siwak and func-
tionless or threatened KW Secretaries such as Bryk,
Kusiak and Grabski rose at 5 p.m. to press home the
challenge to Kania. He was short and to the point,
accepting the validity of the Soviet charges concerning Kania's feeble policy of 'concessions, compromise and opportunism'. Grabski claimed that
the Politburo had not been united and that many decisions (such as the agreements with the students
and the peasants and the condemnation of the Katowice
Forum) had been taken outside it without his personal knowledge. He concluded that the present
Politburo under Kania's leadership was not capable
of leading the country out of the crisis. Zygmunt
Rybicki, the Government Cabinet Secretary, then

moved a suspension of the plenum's proceedings in
order to allow the Politburo to prepare a reply to
Grabski's charges, but not before Barcikowski had
put in some well timed blows in the leadership's
defence.

   We do not know what then transpired at the long
Politburo session but probably Olszowski, who had
remained silent in a deal with Kania ensuring his
long-term survival, tilted the balance in favour of
the status quo.   Kania was also supported by the KW
Secretaries elected since September 1980, who made
it clear that their organisations backed Kania and
the renewal line;   as their reactions to the Katowice
Forum showed, they would have nothing to do with the
unconditionally pro-Soviet hardliners.   Finally,
as the Nowe Drogi report indicated (July 1981), the
Army CC members, whose standpoint was expressed at
this plenum by Chief of Staff Siwicki and deputy
Defence Minister Molczyk, expressed their full backing for the Kania-Jaruzelski team.

   Kania moved that the CC should have a vote of
confidence individually on himself and his Politburo
colleagues and that anyone who received less than
half the votes should resign.   The CC backed down
from this challenge, although the wording meant that
Kania's friends should vote against the proposal and
his opponents in favour of it.   So the vote went
89 to 24 (with 5 abstentions) against having the vote
of confidence.   This was a resounding defeat for
the hardliners and a clear endorsement of Kania.
The plenum's moderately worded final resolution confirmed the party's will to continue the renewal and
the earlier decisions regarding the congress;   but
it condemned the anti-socialist and anti-Soviet activity of the previous weeks.   Warnings that police
and judicial measures would be invoked against inad-
missible political strikes and protests were reinforced in Kania's closing speech.   He promised
the USSR and its allies greater PZPR firmness in the
struggle against anti-socialist and anti-Soviet forces
in both Solidarity and society.

   Rakowski gave a firm intimation of the PZPR's
hardening line at the Bydgoszcz electoral conference
on 7 June.   'The reserves of patience of Poland's
allies were being exhausted' and the policy of dialogue with Solidarity was being threatened by its
radicals (TL, 8.6.81).   On the 9th, though, under
Church pressure and through the good offices of a
Sejm Commission, Solidarity agreed to suspend all
strikes until 3 July.   At the same time a letter of
8 June, signed by 24 intellectuals including Wajda
and Bratkowski, warned of the dangers of abandoning

reform and renewal which 'was the only way out of
the crisis' [12].

Polish political life after the Eleventh Plenum
was therefore highly paradoxical.   The congress
preparations and the democratisation of the PZPR
continued as before, but the leadership's tone became
sombre and the limits of renewal and of co-existence
with Solidarity were narrowed down day by day [13].
The more committed party reformers and radicals continued in good voice but it became clearer that they
need the protection of Kania's centrism against both
domestic hardliners and Soviet pressures.   Having
said that, though, the electoral conferences still
offered venues for significant dialogues between the
leadership and the membership.   The Eleventh Plenum
had confirmed that KW First Secretaries could be
elected directly by the party conference, and not
solely by the KW Executive as in the past.   On the
other hand, the plenum resolution that the limitation
of candidates for the Executives and for congress
delegates solely to mandated conference delegates
violated the party statute largely fell on deaf ears.
So did Kania's plea that a greater degree of continuity be assured by the re-election of more experienced incumbents.   The provincial electoral
report conferences continued very much on the same
lines as before the Eleventh Plenum.   The one possible exception was Lublin, where the invalidation
of the Municipal Conference delegates elected contrary to the Temporary Election Regulations allowed
Kruk to gain a mandate as a conference delegate which
he had been refused the first time around.   This
ensured his re-election as First Secretary and as
a congress delegate.

The delayed and over-controlled Democratisation is completed

The postponed Sejm session of 12 June was an
extremely long one, lasting till well past midnight
[14].   It carried out the customary Ministerial
reshuffle, notably replacing Kisiel as Planning
Chairman with his deputy, Zbigniew Madej.   Zdzisław
Krasiński's appointment as Chairman of the State
Prices Commission met with 27 abstentions and 16
dissentient votes, as he was such a fervent advo-
cate of higher prices.   Bafia's post as Minister
of Justice went to the doyen of Polish state lawyers,
Sylwester Zawadzki, who since 1980 had been the
Founding President of the Supreme Administration
Court.   He had also chaired the Council of State
Commission on the TU Law,whose draft he now presented.
The Sejm, a Communist parliament, held a minute's

silence in Wyszyński's memory and applauded Wojtyła's thanks for their good wishes for his rapid recovery.

In his hour long speech Jaruzelski concentrated on the need for greater social discipline and respect for law and order. He declared that anti-socialist and anti-Soviet activities would now be dealt with severely. His Government would announce an economic reform and measures to save the country from complete economic breakdown soon, although the basic problem was that the Poles were paying themselves more to produce less. Some of the Economic Ministries would be amalgamated to form larger but still far from streamlined ones [15]. The deputies, led by Karol Małcużyński, who pointed to the great social pressure in favour of reform, then supported the policy of dialogue and conciliation. He considered that the Soviet letter's assessment of the Polish situation 'was one-sided in many points' and concentrated overmuch on harmful phenomena to the neglect 'of the achievements of reform'. The Sejm's unanimously supported resolution called on the Government to 'undertake firm actions against all violations of the law',especially against Solidarity extremism which was pushing the country towards 'a national tragedy'.

The harder post-Eleventh Plenum line was stated by Kania at the Kraków electoral conference where he resurrected his Eighth Plenum maxim that 'the counter-revolution will not pass in Poland'. The most important tasks now were to restore the normal functioning of the organs of power responsibility, to restore social discipline and to rebuild 'the credibility of People's Poland as an ally' (TL, 15.7.81). Further support for the leadership directed socialist renewal and the thesis that the main danger was now the anarchy of social and economic life came from the Warsaw Military District Conference. It elected Jaruzelski as a congress delegate with 238 votes out of 241 (TL, 16.6.81). Jaruzelski's main conference themes, notably in Katowice,were to stress the need for economic reform, for officials to gain public support, for a firm but fair relationship with Solidarity and for unflinching loyalty to the USSR (TL, 27-28.6.81).

The moderate wing of Solidary reacted cautiously to the foregoing developments as exemplfied by Wałęsa, who during his trip to Lublin persuaded his supporters to clean the Soviet War Memorial which had been daubed in paint [16]. Although Wałęsa seemed to accept the need for Solidarity to brake the demands of its members in order to establish a co-partnership with the Government in a policy of

austerity designed to lead Poland out of the crisis,
he remained his old caustic self.   His quip that
'the Polish economy resembled the Bermuda Triangle
because everything vanished into it' was particularly
apposite!
     The official press highlighted the spate of
desecrations of Soviet memorials, which continued
throughout June, and played up such events as a riot
by drunks in Katowice railway station which Solidarity
viewed as being organised by the authorities in
order to discredit it.   More significantly, the
trial of the 4 KPN leaders opened at long last on 15
June in the Warsaw Provincial Court, although it was
quickly and quietly adjourned and was to drag on
endlessly [17].   The defendants were charged under
Article 123 of the Penal Code with forming an illegal organisation and with conspiracy against Poland's
political system, alliances, independence and frontiers in terms which could have carried the death
penalty [18].
     In the period between the Eleventh Plenum and
the Ninth Congress it became apparent that there
was no alternative to the Kania-Jaruzelski tandem.
They appeared to have struck the right balance in
riding the PZPR grassroots tide without getting
swamped by it.   They had outfaced the Kremlin and
its domestic allies by demonstrating that the party
would not stand for Grabski and the reversal of renewal.   The Katowice Forum and Grunwald had also
been shown to be mere scum on the surface of Polish
political life.   The emergence of other Stalinist
Forums in Poznań and about a dozen other places, normally in the shadow of the KW apparats which fostered
them, had by now become largely irrelevant.   So
was the Stalinist réplique to Toruń, a meeting in
Poznań in late July of representatives of about 15
of these Forums and discussion groups.
     Although tougher leadership statements on law
and order and the mass media and measures against
the printers and distributors of anti-state leaflets and the daubers of Soviet memorials kept up an
appearance of firmness for the Soviets what was most
important was the post-Eleventh Plenum turn in the
electoral conferences.   Klasa was admittedly demonstratively elected as a congress delegate while
his successor was rejected but the significant fact
for Kania was that most of the outgoing Politburo
and Secretariat were now scraping in as congress
delegates, whereas the Kremlin would have been
publicly humiliated if three-quarters had been
eliminated at the outset, as seemed likely before
the Eleventh Plenum.   All this constituted a policy

of transformation and of safety valves, not a revolution. The new, and often younger, political generation that was now taking over in Poland may have occasionally started off as pro-Solidarity critics of Gierek's régime but more often than not they were reliable lower and middle rankers very similar in outlook to the front runners whom they replaced. Kania knew that they could be relied on to protect the authority which they were inheriting. Moscow thus found itself in the position of either having to accept Kania's achievement or to invade to prevent the congress being held which would confirm the new order. On the other hand, its desire to gain time may have been supplemented by the value of the Polish laboratory in testing, if need be to destruction, many of the reforms required by a developed socialist society, and in particular the techniques of social control required by CPs to survive crisis and reform periods. The main reason for Soviet forbearance, though, was that the Polish leadership and CPA had neither collapsed (as in Hungary in 1956) nor been corroded by revisionism (as in Prague in 1968) in spite of the fact that Kania had allowed Polish developments to go further than he had promised the Soviet bloc in the Spring. The Kremlin must therefore have been confident that the strategy of renewal would rejuvenate the PZPR without turning it into a Eurocommunist revisionist force. Therefore, contrary to some Western interpreations, I do not consider that Kania ever defied the Kremlin on essentials but that he certainly annoyed them with such pinpricks as his handling of the Horizontalists, of political prisoners and of the mass media, which was a cryptonym for Poland's effervescent intellectual and political life.

One should also remember that there was a completely separate chain of command between the Polish and the Red Army and Warsaw Pact High Commands. What went on therein can only be assessed in the light of such decisions as the announcement on 25 June of the holding of Polish-Soviet manoeuvres in Silesia - yet another reminder to the Poles of ultimate military realities. The situation remained complex and highly ambiguous. At the end of the day the Soviet leadership ratified the congress elections by sending the conservative dominated Warsaw party a message through the intermediary of the Moscow party. Moscow's hope that the PZPR would be able to mobilise society in defence of socialism was matched by Warsaw's fervent assurance that Poland would remain a reliable socialist partner (TL, 29.6.81). Gromyko's very discreet visit to Warsaw

on 3-5 July was therefore devoted to an exchange of
views on the final preparations for the congress,
while the communiqué merely expressed unreserved
Polish support for a wide range of Soviet foreign
policy positions (TL, 6.7.81). At the same time
Jaruzelski and Grabski were pleading, without success, at a Comecon session in Sofia for greater
socialist bloc support for Poland.
     The extent to which Polish political life was
changing was pointed up by the official celebration
of the twenty-fifth anniversary of the Poznań uprising. Poznań was thus rehabilitated and much
literature appeared celebrating it as the first justified workers' revolt in Poland and a precursor of
the wider 1970 and 1980 upsurges [19]. On the other
hand, in spite of strong pressures the leadership refused to accept an inquest on 1968 [20]. It also
managed to contain the settlement of accounts for
1976 to the local Radom level [21]. Another sign
of the times was Wałęsa's call on TV on 20 June for
moderation and for the Government to rule with
Solidarity's negotiated support. The democratically
elected Rector of Warsaw University, the history
Professor Henryk Samsonowicz, also caused resentment
amongst his anti-Catholic party colleagues by agreeing to chair the committee raising funds for Wyszyński's
memorial, although this made him a bit of a hero in
the eyes of liberal and Western opinion [22].
     The Sejm on 2-3 July was dominated by Planning
Chairman Madej's unrelievedly grim report on the
economic situation [23]. Poland's foreign debts
continued to rise as imports remained much higher than
exports but the domestic indicators were even more
shattering. GNP was likely to fall by 15% compared
with the previous year, industrial production had
fallen 10% by January and 18% by May and the slide
was worsening. A Bank of Poland official later
supplied extra statistics glossed over by Madej.
There had been a year-on increase of 25% in wages
and this formidable inflationary pressure had caused
the collapse of the retail system. Cigarettes,
alcohol, soap and soap-powder would now need to be
rationed along with meat, flour, butter and sugar
[24]. Madej implicitly accepted the collapse of
socialist economic planning in Poland by presenting
2 variants of the proposed changes to the plan and
budget. He hoped that the Economic Reform, concentrating central planning decisions on essentials
and based on self-managing, self-financing enterprises, would be introduced on 1 January 1982 and
that it would be accompanied by a sweeping price
reform. Madej also made it clear that rehabilitating

the economy, in terms of achieving pre-crisis output,
would take 2-3 years in agriculture, 3-4 years in
industry and 5-6 years as far as overall GNP was
concerned. The draft bills on Enterprise Autonomy
and Workers' Self-Management were then read for the
first time. The following day the Sejm confirmed
the reorganisation of industrial Ministries and
carried out the consequent appointments and dismissals.
Most notably General Czesław Piotrowski, the ex-
commander of Poland's sappers, took over Mining and
Energy, while Władysław Baka was upgraded to Minister
for the Economic Reform. An interesting form of
spurious democracy was the opportunity for deputies
to express dissent over dismissals; for example, the
outgoing Chemicals Minister, Jan Klęka, found 51
deputies to vote for his retention while another 23
abstained. Another new departure was that the
appropriate Sejm Commission was consulted beforehand
on proposed ministerial changes and in Klęka's case
had expressed much opposition.
      The announcement on 7 July that Józef Glemp
(born 1929), the bishop of Warmia in Olsztyn since
1979, was to succeed Wyszyński as Primate met with
official best wishes from Kania, Jaruzelski and
Jabłoński and assurances that the dialogue with the
Church would continue. Glemp had collaborated
closely with Wyszyński and was known as his disciple,
so it was expected that he would continue his patron's
policies [25]. He owed his election partly to this
factor but also to the weakness of his competitors.
Cardinal Macharski of Kraków was too weak and academic
a personality,while Archbishop Gulbinowicz of Wrocław
was notoriously too aggressive towards the Communist
régime to be able to lead the Church successfully.
      Although I am concentrating on élite level de-
velopments it may, again, be interesting to examine
the state of public opinion at this time. A late
May poll showed that the Poles had the greatest confidence in the Church followed by Solidarity, the
Army, the Sejm, the Council of State and only then
the Government. A Centre for the Study of Public
Opinion (TV) poll also showed the extent to which
the renewal was a party and élite matter without
much popular enthusiasm: 41% had not noticed the
renewal, 39% barely so, while only 16% had noticed
its effects on freedom of information and Church-
state relations. Just a fortnight before the
congress 67% did not know the date on which it would
open and 8% did not even know that it was going to
be held. Undue optimism as to its results was
noticeably absent: 37% did not think that it would
bring significant changes, 4% thought that it would

have negative effects, while only 32% considered
that it would be a positive event [26].

If public opinion were largely apathetic two
social conflicts spoilt the political atmosphere
just before the congress. About 40,000 Baltic
dockers held a one hour warning strike on 9 July in
support of their demands for higher salaries, longer
holidays and better working conditions. It was
feared that the unrest would spread to the miners
and other discontented groups. The 6,000 LOT
(Polish airline) workers, three-quarters of whom belonged to Solidarity, also stopped work for 4 hours
for a potentially more explosive reason. The LOT
workers had in a secret vote on 3 good candidates on
27 May chosen Bronisław Klimaszewski to be their
new Director-General [27]. The procedure, in principle at least, seemed to be justified by the Self-
Management Bill but the Government, using the argument that LOT had military significance, refused to
accept the appointment. In spite of being threatened
with an unlimited strike for 24 July it appointed
Air Force General Józef Kowalski to take over LOT.

Official comment appraised the congress election
campaign very positively. It was argued that in
spite of some excesses due to inexperience with
democratic forms it had consolidated the party on
the basis of 'unity in diversity' [28]. On 29 June
Kania and Barcikowski gave the Central Delegates'
Working Group (made up of 3 representatives for each
province) a pep talk about the need for agreement to
be reached on how the candidates for the main party
committees should be produced. In the past the CC
Organisation Department had drawn up a list for the
Politburo to confirm, but this traditional Leninist
technique would no longer do. Kania also felt
that more work was needed on the party programme and
on the final resolutions before the congress opened
(TL, 30.6.81). The delegates then went home and
formed themselves into provincial working groups
which set to work to agree standpoints on the questions put to them by Kania. The particularly lively
Gdańsk conference in the Lenin Shipyard allowed
Rakowski to answer charges of political opportunism
and to set out the policies for economic recovery.
Revolution or not, our old friend Klemens Gniech
still remained as the Shipyard's director. One
read without surprise his call for an end to
rozliczenie which he considered had paralysed effective decision-making since August. In a very
sophisticated political tutorial in Kraków Rakowski
again had the opportunity to praise Kania's reform
consensus which was being threatened by Solidarity

extremists outside the party and by ultras such as
the Katowice Forum and Grunwald within it (TL,
7.7.81).

Rozliczenie and the Problem of Leadership Change

As we have seen, one of the great 'historical
alibis' in post-August reform Communist politics was
the theme that as socialism and the PZPR were intrin-
sically good all that was necessary to correct the
deformations of the Gierek period was to cleanse the
PZPR of its leaders and members guilty of the personal and political corruption and mistakes which
had caused the crisis.   All non-Gierekite incumbents
from ex-Partisans such as Moczar to technocrats such
as Grabski right through the political spectrum to
committed democratic reformers such as Fiszbach
agreed,on the basis of the October Sixth Plenum analysis of Gierek's responsibility for the crisis,
that what was required was the removal of the directing cadres of the Gierek period.   This would also
have the advantage of allaying the generational crisis
within the PZPR.   The humiliation, removal and, where
appropriate, punishment of the Gierek élite were designed to appease the PZPR grassroots and the more
backward sections of Polish society by supplying them
with scapegoats and very necessary emotional safety
valves for the feelings of revenge against individuals in order to protect the system.   There were
also admittedly some genuine elements of Communist
moral puritanism, revolutionary asceticism and a real
working class reaction against Gierek's amiable
policy of 'enrichissez-vous' and favouritism of the
educated and professional classes.   Leadership and
personnel change for the democratisers was only an
essential preliminary to the implementation of their
policies;   but the nationalist, managerial and CPA
survivor wings viewed it as an essential demagogic
substitute for real reforms and democratisation.
Both sides, however, knew that without a moral and
political renewal of the PZPR confirmed by the Ninth
Congress there would be no question of regaining
society's confidence and of re-establishing the
PZPR's legitimacy.

The preceding chapters have explained why leadership change, although very sweeping, when viewed from
the perspective of the months since August, had had
to be balanced against Kania's desire to preserve
the fundamentals of Leninist party rule.   The gradual changes in the Politburo and Secretariat, at KW
Secretariat and Governor's level, spreading down to
local levels in the New Year, were cumulatively very
important;   they moved the PZPR gradually towards

Kania's reform consensus of the early Summer, but
the hardline and Soviet counter-attacks designed to
control and to stem these currents robbed the personnel changes of much social credibility, especially
as in Częstochowa, Bielsko-Biała and elsewhere local
leadership changes were effected under direct social
pressure.   By the Ninth and Tenth Plena Kania,
Barcikowski and Jaruzelski were ready to renew the
PZPR through the democratic processes of free election and debate and to confirm the new policy and
leadership consensus at the congress.   This brilliant
feat of CP politics was a complete success viewed
from the top levels but it fell as flat as a stone,
for a variety of economic and psychological reasons,
as far as Polish society was concerned.

Individual responsibility for the crisis could
take two major forms.   The leadership emphasised,
from the outset, that political mistakes should carry
political sanctions such as loss of office or expulsion from the party.   Corruption should carry the
foregoing penalties initially and then be dealt with
through the judicial process like any other criminal
acts.   The problem was that the distinction was
rarely a clear one.

The Ninth Congress received three reports from
the Grabski Commission, the CKKP and the Central
Appeals Commission (CKR) which summed up the settlement of accounts with Gierek and his officials.
From April onwards a series of CKKP communiqués and
the accounts of the work of the Grabski Commission
had revealed the detail of the most glaring cases
of corruption as well as the global proportions of
the cleansing process.   These were supported by
procuracy communiqués on the progress of their preliminary investigations and by full press reports
of the scabrous details emerging from the trials of
those accused of corruption, such as Szczepański and
his radio/TV associates.   By then the main individuals expelled from the party with much publicity
were an ex-Premier (Jaroszewicz), 6 Ministers (Kaim,
Glazur, Lejczak, Wrzaszczyk, Barszcz and J.
Olszewski), various deputy Ministers, Departmental
Heads, Chairmen and officials of state agencies,
Provincial Governors, their deputies, local officials,
as well as a sprinkling of KW Secretaries and officials.   The most frequent charges of corruption
concerned the misuse of public office and resources
for building or improving private housing, the acceptance of bribes in exchange for allocating flats,
car vouchers and the like, and such oddities as
the case against the KW First Secretary and Governor
of Piła for the abuse of deer hunting.   Comparative

judgements may take us on to a different tack, but
it is not proven that Gierek's élite was any more or
any less corrupt than equivalents elsewhere in Eastern
Europe.   Certainly the peccadilloes of the top
leadership were small beer compared with the notorious Byzantine extravagances of the Communist rulers
of Romania, Albania and North Korea.   The general
level of corruption only seemed to be more striking
to a badly informed Western public opinion in 1980-
1981 because the more 'closed' societies such as
the USSR masked this problem rather better except
in Georgia [29].   Although the opportunities for
corruption in Poland were potentially greater because
of its large private economic sector and wider Western links greater social brakes, rather than the
more normal type of Soviet police controls, existed
in the form of public opinion and envy as the Poles
notoriously cannot keep a secret.

The CKKP and CKR reported that Gierek had gone
for quantity rather than quality in party membership
[30].   The PZPR had accepted 1,560,000 candidates
between 1970 and June 1980, mainly after 1976.
About half a million members had left the PZPR in
this period, of whom 58,000 had been expelled,
1,566 of the latter being in directing positions.
What was notable about the post-August 1980 work of
the CKKP in cleansing the PZPR of individuals who
had abused their offices for private gain was not
the quantitative number of the sanctions but the
eminence of the people against whom they now moved,
whereas during the 1970s small fry were dealt with
while notables had sufficient influence to brush off
enquiries.   Between the Sixth Plenum and 10 June
1981 party control commissions, both central and
local, had received over 16,000 denunciations or
'signals' (1,000 against top leadership personnel).
They had confirmed the accusations, wholly or in
part, against 4,990 individuals.   They had caused
956 persons to be expelled for corruption (note that
the figure had been on average 580 p.a. during the
1970s), 565 of whom had been in directing positions.
They had also reprimanded another 1,531 and warned
9,907 (Nowe Drogi, August 1981).   Its second main
line of activity, apart from weeding out cases of
alleged corruption, was, however, to maintain party
discipline.   175 individuals had been expelled, 378
censured and 7,391 warned in this effort to maintain
the PZPR's ideological and organisational unity.
NIK, in the same period, had investigated 7,149
persons (2,819 in directing positions) and had confirmed accusations either wholly, or in part, in just
under half the cases.   Its investigations had

resulted in 427 dismissals from directing positions, while another 918 cases had been referred to the CKKP and 531 to the procuracy. The judicial system, as is customary in a procuratorial system, was infinitely slower than that of the party and state control commissions. By the time of the congress only 59 individuals had been charged while the pre-liminary investigation of 146 cases involving 285 persons (85 of whom, all officials, were under provisional arrest) was still in train.

The Grabski Commission's report summarised the decisions taken against various individuals so far. It set out what by now had become the fairly stock explanation of the causes of the crisis, although it did so in a sharp, publicly comprehensible form [31]. On the surface this Communist equivalent of a Select Committee of Enquiry had been very busy in its 8 sessions interviewing the key figures of the Gierek period and it had drawn on a wide range of party, NIK, judicial and academic evidence. In practice it had done little more than to recapitulate, summarise and publicise the work of the other agencies. Its proceedings were yet one more PZPR smokescreen. Its only real initiative led to the congress expell-ing Gierek, Babiuch, Łukasiewicz, Pyka, Szydlak and Żandarowski from the party and to the Council of State's depriving them of their official decorations which entailed the loss of certain pension rights. It also recommended that Jaroszewicz's glaring mis-takes in running the economy should be investigated by the procuracy to see if he had infringed Article 246 of the Criminal Code and that Gierek's house in Katowice should be returned to the public treasury.

Grabski stated at the Twelfth Plenum that all told 26,000 individuals had been investigated and that charges had been confirmed against 12,000, 3,400 of whom had been in directing positions (TL, 11-12.7.81). The rozliczenie process was carried out in a fair, judicial manner and spread out over the whole period before and after the congress [32]. It therefore failed to catch, let alone satisfy, the public mood, but then perhaps nothing short of tumbrils and guillotines would have done so. On the other hand, if the process is viewed in the con-text of the staggeringly high turnover in main leadership positions achieved by the end of the Ninth Congress, one can say that the PZPR really had re-newed itself in personnel terms in a most dramatic fashion; however, the policy of rozliczenie and leadership renewal could not really rebuild the Communist élite in structural terms short of a real social revolution. Most Solidarity and working

class activists therefore considered the process
which had taken place to be irrelevant to their interests as it did not widen the limits of élite recruitment very significantly.   This was accentuated
by another factor.   Gierek's élite to a large extent merely reflected, on a grander scale, the
faults of Polish society.   The top layers of Gierek's
élite were perhaps no more corrupt than their con-
frères in other socialist states.   What was exceptional about the Polish case was the extent to which
the absence of strong state and police controls and
the existence of large private agricultural, handi-
craft, retail and housing sectors allowed the middle
and lower levels of officialdom to join in and from
thence for the process to spread to almost every
layer of Polish society.   In the factories, in the
shops, in offices and even in schools and universities everyone took bribes or stole from the state,
or at least was suspected of doing so.   The problem
was discussed openly in the official press during
the Gierek period.   It, and alcoholism, was regarded by the spokesmen for the Polish counter-
community in 1980-1981 to be a purposive form of
social demoralisation encouraged by the élite,but
their argument put the cart before the horse [33].
     The very business-like Twelfth Plenum on 10
July put the finishing touches to the congress preparations.   The speeches by the major politicians
were written into the congress record so the plenum
was an integral curtain raiser to it (Nowe Drogi,
August 1981).   Barcikowski noted with pleasure
that only a few extremists had been elected to party
office.   The changes were roughly comparable to
what had occurred in late 1956-early 1957 with about
half the cell secretaries, 38% of the first level
secretaries and higher percentages of provincial
secretaries and Executives being changed.   Olszowski
presented the CC, CKKP and CKR reports on their
activities since the Eighth Congress as well as the
draft programme and statutes, the proposed resolution on the Centenary of the Polish Labour Movement
and the Government report on the economy.   The
Communist veteran, and long-time Minister under
Gomułka, Eugeniusz Stawiński, intervened in the
controversies which were rumbling on extra muros
over whether there should be an enlarged Politburo
as well as an Executive Presidium and who should
elect these bodies by saying that the CC should do
so.   Grabski presented the Report on Responsibility,
which has just been discussed, in terms which indicated that all that needed to be done had been done
and that criticism should cease herewith.   The

Report's conclusions were incorporated into the plenum's resolution but this did not prevent the matter being reopened at the congress. Moczar gave numerous examples of how the Gierek régime had prevented NIK from functioning and from publicising the economic and social shortcomings of the late 1970s. The problem of the leaders on the fringe of Gierek's inner team was then raised. Kania gave Karkoszka a friendly hand but left Kępa and Ryszard Frelek to fend for themsleves. While no one was looking Kania also cleared Prokopiak of all blame for the 1976 events in Radom. Prokopiak, it will be remembered, had demanded Kania's head only 6 weeks previously, so either Kania was a remarkably forgiving soul or he wanted to signal that the party had had enough inquests. Alternatively, Prokopiak had merely been playing charades for Kania's benefit in order to mislead the Russians. At any rate Kania gave the outgoing CC, which was about to find itself in the rubbish bin of history, a few commendatory pats for having at long last worked out the line of socialist renewal.

A new Leninist Party emerges at the Ninth Congress. Society yawns!

The Extraordinary Ninth Congress which met in Warsaw between 14 and 20 July, amidst great expectations in party circles, confirmed the Sixth Plenum analysis of the causes of the 1980 crisis and the renewal strategy which had evolved, slowly, painfully and erratically after that. As foreseen, the delegates swept away the old leadership. The congress, however, marked the summing up of the democratisation process rather than being a springboard for further advance. Although Kania had some difficult and uncertain moments at the congress it eventually restored the initiative to the leadership institutions within the PZPR, albeit in a better way than previously. The cost of this internal party stabilisation was that the process failed to gain much credibility or to legitimise the PZPR in the eyes of Polish society so that the party could tackle the political and economic crisis.

The congress proceedings may be examined under the following headings [34]. Firstly a genuine spontaneous debate took place over the methods of nomination and election for all the leadership bodies and a real struggle for power then occurred in the elections themselves. Secondly, the congress was in many respects a 'working' one, as the reformists had wanted, with problem commissions honing up and incorporating radical and democratic ideas in the

party programme and statutes.   Thirdly, the speeches
and general debate at the congress were not so
choreographed as in the past.   The major personalities - notably Rakowski, Fiszbach, Siwak and
others - used it as a genuine forum of appeal for
support to the delegates and to publicise their
competing political attitudes.   Lastly, the top
men (Kania, Barcikowski and Jaruzelski) used their
control of the main Congress Reports to guide the
party towards their new consensus.
    Kania, Barcikowski and the CC Secretariat had
worked very hard on the provincial delegates' groups
in order to achieve agreement on procedures before
the congress.   They failed signally, however, to
close the debate over electoral processes before
the congress assembled for its first closed session
on the morning of Tuesday, 14 July.   Preliminary
soundings had made it clear that the previous method
of producing the First Secretary by the congress
electing a new CC, which then elected the Politburo
and First Secretary at its First Plenum, was unacceptable.   The problem was that Kania wanted to
have himself re-elected by acclamation by the whole
congress at the start.   Hardly surprisingly, this
smacked too much of the old methods of manipulation.
After long and protracted procedural wrangling,
which carried over into another closed session the
following morning, Kania was refused his blank cheque
and had to climb down.   It was decided instead by
925 votes, against the 862 who favoured immediate
and direct election, that the congress would elect
a new CC composed of 200 full and 75 candidate members first, while the First Secretary would be voted
on from among its members by the whole congress
towards the end of its proceedings.   The CC would
elect the Politburo from among its members, as in
the past.
    The third day, 16 July, was again dominated by
electoral procedural matters.   The previous day's
decision to allow delegates an almost unlimited
right of nominating their fellows for the CC slates
produced no less than 618 preliminary nominations
(31% of all delegates).   After questioning major
CC candidates, such as Kania, Jabłoński and
Jagielski, the delegates then elected a 130-strong
Scrutiny Commission and voted for the CC, the CKKP
and the CKR last thing that day [35].   As 1,909
delegates voted the provision that all CC members
should receive 50% of the votes indicated that 955
would be the minimum required for election.   In
practice,because of the odd distribution of votes,
the least popular (270th) elected candidate needed

over a hundred votes more.   The results, announced
on the afternoon of 17 July, represented one of the
most sweeping leadership turnovers ever experienced
by a ruling CP [36].   Just over 90% of the CC were
new with only Jaruzelski, who won the most votes
(1,615), Kania (1,338), Barcikowski (1,269),
Olszowski (1,090) and 14 other full outgoing CC
members and 5 candiates being elected to the new
one.   What was equally striking was that both the
reformers (Fiszbach 951, Klasa 484 and the likes of
Dąbrowa and Ney) were rejected as well as conservatives of various hues (Moczar 764, Grabski 889,
Czubiński 769, Kociołek 601).   Rakowski only just
scraped in with 1,085 votes, while all the other
outgoing notables were mown down (Jabłoński 645,
Jagielski 650).   The newcomers were a mixed bunch
with unknowns appearing alongside those who had
achieved prominence in the previous months - like
Opałko, Porębski, Kubiak and Zofia Grzyb.   Siwak's
1,227 votes against Łabecki's 1,168, however, indicated the way the congress wind was blowing against
the party reformers and pro-Solidarity forces.
Only a handful of Horizontalists, such as Marian
Arendt and Zbigniew Ciechan, scraped in.   The
congress delegates, as during the electoral report
campaign, definitely wanted a break with the past.
But these long time,middle rank party activists
also distrusted both the conservative and reformist
extremes as well as all strong personalities, irrespective of political viewpoint.   The plain, somewhat inarticulate, apparently humble and non-domineer-
ing Kania was their man and they were his majority.
So alongside the charismatic figures all office
holders, especially national ones, suffered heavily,
as only 9 KW First Secretaries and 5 Ministers
found themselves on the new CC,compared with the
normal practice of electing all KW First Secretaries
and most major office holders [37].
    On the afternoon of 18 July the First Plenum
of this new CC considered the nominations of Kania,
Barcikowski, Rakowski and Olszowski for First
Secretary.   The latter two's poor showing in the
CC elections and socialist bloc considerations,
however, determined that only Kania and Barcikowski
should be presented and that the congress should
have the privilege of choosing between the
Tweedledum and the Tweedledee of socialist renewal.
The congress then proceeded to elect Kania by 1,311
votes to Barcikowski's 568 with 60 delegates cross-
ing off both names.
    Although Kania did not get as rousing a triumph
as he had originally hoped he was now in a very

strong position to dominate the minor, disorganised
and disorientated CC figures at its meeting on
19 July.   They confirmed through open voting Kania's
proposals for the additional 14 full Politburo members and two candidates and 7 Secretaries.   An
additional 6 nominations from the floor did not
muster sufficient support to get elected.   Only
Kania, Barcikowski, Jaruzelski and Olszowski survived
from the Gierek period and assured a minimum degree
of continuity.   Rakowski suffered from the residual
apparat and second rank anti-intellectual militants'
backlash and, most surprisingly, failed to get
elected to the Politburo.   Of the rest, Czyrek
represented Foreign Affairs and Milewski the police.
In spite of all the fuss on the subject there were
only 4 clear worker representatives: Łąbecki from
Gdańsk and Romanik, the Silesian coalminer, represented the 1980 Workers' Upsurge [38].   Zofia Grzyb,
the Radom leatherworker and first woman ever to
enter the Politburo, was the only bigamous PZPR-
Solidarity member [39].   Siwak emerged to voice the
hard populist tones of the Polish working class.
Post-August developments had catapulted numerous
academics into leading party positions in place of
discredited apparatchiks.   The most striking of
the three was Hieronim Kubiak, a UJ sociology Professor and a prominent reform spokesman for Kuźnica
and the Kraków party.   Tadeusz Porębski, Rector of
Wrocław Polytechnic, had become the KW First Secretary and presided very capably over the lively
reform movement there.   Zbigniew Messner, the
Rector of the Katowice Higher School of Economics,
had become the Chairman of the Katowice People's
Council in November 1980.   A more traditional
path to the top had been followed by Włodzimierz
Mokrzyszczak from the Baltic railways to party
work in Olsztyn and eventually in November 1980 the
KW First Secretaryship there.   The remaining
figures had achieved secondary levels of prominence:
Jan Główczyk as Editor of Życie Gospodarcze for many
years, Tadeusz Czechowicz as a textile union functionary and from November 1980 KW First Secretary
in Łódź, while Stanisław Opałko, at 66 the oldest
member of the new team, had been an industrial manager
of PPS origins who was brought out of retirement
to become KW First Secretary in Tarnów.   The two
non-Politburo Secretaries contrasted markedly.
Marian Woźniak had been a Planning official and then
Governor in Siedlce, while Zbigniew Michałek, an
unknown PGR Director from Opole, seems to have been
brought in solely for his agricultural expertise.
     The new leadership of personally highly competent

but politically second rank newcomers represented
the new consensus of attitudes and skills which the
Kania-Jaruzelski condominium considered they would
need to tackle Poland's political and economic problems after the congress.   Apart from the reserved
position of Olszowski both the Politburo and the
Secretariat were designed to produce the politically
united leadership team which Kania had been lacking
since September 1980.
      The party programme and statutes were discussed
and worked over in a number of closed sessions by
the delegates who, together with about 600
invited guests and specialists, formed themselves
into 16 working commissions which heard no less than
761 speeches [40].   The party programme covered
the well trodden Sixth Plenum analysis of the causes
of the crisis and how to overcome it (Nowe Drogi,
August 1981).   Its inadequacies were admitted in a
congress resolution which bound the new CC to
establish a commission to work out a better and
more credible 'perspective programme'.   This, along
with discussion of the new statute which embodied
many of the democratisation proposals and which was
passed with only 38 delegates against and 53 ab-
staining, dominated the congress proceedings on its
last day [41].
      The open proceedings of a Communist congress
are normally a mixture of long reports by the Communist leaders, shorter interventions by ordinary
delegates and medium length contributions by secondary
ranking party-state apparatchiks.   These long proceedings are padded out to an even greater extent
by the speeches and good wishes of the guest delegations of the world CPs.   In this instance the
CPSU sent Viktor Griszin, First Secretary of the
Moscow party, flanked by Rusakov, their CC Secretary,
for relations with ruling CPs and the First Secretary
of neighbouring Byelorussia.   Griszin's very
moderate speech on the first day indicated that the
Kremlin expected the congress to rebuild the PZPR
on a more combative and cohesive Marxist-Leninist
basis, which would correct the deformations of the
past, rebuff Western Imperialist interference and
lead Poland out of the crisis.
      The main speeches and the major highlights of
the congress came from the following.   Kania's
fairly dull, but firm, CC Report on the first day
repeated the Sixth Plenum analysis and the strategy
of renewal coupled with a sharper definition of the
coming struggle against anti-socialist forces in
Solidarity and society and undisciplined elements
within the PZPR [42].   Rakowski's resolutely

reformist speech on the second day gained an enthusiastic ovation as it contrasted with Kania's limited
and disappointing performance, but the votes of
Communist delegates are not swayed by mere speeches.
Rakowski accepted that the party had not been bold
and rapid enough in producing the required political
and economic reforms.   There was a way out of
Poland's vicious circle of passivity and disbelief
and Rakowski presented the 9 principles which should
be acted upon by the new credible and courageous
leadership which he hoped the congress would produce
[43].   In his Government Report at the end of the
congress Jaruzelski made it clear that the time for
concessions had passed [44].   The PZPR would now
defend its power against Solidarity and other ex-
temists.   Renewal and democratisation would continue
after the congress but within socialist limits acceptable to Poland's allies.   He promised an Economic Reform, loosening up central planning and
permitting workers' Self-Management.   As usual he
painted a realistically bleak picture of the state
of Poland's economy in order to remind delegates that
this was what really mattered to Polish society.
The main points of his litany of woe was that the
external debt had reached $26 milliard, that GNP
had fallen 15% over the year, that market supplies
had fallen 10% while wages had risen by 23%.   The
inflationary situation required a more than twofold
increase in food prices.   Lastly, in a speech enrolled on the Congress Record, Czyrek, the Foreign
Minister and CC Foreign Affairs Secretary, paid
tribute to Soviet economic and foreign policy support and showed how the domestic crisis had affected
Poland's international standing.
   It would be a tendentious and unprofitable
exercise to attempt to cover all the speeches in
the general debate here, but one can point to a few
which illustrated the diverse political currents
aired at the congress.   As at earlier plena, the
matter was more complicated than just being a matter
of conservatives versus reformers with a large and
dominant Kania centre.   The former were divided
into a number of tendencies - nationalist, apparat,
unreservedly pro-Soviet, technocratic, hard-populist
working class - while the latter were split between
the voices of the Workers' Upsurge, the pro-Solidarity
workers, the provincial apparat reformers and the
Communist intelligentsia.
   Taking the conservatives first, two strands
were introduced right at the beginning by Bednarski
(Bydgoszcz KW First Secretary).   He called for the
party to move from its sackcloth and ashes acceptance

of responsibility for the August crisis to a more
determined defence of its values and interests.   He
wanted the settlement of accounts to be terminated
and his attack on Rulewski's openly oppositionist
and anti-socialist activities suggested that he
wanted sterner judicial measures against the organisers of strikes and political demonstrations.
Bednarski's attack on Solidarity was supported by
some of the KW Secretaries (such as Niedźwiedź,
Piła) but they were clearly in a minority.   The
military's position was stated by Baryła, who called
for party unity and the establishment of order and
discipline in both society and the economy.
Szyszka inveighed against technocratic-bureaucratic
proposals for structural unemployment and, as
befitted the Chairman of the Branch Unions, defended
the pre-1980 unions.   He considered that the workers' protest in Summer 1980 had been directed primarily against the party and state and only thirdly
against the official TUs.   He denounced the Fourth
Plenum analysis as an unjustified calumny which had
opened up the floodgates to the development of
Solidarity.   The most controversial speech for the
hardliners came from the ebullient Siwak.   For him
all the PZPR's problems arose from its post-1956
move away from a working class character and composition.   For Polish Communists the keypoint was
his successful demolition of the optimistic woolly-
mindedness of Rakowski's and Fiszbach's reform slogans.   The party, said Siwak, must admittedly carry
out the policy of conciliation and social understanding, but first of all it must establish the accep-
tability and good intentions of its partners;
otherwise its political paralysis would deepen, anti-
socialist forces in KOR and Solidarity would continue
to grow in influence and the crisis would deepen
[45].   This analysis, and the violent earthy language in which it was couched, might not appeal to
the Western reader,but its trenchant tone was what
the majority of delegates wanted to hear.   That is
why they voted Siwak,not Fiszbach, on to the CC,
although admittedly Siwak earned the hatred of the
reformers and Communist intelligentsia who had always regarded him as a bogey figure.
     Although reforming and critical workers'
speeches were in the majority at the congress their
impact was dulled as they were largely a repetition of the Tenth Plenum themes.   Firstly, all the
reformers opposed Bednarski and backed Mróz's
(Opole KW First Secretary) plea for more not less
rozliczenie.   Jarmala, a coalminer from Turów,
told Grabski to his face that his commission had

not done the job which it was set and that society
had had enough of the carousel of top offfice holding.   Grabski's Report was heavily criticised at
the closed session on the second day.   A major row
was only headed off by Moczar's promising that NIK
and the new CKKP would complete their enquiries with
renewed vigour, as would the judiciary.   The delegates also blew off steam by voting to expel Gierek
and his lieutenants from the PZPR there and then.
Secondly, workers such as Kazimierz Miniur from Nowa
Huta praised the energies unleashed by the new style
of inner party democracy and contrasted it with the
Government's passivity and failure to produce a
programme offering a way out of the crisis.   The
voice of the Horizontalists was now extremely muted
but Ciechan, a KZ First Secretary from one of their
Toruń strongholds, set out their conception of the
new balance between the CPA organs and grassroots
democracy.
      These primary themes recurred continually in
various other forms, such as Janicki's demand for
credible guarantees, Łudos' diagnosis of the crisis
as having been caused primarily by Gierek's faulty
cadres policy and in Gdula's (Bielsko-Biała KW First
Secretary) assertion that the crisis was 'above all
a crisis of the ruling Marxist-Leninist party'.
Thirdly, there were very few clear and coherent
critiques of the emerging Kania consensus.   Henryka
Kubiak, a Łódź clothing worker, attacked the delayed
holding of the congress and the unconvincing character of rozliczenie.   Half hearted and insufficient
reform had had to be extorted by workers striking in
defence of their rights, as the Baltic dockers were
now doing and as the bitter textile workers might
have to do if something were not done for them in
time.   Fiszbach, in contrast, was more reserved,
although his reform line was supported by new figures
who had emerged during the election campaign, such
as Skrzypczak.   Fiszbach reiterated his call for
the political resolution of conflicts, for an understanding with Solidarity in spite of its extremists
and for the defence of living standards.   His
criticism of party indecision and his general programme did not, however, convince the bulk of delegates.   Lastly, many delegages - such as the Radom
City President, Łębecki, who wanted a commission to
establish the responsibility for the December 1970
events, or Kaleta, who wanted the Economic Reform
speeded up - expressed a wide variety of local and
sectional demands.
      This largely unchoreographed congress was
enlivened by a number of side issues.   Bek, the

Government spokesman, had to issue an official denial
that Iwanow was a guest of the Toruń delegation to
the congress. A row blew up over Siwak's attack on
Bratkowski for allegedly calling congress delegates
'mud' whereas, as befits a literary gent, Bratkowski
had used the word 'magma', a geological term describing the molten rocks below the earth's surface, to
describe the politically formless character of the
delegates. The Katowice Forum circulated delegates
with their standpoint while more seriously a document, allegedly written by Gomułka and dated 1 July,
was distributed among the delegates by persons unknown. In this Kania was accused of full knowledge
and responsibility for the Baltic shootings of
December 1970.

The Ninth Congress had elected entirely new
leadership organs and ratified the new party programme
and statutes. It also passed a number of resolutions, including an Appeal to the Polish Nation setting out its political stall around the hope that
its proceedings 'would mark a turning point in the
struggle to emerge from the crisis'. In his closing
speech Kania sketched out the political significance
of the congress. It had confirmed socialist Poland's
fidelity to her allies and had strengthened the
PZPR's leading role by renewing the worker and peasant
character of the new CC while producing an almost
entirely new leadership. The new party statute
would guarantee disciplined Leninist democracy against
future deformations. The support accorded to
Premier Jaruzelski and the increase in Army men
elected to the new CC from 5 to 9 indicated that,
while the socialist renewal would continue, the
party would now deal with its anti-socialist and
counter-revolutionary enemies. The threat was
clear but was not appreciated sufficiently at the
time as were the political alternatives - if the
class enemy backed down a peaceful solution would
be carried through; if not the Army would do its duty.

So, in spite of all the hopes of the early
Summer, the congress did not act as a cure for all
Poland's ills. How could it? But it marked, as
did Gomułka's assumption of office in October 1956,
the end of real pluralist debate and conflict over
rival political strategies within the party. The
PZPR renewed and democratised itself in Leninist
terms and decentralised power to some extent from
its central to its lower levels. What was acceptable to the party's inner membership ring, though,
was unlikely, by itself, to prove particularly
alluring to the remaining bulk of the Polish nation
[46]. This was demonstrated clearly, within a

few days of the congress, by strikes, hunger marches and a hardening of attitudes within Solidarity as well as the PZPR. The unequivocal historical verdict must therefore be that the congress was a short term success for the party, especially for its wider and lower level élites, but that it proved an unqualified damp squib as far as the expectations and demands of Polish society were concerned.

Notes

1. Zbigniew Sufin, 'Nie chcę czy nie są wybierani', Życie Warszawy, 3.6.81; English version, Contemporary Poland (June 1981), pp. 1-4.   See the réplique by Marian Arendt in TL, 16.6.81.
2. For descriptions of some of these and the earlier municipal ones, see Polityka, 11 & 18 April, 6 & 20 June 1981.
3. 'Sprawozdanie KC PZPR za okres od VIII Zjazdu do IX Nadzwyczajnego Zjazdu PZPR', Nowe Drogi (August 1981), p. 80.
4. Manual workers had composed 45% of the Eighth Congress delegates while the representation of teachers and academics which had been 4% now increased to 12%.   See J. Szadek, 'Zjazd Funkcjonariuszy', Aneks, No. 23 (1980), pp. 108-120.
5. See the preliminary analysis by G. Kolankiewicz, Times, 13.7.81.
6. Full text in Sztandar Młodych, 28.5.81 and Le Monde, 4.6.81.
7. On the latter course of police trade-unionism, see ICPA News Bulletin, 81/10, pp. 4-5.
8. See the critique by the radical defence lawyer, Janusz Taylor,'Więzienia PRL - rok 1980', Zeszyty Historyczne, No. 59 (1982), pp. 205-209.   An organisation to help prisoners called 'Patronat' was animated by Taylor, Siła-Nowicki,Gieysztor, Halina Auderska and others, but its registration was refused by the Warsaw Court on 6.2.81.   The problem was aggravated by the fact that Poland with a 36 million population had 200,000 in its prisons, while the UK with 55 million people only had 48,000.   See ICPA News Bulletins, 81/7, p. 12; 81/9, pp. 9-10; 81/10, p. 6.
9. 'List Komitetu Centralnego KPZR do Komitetu Centralnego PZPR', Nowe Drogi (July 1981), pp. 29-32.   English text, ICPA News Bulletin, 81/9, pp. 1-3.
10. See Klasa's qualified defence, Polityka, 11.7.81, p. 5.
11. XI Plenum PZPR, 9-10 czerwca 1981r (Warsaw, KiW, 1981). References to Nowe Drogi (July 1981); Kania, pp. 8-18 and 24-28; Najdowski, pp. 33-35; Łabus, pp. 35-38; Żabinski, pp. 48-52; Prokopiak, pp. 45-48; Nowakowska, pp. 65-66; Jarzębek, pp. 58-61; Rakowski, pp. 76-80;

Jaruzelski, pp. 135-139; Grabski, pp. 120-122; Ney, pp. 81-84; Barcikowski, pp. 122-124; Wasilewski, pp. 91-92; Siwak, pp. 87-92; Nowak, pp. 92-94.

12. Cf. Wajda's interview, Polityka, 30.5.81 and the award of the Golden Palm to him at the Cannes Film Festival for his 'Man of Iron', ibid., 6.6.81.

13. National arguments now prevailed against the post-August sectional trend. Cf. A.K. Wróblewski, 'Kłocki w narodowym pudełku', Polityka, 20.6.81.

14. SSS, VIIIth Sejm, 13th sitting of 12.6.81; esp. cols. 5, 62, 104-119, 137-139.

15. An acrimonious debate had preceded the decision to create the following: Agriculture, Food Industry & Fisheries; Mining & Energy; Metallurgy & Machine-Engineering; Chemical & Light Industry; the turbulent Baltic sea coast had its particularist demand for a separate office for the Maritime Economy conceded. See Szeliga, Polityka, 4.4.81 and D. Zagrodziński, ibid., 27.6.81.

16. For the Solidarity National Conference in Łódź, ICPA News Bulletin,81/10, p. 3.

17. The trial did not finish until October 1982, when Moczulski received a 7 year sentence, Stański and Szeremetiew 5 years and Jandziszak a suspended 2 year sentence.

18. The proposal to abolish the often used death penalty was included in the amended Penal Code published in August 1981, but was not implemented as it met with strong opposition from legal circles. Cf. Wł. Męcior, 'Kara śmierci jako ultima ratio', Państwo i Prawo, XXXVI, No. 9-12 (September-December 1981), pp. 91-95. Even he accepted, though, that the death penalty should not be applied in political cases.

19. See J. Maciejewski and Z. Trojanowicz (eds.), Poznański czerwiec (Poznań, Wydawnictwo Poznańskie, 1981). The main journalistic thesis was that the Poznań events accelerated the PZPR's acceptance of fundamental changes in 1956: Z. Rykowski and W. Władyka, 'Poznań 1956', Kultura, 28.6.81.

20. Cf. J. Holzer, 'Doświadczenie marca 1968r', Kierunki, 17.5.81; commented on by Polityka, 23.5.81.

21. See Marian Turski, 'Radom 1976', Polityka, 27 June and 4 July 1981. For the Solidarity view, see M. Chojecki, Robotnik, No. 51-52, 11.6.81.

22. Samsonowicz's interview, Polityka, 18.4.81.

23. SSS, VIIIth Sejm, 14th sitting of 2 & 3 July 1981; refs. to cols. 6-14, 141-173, 173-180, 180-190.

24. On rationing, see K. Rzemieniecki, Contemporary Poland (October 1980), pp. 9-11.

25. For his views, see Tygodnik Powszechny, 21.6.81.

26. Kultura, 7 and 14 June 1981 and the late May Ruch poll of 800 respondents; Fikus, Polityka, 18.7.81.

27.   J. Maziarski, 'To nie był zamach stanu', Kultura, 5.7.81.
        Solidarność, 17.7.81.   AS 81/23, p. 207, and 81/25,
        p. 205.   TL, 3.7.81.
28.   W. Rogowski, 'Jedność w różnorodnośći',TL, 7.7.81.   See
        also the views of KW First Secretaries in Polityka,18.7.81.
29.   M. Matthews, Privilege in the Soviet Union (London,
        George Allen & Unwin, 1978).   Simis' testimony in
        Sunday Times, 12.9.82.
30.   'Sprawozdanie CKKP PZPR za okres od VIII Zjazdu do IX
        Nadzwyczajnego Zjazdu PZPR', Nowe Drogi (August 1981),
        pp. 83-91, and 'Sprawozdanie CKR PZPR ...', ibid.,
        pp. 93-101.
31.   Nowe Drogi (August 1981), pp. 102-111.
32.   The judicial process was speeded up under the State of
        War.   By August 1982 about 200 persons had been tried
        and imprisoned (including 2 Ministers, 2 deputy Ministers,
        6 Governors, 5 deputy Governors, 7 KW Secretaries and
        numerous other types of official.   All told, 11 received
        severe sentences over 5 years, the highest being 10
        years for the deputy President of Płock.
33.   On alcoholism, see H. Malinowska, 'Extent and effect of
        alcoholism in People's Poland', Survey (Winter 1980),
        pp. 53-57.
34.   IX Nadzwyczajny Zjazd PZPR, 14-20 lipca 1981r.   Podstawowe
        materiały i dokumenty (Warsaw, KiW, 1981).   Nowe Drogi
        (August 1981).   Unusually these are not full records,
        so for the individual speeches refer to Trybuna Ludu.
35.   By which time the nominations had been slimmed down to
        275 for the 200 full and 105 for the 70 candidate CC
        places.
36.   Quite apart from the CC all the CKKP and all bar one of
        the CKR were new.
37.   The new CC had only 22 central and provincial party
        functionaries, 21 KZ Secretaries, 12 Ministers and deputy
        Ministers, 2 local and 3 mass organisation officials.
        White collar professionals totalled 35 (15 University
        Professors, 7 teachers and 10 doctors) and were
        strikingly over-represented.   Industry had 102 (6
        managers, 37 foremen, supervisors and clerical staff and
        59 workers) and agriculture 40 (31 peasants, 7 PGR
        and collective farm officials and 2 labourers).   See
        Z. Szeliga, Polityka, 25.7.81.
38.   For official biographies of Politburo and Secretariat
        members, see TL, 18-19.7.81; Contemporary Poland
        (August 1981), pp. 4-15.
39.   Solidarity claimed the following representatives on the
        main PZPR committees after the congress: one on the
        Politburo, 40 full and 14 candidate CC members, 12 on the
        CKR and 17 on the CKKP.   Out of a total of 430 on these
        bodies, Solidarity claimed 83 (19.3%), AS 81/25, p. 205.

40. See 'Trzy dni w zespołach', Polityka, 25.7.81.
41. For the text of the statute, see Nadzwyczajny Zjazd, op. cit., pp. 169–211. For an English language translation and commentary, see G. Sanford in S. White and W.B. Simons, The Party Rules of the Communist World (The Hague, Martinus Nijhof, forthcoming, 1984).
42. Nowe Drogi (August 1981), pp. 17–52; Contemporary Poland (August 1981), pp. 20–61.
43. Polityka, 25.7.81.
44. Nadzwyczajny Zjazd, op. cit., pp. 76–100.
45. See Moszyński's commentary on Siwak's speech, Polityka, 25.7.81.
46. Janusz Rolicki, 'Zjazd historyczny', Kultura, 19.7.81, argued the historical significance of the attempt to create institutional guarantees against the repetition of crises. The other side of the coin was Urban's assertion that 'the PZPR as a reborn and consolidated whole will move on to sharper competition with Solidarity for power in the state as a whole as well as in each factory, commune and town', Polityka, 25.7.81.

CONCLUSION: TOWARDS THE STATE OF WAR

Liberal Communists had hoped the Ninth Congress would allow fresh Communist leadership and a democratised PZPR to introduce the reform programme required to pacify society. And yet within a few days widespread hunger marches and street demonstrations occurred for the first time. A vast cavalcade of Solidarity buses, trams and lorries blocked the centre of Warsaw from 3 to 5 August. A great humiliation for the authorities, it demonstrated publicly that the Ninth Congress had failed to achieve the necessary response for a peaceful settlement on PZPR terms. The leadership's increasingly hardline reaction was expressed at the Second Plenum on 11 August while Kania's meeting with Glemp failed to save the policy of national reconciliation [1].

Kania and Jaruzelski, in mid August in the Crimea, finally accepted the Soviet analysis, which had never really changed, that Solidarity and all that it stood for was the enemy, not just a hostile current within it. They genuinely promised the Soviet leaders a full blooded struggle against anarchy, counter-revolution and anti-Sovietism (TL, 17.8.81). Główczyk at the Third Plenum on 2-3 September confirmed that the PZPR would not abandon its leading role in the large factories after the introduction of self-management while it would continue to appoint their managers [2]. The official state-socialist version of self-management was criticised at the first round of the Solidarity Congress on 5-9 September which demanded a workers' referendum on the issue [3]. Amidst much publicity it also sent an Address expressing its solidarity with fellow workers in Eastern Europe, especially those struggling for free TUs [4]. The Soviet response was immediate. A CPSU CC and Soviet Government letter demanded 'immediate and energetic' measures against anti-Sovietism in Poland (TL, 18.9.81). Although the hardliners such as Siwak wanted to outlaw Solidarity and to declare a State of Emergency the pragmatists again gained time. The fiercely worded Politburo communiqué of 16 September cast Solidarity beyond the ideological pale but, for the last time, stopped short of action [5]. Motivated by the increasingly impatient and hardline reaction within the CC against the obvious failure of Kania's Ninth Congress strategy, the communiqué set out the PZPR's political stall for the next 3 months. It aimed to use the threat of naked force to persuade the Church and the Solidarity moderates to accept the PZPR's limited conception of a Front of National Understanding (FPN).

This last ditch attempt to preserve the party's hegemony through negotiation was relaunched by Olszowski. The other arm of this strategy was stronger police and judicial measures against opposition activity and a growing role by the military in political, economic and administrative life. Behind the scenes highly secret step-by-step preparations for the Army takeover were mounted under cover of various highly successful subterfuges.

The second round of the Solidarity Congress from 26 September to 7 October criticised the self-management bills passed by the Sejm on 25 September, re-elected Wałęsa with 55% of the votes cast and elected a radical majority to the KKP. The Congress adopted a new programme enshrining the demands for domestic reform and pluralism designed to transform Poland into the 'Self-Governing Republic' [6]. The PZPR responded at its Fourth Plenum on 16-18 October by forcing its 'bigamous' members, such as Zofia Grzyb and 11 CC members, to resign from Solidarity. The desire for an ideologically and organisationally united party to confront Solidarity was typified by Marian Orzechowski's bon mot that ideological diversion should be combatted 'not only with the force of argument but with the argument of force' [7]. In the face of such a hardline offensive Kania's resignation was accepted by 104 votes to 79 and Jaruzelski was elected in his place by 180 votes to 4 [8]. All political, administrative and military power was thus centralised in the latter's hands. He sent Operational Army Groups into the countryside in late October and into the towns a month later. On 30 October Jaruzelski introduced an Emergency Powers Bill suspending strikes but for the moment he left it hanging as a threat [9].

Were the last chance November negotiations over the PZPR's proposed 'Historic Compromise' with society in the form of the FPN and various consultative councils really genuine or part of a plot to lull suspicions as the preparations for the State of War entered their final phase? The unprecedented Jaruzelski-Glemp-Wałęsa meeting of 4 November raised hopes that the PZPR would be willing to accept a reduction of its leading role in order to make social agreement possible, as in 1956 [10]. In exchange Solidarity, backed by the Church, would support the institutional modus vivendi with sufficient safeguards to prevent the free play of pluralist forces from sweeping away the unpopular Communist order. The arduous negotiations of mid to late November, however, revealed the irreconcilable gap between what Solidarity might grudgingly accept and what the

USSR and its Polish Communist supporters would stand
for: the PZPR offer was no more than a more flexibly
exercised PZPR leading role maintaining the party's
hegemony in all bar a few insignificant areas but
including a greater role for its fundamentally loyal
SD and ZSL partners with the possibility of a rever-
sion towards greater monopoly control when the situation quietened down. The key issues of power and
control over the new bodies were never resolved. By
the Sixth Plenum on 27-28 November the PZPR came out
openly with its hardline FPN conception designed
solely to defeat the anti-socialist opposition [11].
Jaruzelski crossed a new political frontier. He
made it clear that the anti-strike bill would soon
be passed, thus clawing back one of the two main
institutional guarantees of August 1980 for the Communist reaction.

     After this there was no room left for manoeuvre,
as was shown by the forcible reoccupation of the
Firemen's School in Warsaw on 2 December. There is
no evidence that the Solidarity leaders, despite the
colourful language used at the bugged Radom KKP session, were really planning a final showdown with the
régime; but the threatened general strike and demands for free elections to both the Sejm and the
People's Councils and for a referendum on self-
management took the movement to the brink [12].
Following Kulikov's Warsaw visit on 25 November, when
the 'green light' for the State of War was given,
the Politburo probably took the fateful decision on
5 December. Their political analysis was that the
'Radomgate' revelations confirmed that Solidarity
was now in total opposition to the Communist system.

     In the early hours of 13 December Jaruzelski
announced that the Council of State had declared a
State of War, that a 21 strong Military Council of
National Salvation (WRON) was taking over to fore-
stall a Solidarity coup and that a mass of police
and legal restrictions, including internment of
opposition individuals, would be instituted [13].
There would be no return to pre-1980 conditions
and the Ninth Congress reforms would be implemented
in a disciplined manner. Jaruzelski appealed to
traditional Polish patriotism while the WRON declaration played on the realpolitik argument that military rule provided the Poles with their last chance
to restore order without foreign interference (TL,
14.12.81).

     The historical significance of the 1980-1981
crisis was not the failure to transform the Soviet
type of Communist system in a more pluralist and
democratic direction.   It was that the Polish

Conclusion

Communist élite proved strong and determined enough to preserve its rule without direct Soviet intervention. The Polish 'War' saved the Communist hegemony by shifting power from the CPA proper to the military; but the amount of force and repression used and the number of lives lost were extremely moderate given the circumstances. In this way the Communist system gained time to work for the economic upturn of the mid 1980s when it would be able to rebuild its political and social bases, perhaps on the lines which Hungary had done after 1961*.

Notes

1. II Plenum KC PZPR, 11 sierpnia 1981r (Warsaw, KiW, 1981).
2. III Plenum KC PZPR, 2-3 września 1981r. Samorząd załóg socjalistycznych przedziębiorstw w warunkach reformy gospodarczej (Warsaw, KiW, 1981).
3. For its proceedings, AS/36 of 5-10 September 1981.
4. ICPA News Bulletin, 81/14, pp. 3-4.
5. TL, 17.9.80; Contemporary Poland (October 1981), pp.18-20.
6. Its entire proceedings in AS, Nos. 38, 39 and 40; resolutions, ICPA News Bulletin, 81/16.
7. IV Plenum KC PZPR, 16-18 października 1981r (Warsaw, KiW, 1981). General Florian Siwicki, the Army Chief of Staff, was also appointed a Politburo candidate at the low key Fifth Plenum of 28 October which took place at the same time as a one hour Solidarity warning strike.
8. Jaruzelski's official biography, TL, 19.10.81; cf. interview in Guardian, 15.11.82.
9. SSS, VIIIth Sejm, 17th sitting of 30 October 1981.
10. As late as early December Wiatr talking to Kuźnica considered this the 'best and most likely' outcome preferable to a return to pre-1980 conditions, the collapse of socialism or military rule; Gazeta Krakowska,10.12.81.
11. VI Plenum KC PZPR, 27-28 listopada 1981r (Warsaw, KiW, 1981).
12. Numerous factory referenda had already been held during the Autumn. 88% in 2 Silesian factories opposed the anti-strike law on 28 October, AS 48/5. At the same time 3 factories in Wrocław overwhelmingly voted no confidence in Jaruzelski's Government (81.5% on a 71.8% turn-out in PAFAWAG, while 86% wanted a new electoral law and the Sejm dissolved), AS 48/5.
13. Council of State decree, DzU, No. 29, pos. 154; Jaruzelski's speech, ICPA News Bulletin, 81/20, pp. 4-11; WRON proclamation, ibid., pp. 11-12.

*   I should like to express my deep gratitude to Mrs. Anne Merriman for her skill in typing the whole of this study and for her invaluable assistance in helping me to prepare the final 'Camera Ready' text.

BIBLIOGRAPHY

Official publications and reference sources

Biuletyny Prasowe Sejmu (Warsaw, Sejm Library, 1952-).
Concise Statistical Yearbook of Poland (Warsaw, GUS, 1959-).
Druki Sejmowe (Warsaw, 1952-).
Dziennik Ustaw (Warsaw, 1952-).
Monitor Polski (Warsaw, 1952-).
Polska Informator (Warsaw, Interpress, 1974 and 1977).
Polska 75 (Warsaw, PWN, 1975).
Polska. Zarys Encyklopedyczny (Warsaw, PWN, 1974).
Rocznik polityczny i gospodarczy (Warsaw, PWE, 1958-).
Rocznik Statystyczny (Warsaw, GUS, 1947-).
Sprawozdanie Stenograficzne z posiedzeń Sejmu PRL (Warsaw,1952-)
The official records of PZPR Congresses and Plena as published
by KiW are too numerous to set out here but they are quoted in
the text. The reader is also referred to the chapter on
'Poland' by G. Sanford in G. Walker (ed.), Official Publications
of the Soviet Union and Eastern Europe, 1945-1980. A Select
Annotated Bibliography (London, Mansell, 1982).

Background to pre-1980 Poland

The secondary literature on Poland is vast. The following is therefore a somewhat selective list, although I have
included most of the works of any value in English.

Adamski, W.	Dwa pokolenia pracowników przemysłu (Warsaw, IW, CRZZ, 1980)
Banas, J.	The Scapegoats. The Exodus of the Remnants of Polish Jewry (London, Weidenfeld and Nicolson, 1979).
Bauman, Z.	'Twenty years after: the crisis of Soviet type systems', Problems of Communism, XX, No. 6 (June 1971), pp. 45-53.
Bethell, N.	Gomułka. His Poland and his Communism (London, Penguin, 1972).
Bieńkowski, W	Rewolucja ciąg dalszy (Warsaw, KiW, 1957). Motory i Hamulce Socjalizmu (Paris, Instytut Literacki, 1969) Socjologia klęski (Paris, Instytut Literacki, 1971) Droga wyjścia (Paris, Instytut Literacki, 1971)
Blazynski, G.	Flashpoint Poland (London, Pergamon,1979)
Bobrowski, C.	Planowanie gospodarcze. Problemy podstawowe (Warsaw, PWN, 1965)
Bromke, A.	Poland's politics; idealism v realism (Cambridge, Mass., Harvard UP, 1967) 'Poland under Gierek', Problems of Communism, XXI, No. 5 (Sept.-Oct. 1972),pp.1-19 'A new juncture in Poland', Problems of Communism, XXV,No.5 (Sept.-Oct.1976),pp.1-17.

Bibliography

Bromke, A.   'Poland at the crossroads', World Today,
                             XXIV, No. 4 (April 1978), pp. 147-156.
                             'The Opposition in Poland', Problems of
                             Communism, XXVII,No.5 (Sept.-Oct. 1978),
                             pp. 37-57.
& Strong, J. (eds.)   Gierek's Poland (New York, Praeger, 1973)
Brus, W.   Economics and Politics of Socialism (London,
                             Routledge and Kegan Paul, 1973)
Burda, A. (ed.)   Sejm PRL (Wrocław-Warsaw, Ossolineum,1975)
Cieplak, T. (ed.)   Poland since 1956. Readings and Essays on
                             Polish Government and Politics (New York,
                             Twayne Publishers, 1972)
Costello, M.   'Political prospects', Survey, XVIII,
                             No. 3 (Summer 1971), pp. 53-73.
-/-   Czarna Księga Cenzury PRL (London, Aneks,
                             2 vols., 1977 and 1978)
Czubiński, A. (ed.)   Polski Ruch Robotniczy. Zarys Historii
                             (Warsaw, KiW, 1974)
Davies, N.   'Poland' in M. McCauley (ed.), Communist
                             Power in Europe, 1944-1949 (London,
                             Macmillan, 1977)
Dean, R.W.   'Gierek's three years', Survey, XX, No.2-3
                             (Spring-Summer 1974), pp. 59-79
Dobieszewski, A.   Organizacja polityczna społeczeństwa
    (ed.)   socjalistycznego w Polsce (Warsaw,KiW,1977)
& Gołębiowski, J. (eds.)   PZPR, 1948-1978 (Warsaw, PWN, 1978)
Drewnowski, J.   Władza i opozycja (London, Veritas, 1979)
Dziewanowski, M.   The Communist Party of Poland (Cambridge,
                             Mass., Harvard UP, 1976)
Erard, Z. and   La Pologne. Une Société en dissidence
    Zygier, G. (eds.)   (Paris, Maspero, 1978)
Fiszman, J.   Revolution and Tradition in People's Poland.
                             Education and Socialisation (Princeton UP,
                             1972)
Flemming, G.   Polska mało znana (Paris, Instytut
                             Literacki, 1966)
Gati, C. (ed.)   Politics of Modernisation in Eastern
                             Europe (New York, Praeger, 1974)
Godlewski, J.   Kościół rzymsko-katolicki wobec sekulary-
                             zacji życia publicznego (Warsaw,PWN,1978)
Gomułka, W.   'Letter of 17 November 1971 to the Chair-
                             man of the PZPR deputies' Club', Nowe
                             Drogi (April 1981), pp. 179-184.
Góra, Wł.   PRL, 1944-1974 (Warsaw, KiW, 1976)
                             PZPR, 1948-1978 (Warsaw, MON, 1978)
& Gołębiowski (eds.)   Ruch Robotniczy w Polsce Ludowej (Warsaw,
                             Wiedza Powszechna, 1980).
Grabski, T.   'Wystąpienie na IX Plenum KC PZPR', Nowe
                             Drogi (May-June 1981), pp. 283-288.
Gross, J.   'Thirty years of crisis management in Poland'
                             in T. Rakowska-Harmstone (ed.), Perspec-
                             tives for Change in Communist Societies
                             (Boulder, Colorado, Westview Press,1979)

Bibliography

Haraszti, M.   A Worker in a Workers' State (London,
                      Penguin, 1977)
Hirszowicz, M.   The Bureaucratic Leviathan (Oxford, Martin
                      Robertson, 1980)
Hiscocks, R.   Poland. Bridge for the Abyss? (Oxford UP,
                      1963)
Hochfeld, J.   Studia o marksowskiej teorii społeczaństwo
                      (Warsaw, 1963)
Ionescu, G.   The Politics of the European Communist
                      States (New York, Praeger, 1967)
Janos, A. (ed.)   Authoritarian politics in Communist Europe
                      (Berkeley, 1976)
Jedlicki, W.   Klub Krzywego Koła (Paris, Instytut
                      Literacki, 1963)
Johnson, A.R.   'Polish perspectives', Problems of Commu-
                      nism, XX, No. 4 (July-August 1970),
                      pp. 59-72.
Kołakowski, L.   'Responsibility and history' in E. Stillman
                      (ed.), Bitter Harvest. The Intellectual
                      Revolt behind the Iron Curtain (London,
                      Thames & Hudson, 1958), pp. 94-125.
                      Świadomość religijna i więż kościelna
                      (Warsaw, PWN, 1965)
                      Rozmowy z diabłem (Warsaw, PIW, 1965)
                      Notatki o wspołczesnej kontrreformacji
                      (Warsaw, KiW, 1965)
                      'Hope and Hopelessness', Survey, XVII,
                      No. 3 (Summer 1971), pp. 37-52.
Kolankiewicz, G. &   'Socialism for Everyman' in A. Brown and
Taras, R.   J. Gray (eds.), Political Culture and
                      Political Change in Communist States
                      (London, Macmillan, 1977)
Konrad, G. and   The Intellectuals on the Road to Class
Szelenyi, I.   Power (Brighton, Harvester Press, 1979)
Kozik, Z.   PZPR w latach 1954-1957 (Warsaw, PWN, 1982)
Kuczyński, W.   'Planning and economic reforms under
                      socialism', Soviet Studies, XXXI, No. 4
                      (October 1979), pp. 505-522.
Kuroń, J.   Zasady ideowe (Paris, Instytut Literacki,
                      1978)
                      'The situation in Eastern Europe and the
                      programme of the Opposition', Labour Focus
                      on Eastern Europe (July-August 1979).
& Modzelewski, K.   Open Letter to the Party (London, Inter-
                      national Socialist Publications, 1969)
Lane, D. &   Social Groups in Polish Society (London,
Kolankiewicz, G.   (eds.) Macmillan, 1973)
Leslie, R.F. (ed.)   History of Poland since 1863 (Cambridge
                      UP, 1980)
Łętowski, J. (ed.)   Administration in People's Poland (Wrocław-
                      Warsaw, Ossolineum, 1980)

231

Bibliography

Kopatka, A.   Kierownicza rola partii komunistycznej
                         w stosunku do państwa socjalistycznego
                         (Poznań, Wyd. Poznańskie, 1963)
Maciejewski, J. &   Poznański Czerwiec (Poznań, Wyd.
  Trojanowicza, Z.   (eds.) Poznańskie, 1981)
Matejko, A.   Social change and stratification in Eastern
                         Europe. An analysis of Poland and her
                         neighbours (New York, Praeger, 1974)
Maziarski, J. (ed.)   The Polish Upswing, 1971-1975 (Warsaw,
                         Interpress, 1975)
Michnik, A.   'The New Evolutionism', Survey, XXII,
                         No. 3-4 (Summer-Autumn 1976)
                         L'Eglise et la Gauche. Le dialogue polo-
                         nais (Paris, Seuil, 1979)
Mieczkowski, B.   'Relationship between consumption and
                         politics in Poland', Soviet Studies, XXX,
                         No. 2 (April 1978), pp. 262-269.
Mieroszewski, J.   Ewolucjonizm (Paris, Instytut Literacki,
                         1964)
Millard, L.F.   'The health of the Polish health service',
                         Critique, No. 15 (1981), pp. 57-67.
Młynař, Z.   Night Frost in Prague (London, Hurst,1980)
Moczulski, L.   'Rewolucja bez rewolucji', Droga, No. 7
                         (1979)
Narkiewicz, O.   The Green Flag. Polish populist politics,
                         1867-1970 (London, Croom Helm, 1976)
Osnos, P.   'The Polish Road to Communism', Foreign
                         Affairs, 56, No. 1 (October 1977),pp.209-220.
Ostaja-Ostaszewski,A.   Dissent in Poland. Reports and Documents,
  (ed.)   December 1975-July 1977 (London, Veritas
                         Press, 1977)
Ozdowski, S.   'The Polish industrial enterprise',
                         Critique, No. 12 (Autumn-Winter, 1979-1980),
                         pp. 55-80.
Piasecki, B.   Patriotyzm Polski (Warsaw, PAX, 1958)
                         Siły rozwoju (Warsaw, PAX, 1971)
Piekalkiewicz, J.   Communist Local Government (Athens, Ohio
                         UP, 1975)
Pienkos, D.   'Party élites and society. The shape of
                         the Polish Communist Central Committee
                         since 1945', Polish Review, XX, No. 4
                         (1975), pp. 27-42.
Pirages, D.   Modernisation and political tension-manage-
                         ment. A socialist society in perspective;
                         case-study of Poland (New York,Praeger,1972)
Polonsky, A.   Politics in Independent Poland, 1921-1939
                         (Oxford UP, 1972)
Pravda, A.   'Gierek's Poland; five years on', World
                         Today, XXII, No. 7 (July 1976),pp.270-278
Preiss, P. (pseud.)   Biurokracja totalna (Paris, Instytut
                         Literacki, 1969)

Bibliography

Raina, P.   Władysław Gomułka. Zyciorys polityczny
                             (London, Polonia, 1969)
                             Political Opposition in Poland, 1959-1977
                             (London, Poet & Painters' Press, 1978)
Rakowski, M.F.   Przesilenie grudniowe (Warsaw, PIW, 1981)
Reynolds, J.   'Communists, Socialists and Workers.
                             Poland, 1944-1948', Soviet Studies, XXX,
                             No. 4 (October 1978), pp. 516-539.
Rozmaryn, S.   Konstytucja jako ustawa zasadnicza PRL
                             (Warsaw, PWN, 1967)
Sakwa, G.   'Gierek's Poland', European Review, XXII,
                             No. 4 (Autumn 1972), pp. 22-26.
                             The Organisation and Work of the Polish
                             Sejm, 1952-1972, CREES Discussion Paper,
                             Series RC/C, No. 12 (Birmingham University,
                             1976)
    & Crouch, M.   'Sejm elections in Communist Poland; an
                             overview and a reappraisal', British Jour-
                             nal of Political Science, VIII (1978),
                             pp. 403-424.
Sanford, G.   'Polish People's Republic' in B. Szajkowski
                             (ed.), Marxist Governments. A World Survey
                             (London, Macmillan, 1980)
Shapiro, I.   'Fiscal crisis of the Polish state; genesis
                             of the 1980 strikes', Theory and Society,
                             X (1980), pp. 469-502.
Siemieński, F.,   Konstytucja i podstawowe akty
    Skrzydło, W. &   ustrojowe PRL (Warsaw, Wyd.
    Ziembiński, J.   Prawnicze, 1980)
Simon, M. &   Background to Crisis. Policy and Politics
    Kanet, R. (eds.)   in Gierek's Poland (Boulder, Colorado,
                             Westview Press, 1981).
Sokolewicz, W.   Konstytucja PRL po zmianach z 1976r
                             (Warsaw, PWN, 1978)
Skrzydło, W.   Ustrój Polityczny PRL (Warsaw, KAW, 1979)
Staar, R.F.   Poland, 1944-1962. The Sovietisation of a
                             Captive People (Baton Rouge, Louisiana UP,
                             1962)
Staliński, T.   Widziane z góry (Paris, Instytut
                             Literacki, 1967)
                             Romans Zimowy (Paris, Instytut Literacki,1972)
Staniszkis, J.   'On remodelling of the Polish economic
                             system', Soviet Studies, XXXI, No. 2 (April
                             1979), pp. 167-187.
Syrop, K.   Spring in October. The story of the Polish
                             Revolution of 1956 (London, Weidenfeld and
                             Nicolson, 1957)
Szafar, T.   'The political opposition in Poland',
                             Polish Review, XXIV, No. 1 (1979),pp.70-81
Szczepański, J.   Polish Society (New York,Random House,1970)
                             Odmiany czasu teraźniejszego (Warsaw, KiW,
                             1973)

233

Bibliography

Szczypiorski, A.   'The limits of political realism', Survey,
                    XXIV, No. 4 (1979), pp. 21-32.
Szporluk, R.   'Poland' in R. Grew (ed.), Crises of poli-
                    tical development in Europe and the US
                    (Princeton UP, 1978)
Szeliga, Z.   Polska. Dziś i jutro (Warsaw,KiW, 1978)
Taras, R.   'Democratic centralism and local government
                    reform', Public Administration, 53 (Winter
                    1975), pp. 403-424.
Tarniewski, M.   Krótkie spięcie (Paris, Inst. Lit., 1975).
                    Porcja wolności (Paris, Inst. Lit., 1977).
Tyrmand, L.   The Roza Luxembourg contraceptive. A primer
                    on Communist civilisation (London,
                    Macmillan, 1971)
Vale, M. (ed.)   Poland. Report on the state of the nation
                    based on a social and economic survey by
                    the Experience and Future Group (London,
                    Pluto Press, 1981)
Wacowska, E.   Rewolta Szczecińska i jej znaczenie
                    (Paris, Instytut Literacki, 1971)
Wesołowski, W.   Klasy, warstwy i władza (Warsaw,PWN,1966)
                    Marksizm i procesy rozwoju społecznego
                    (Warsaw, KiW, 1979)
Weydenthal, J.   The Communists of Poland (Stanford, Hoover
                    Institution, 1978)
Wiatr, J.   'Wybory Sejmowe 1957r w świetle wstępnej
                    analizy', Studia Socjologiczno-Polityczne
                    (1958), No. 1, pp. 163-198. Also ibid.
                    (1959), No. 2, pp. 3-50; (1959), No. 3,
                    pp. 59-94; (1959), No. 4, whole issue.
Woodall, J.   The Socialist Corporation and Technocratic
                    Power (Cambridge UP, 1982)
Zawadzki, S.   'Partia a aparat państowy', Państwo i Prawo,
                    XXVI, No. 11 (November 1971), pp.707-718.
Zieliński, J.   Economic reforms in Polish industry
                    (Oxford UP, 1973).

Material relating directly to the 1980-1981 crisis
a.   Official documents
KKP NSZZ Solidarność. 'Kierunki działania związku w obecnej
sytuacju kraju. Tezy do dyskusji', Offprint to Solidarność,
No. 3, 17 April 1981.
Polska reforma gospodarcza. Główne przesłanki,założenia
modelowe i stan realizacji (Warsaw, MSZ, Biuro Prasowe Rządu,
1982.
Projekt. Tezy projektów ustaw; o związkach zawodowych; o
samorządzie załogi przedsiębiorstwa państwowego; o przedsię-
biorstwa państwowych
(Warsaw, KiW, 1981).
Protokóły porozumień Gdańsk, Szczecin, Jastrzębie. Statut
NSZZ Solidarność. Zaŀozenia ustawy o Związkach Zawodowych
(Warsaw, KAW, 1981).

Bibliography

Protokóły porozumień; rząd-służba zdrowia (Warsaw,IW ZZ,1981)
IX Nadzwyczajny Zjazd PZPR, 14-20 lipca 1981r. Podstawowe
dokumenty i materiały (Warsaw, KiW, 1981).
Rada Ministrów PRL. Rządowy program przezwyciężania kryzysu
oraz stabilizowania gospodarki kraju (Warsaw, Gryf, 1981).
'Sprawozdanie KC PZPR, CKR PZPR, CKKP PZPR za okres od VIII
Zjazdu do IX Nadzwyczajnego Zjazdu PZPR' (Warsaw, Nakładem
TL, July 1981).
Ustawy; o przedsiębiorstwach państwowych; o samorządzie
załogi przedsiębiorstwa państwowego; uchwalone przez Sejm
25 wrzesnia 1981r (Warsaw, KiW, 1981).
'Założenia programowe rozwoju socjalistycznej demokracji,
umacniania przewodniej roli PZPR w budownictwie socjalistycznym
i stabilizacji społeczno-gospodarczej kraju. Założenia pro-
gramowe na IX Nadzwyczajny Zjazd PZPR', KC PZPR (Warsaw, Nakł.
TL, April 1981).
Założenia ustawy o Związkach Zawodowych (Warsaw, KAW, 1981).

b.   Secondary (Non-Polish)

Anderson, R.   'Soviet decision-making and Poland',
                       Problems of Communism (March-April 1982).
Ascherson, N.   The Polish August. The Self-Limiting Re-
                       volution (Harmondsworth, Penguin, 1981).
Ash, T.G.   Articles in Spectator, especially 30.8, 6.9,
                       8 & 29.11 in 1980 and 4.4, 9.5, 13.6, 10.10,
                       19.12 in 1981.
Bromke, A.   'Poland. The cliff's edge', Foreign Policy,
                       XL (Winter 1980-1981), pp. 154-162.
                       'Poland's upheaval - an interim report',
                       World Today, XXXVII, No. 6 (June 1981),
                       pp. 211-218.
                       'The revival of political idealism in
                       Poland', Canadian Slavonic Papers (December
                       1982).
Blazyca, G.   'Comecon and the Polish crisis', World
                       Today, XXXVII, No. 10 (October 1981),
                       pp. 375-379.
Brus, W.   'Lessons of the Polish Summer', Marxism
                       Today (November 1980).
Danecki, J. (ed.)   Towards Poland 2000. Problems of Social
                       Development (Wrocław, Ossolineum, 1980).
Drewnowski, J. (ed.)   Crisis in the East European Economy. The
                       spread of the Polish disease (London,
                       Croom Helm, 1982).
Galtung, J.   'Poland, August-September 1980. Is a
                       socialist revolution under state capitalism
                       possible?', Journal of Peace Research,
                       XVII, No. 4 (1980), pp. 281-290.
Garlicki, L.   'Polish constitutional development in 1980'
                       in W.E. Butler (ed.), Anglo-Polish Legal
                       Essays (New York, Transnational Publishers,
                       1982).

Bibliography

Hirszowicz, L.   'The current Polish crisis and the 1968
                        Anti-Semitic Campaign', Research Report of
                        the Institute of Jewish Affairs (London,
                        December 1980).
Kolankiewicz, G.   'Bureaucratised political participation
                        and its consequence in Poland', Politics,
                        I, No. 1 (April 1981), pp. 35-40.
                        'Reform, Revision or Retreat', World Today,
                        XXXVII, No. 10 (October 1981), pp.369-375.
Lewis, P.   'Obstacles to the establishment of politi-
                        cal legitimacy in Communist Poland',
                        British Journal of Political Science, XII
                        (1982), pp. 125-147.
Luke, T. &   'Soviet subimperialism and the crisis of
    Boggs, C.   bureaucratic centralism', Studies in Com-
                        parative Communism, XV (1982).
Macshane, D.   Solidarity. Poland's Independent Trade
                        Union (Nottingham, Spokesman Books, 1981).
Matejko, A.   'The structural roots of the Polish oppo-
                        sition', Polish Review, XXVII, No. 1-2
                        (1982), pp. 112-140.
Moszcz, G.   'Day the secret police went mad', New
                        Statesman, 27 March 1981.
Nowak, J.   'The Church in Poland', Problems of Com-
                        munism (November-December 1982).
Nuti, D.M.   'The Polish crisis; economic factors and
                        constraints' in The Socialist Register
                        (London, Merlin Press, 1981).
                        'Pay now, live later', New Statesman, 14
                        November 1980.
Pełczyński, Z.   'Poland. Dangers and hopes', New Society,
                        4 December 1980.
                        'Stalemate and after in Poland', New
                        Society, 5 February 1981.
Potel, J-Y.   The Summer before the Frost. Solidarity
                        in Poland (London, Pluto Press, 1982).
Portes, R.   The Polish Crisis. Western economic policy
                        options (London, Royal Institute of Inter-
                        national Affairs, 1981).
Pravda, A.   'Poland 1980. From "premature consumerism"
                        to labour solidarity', Soviet Studies,
                        XXXIV, No. 2 (April 1982), pp. 167-199.
Przeworski, A.   'The Man of Iron and the Men of Power in
                        Poland', Political Science, XV, No. 1
                        (Winter 1982), pp. 18-31.
Rostowski, J.   The political economy of Sarmatia, Kingston
                        Polytechnic Discussion Paper No. 37,
                        August 1981.
Ruane, K.   The Polish Challenge (London, BBC Publica-
                        tions, 1982).

Bibliography

Sanford, G.   'Gierek's downfall and the response of the
                     Polish United Workers' Party to social
                     crisis (August-December 1980)', Paper pre-
                     sented to the annual conference of the
                     National Association of Soviet and Eastern
                     European Studies, Cambridge, 1981.
                     'The response of the Polish Communist
                     Leadership and the Continuing Crisis' in
                     J. Woodall, Policy and Politics in Contem-
                     porary Poland (London, Frances Pinter,1982)

Shapiro, I.   'Fiscal crisis of the Polish state. Genesis
                     of the 1980 strikes', Theory and Society,
                     X (1981), pp. 469-502.

Singer, D.   The Road to Gdańsk. Poland and the USSR
                     (New York, Monthly Review Press, 1981).

Staniszkis, J.   'The evolution of forms of working-class
                     protest in Poland; sociological reflec-
                     tions on the Gdańsk-Szczecin case', Soviet
                     Studies, XXXIII, No. 2 (April 1981),
                     pp. 204-231.

Stehle, H-J.   'Church and Pope in the Polish Crisis',
                     World Today, XXXVIII, No. 4 (April 1982),
                     pp. 139-147.

Szczypiorski, A.   The Polish Ordeal (London, Croom Helm,1982).

Thiboud, P.   'Ce qui a commencé à Gdańsk', Esprit, 10
                     (October 1980), pp. 3-10.

Vale, M. (ed.)   Poland. State of the Republic (London,
                     Pluto Press, 1981).   The two DiP reports
                     are also available in English in Inter-
                     national Journal of Politics (Summer-Fall
                     1981).

Walaszek, Z.   'The Polish crisis and the Communist
                     malaise', Society, XIX, No. 3 (March-
                     April 1982), pp. 36-50.

Weydenthal, J.   'Workers and Party in Poland', Problems of
                     Communism, XXXIX, No. 6 (November-December
                     1980), pp. 1-22.

Windsor, P.   'Can Poland strike a balance?', World Today,
                     XXXVI, No. 9 (October 1980), pp.392-397.

Woodall, J. (ed.)   Policy and Politics in Contemporary Poland.
                     Reform, Failure and Crisis (London, Frances
                     Pinter, 1981).
                     'New social factors in the unrest in
                     Poland', Government & Opposition, XVI,
                     No. 1 (November 1981), pp. 37-57.

c.   Select bibliography of Polish books and articles

Adamski, W.   'Solidarność w oczach opinii publicznej',
                     Kultura, 22 March 1981.

Albinowski, S.   'Partia w nowej scenerii', Kultura, 17
                     May 1981.
                     Alarm dla gospodarki trwa (Warsaw, Inter-
                     press, 1982).

Bibliography

Albrecht, A.   'Głos w dyskusji na temat odnowy', Życie
                      Warszawy, 24.11.80.
Bielecki, J.   Co wydarzyło się w Polsce od Sierpnia 1980r
                      (Warsaw, Wydział Informacji KC PZPR, KiW,
                      April 1982).
Borusiewicz, B.   'Metody walki z opozycją w Polsce',
                      Spotkania, No. 1 (October 1977), pp. 68-77.
Brandys, K.   Miesiące 1980-1981 (Paris, Inst. Lit., 1982).
Bratkowski, S.   'Powrót do starego buldoga', Życie Warszawy,
                      30.10.80.
                      'Życie i Nowoczesność', Życie Warszawy,
                      20.11.80.
                      'Dwie sprawy w których warto coś uzgodnić',
                      Życie Warszawy, 11.3.81.
Buc, M.   'Motory i Hamulce', Życie Warszawy, 23.9.80.
Ehrlich, S.   'Koniec kultu potulności', Życie Warszawy,
                      23.2.81.
                      'Rebelia w ramach systemu i praworządności',
                      Kultura, 29 March 1981.
Frąckowiak, J.   'Prawne znaczenie Porozumienia Gdańskiego
                      jako umowy społeczno-państwowej', Państwo
                      i Prawo, XXVI, No. 7 (July 1981), pp. 81-89.
Garlicki, L.   'Refleksje nad charakterem Porozumienia
                      Gdańskiego', Państwo i Prawo, XXXVI, No. 1
                      (January 1981), pp. 3-13.
                      'Nowa regulacja kontroli państwowej w PRL',
                      Państwo i Prawo, XXXV, No. 11 (November
                      1980), pp. 3-18.
Gebethner, S.   'Konstytucja i praworządność', Polityka,
                      14 March 1981.
                      'Stany szczególnego zagrożenia jako insty-
                      tucja prawa konstytucyjnego', Państwo i
                      Prawo, XXXVIII, No. 8 (August 1982),
                      pp. 39-51.
Giełżyński, L. &   Gdańsk. Sierpień 1980 (Warsaw, KiW,
  Stefański, L.   1981).
Górski, J.   'Pogłębia się kryzys - i co dalej',
                      Kultura, 27 September 1981.
Gułżyński, M.   'Zrozumieć kryzys', Literatura, 18
                      September 1980.
Horodyński, D.   'Dom nasz pozostaje wspólny', Kultura,
                      25 October 1981.
Jankowski, H.   'Z zagadnień sprawiedliwości społecznej',
                      Nowe Drogi (August 1980).
Jarosz, M.   'Nierówność społeczna - w świetle badań',
                      Nowe Drogi, 377/10 (October 1980), pp. 96-
                      107.
Kamiński, J. (ed.)   'Polskie lato; kalendarium wydarzeń',
                      Zeszyty Historyczne, No. 60 (1982),
                      pp. 3-64.
Kleer, J.   'Niektóre problemy stosunków własnościowych
                      w socjaliźmie', Nowe Drogi (March 1981),
                      pp. 144-160.

Bibliography

Klempski, T.   'Pomiędzy euforią a zgrozą', Kultura (Paris,
                      January-February 1981), pp. 59-73.
Kolarska, L. &   'Polacy 80 - Wizja ładu społecznego',
Rychard, A.   Aneks, No. 27 (1982), pp. 101-121.
Konserwatorium   Doświadczenie i Przyszłość. 'Raport Trzeci.
                      Społeczeństwo Polskie po sierpniu 1980r',
                      Kultura (Paris, September 1981), pp. 115-
                      175.
                      'Raport Czwarty. Polska wobec Stanu
                      Wojennego', Kultura (Paris, July-August
                      1982), pp. 143-208.
Kowalski, J.   'Rozkład partii i państwa', Kultura (Paris,
                      October 1981), pp. 74-80.
Kowalski, J.   'Problemy reformy systemu politycznego
                      PRL', Państwo i Prawo, XXXVI, No. 3 (March
                      1981), pp. 3-11.
Koźniewski, K.   'Pluralizm', Polityka, 7 February 1981.
Krajewski, M.   'Nowe doświadczenie, nowe treści',
                      Literatura, 18 September 1980.
Kraus, K.   Polski handel z ZSRR; fakty i mity (Warsaw,
                      Wydział Informacji KC PZPR, KiW, May 1982)
Krzemiński, A.   'Między fasadą a tyłami', Polityka, 4
                      October 1980.
                      'Prymas', Polityka, 6 June 1981.
KSS-KOR   'Oświadczenie o rozwiązaniu się KSS-KORu',
                      Kultura (Paris, November 1981), pp.143-146.
Kuśmierek, J.   Stan Polski (Paris, Inst. Lit., 1982).
Landau, Z.   'Dzieje gospodarcze PRL', Kultura, 18
                      October 1981 & 6 following editions.
Lamentowicz, W.   'Kryteria efektywności działalności publicznej
                      w społeczeństwie socjalistycznym', Studia
                      Nauk Politycznych, No. 6, 48 (1980),
                      pp. 11-30.
                      Articles in Życie Warszawy, 25-26 October,
                      14, 18 & 28 November 1980; 1 December
                      1981; Płomień, 14 December 1980.
Lipski, J.J.   'O niektórych problemach dialogu lewicy
                      laickiej i kościoła', Spotkania, No. 6
                      (January 1979), pp. 332-335.
Lutrzykowski, A. &   'PZPR, ZSL i SD w systemie politycznym PRL',
Zemke, J.   Studia Nauk Politycznych (1980, No. 2),
                      pp. 11-33.
Markiewicz, W.   'Na miecze albo topory', Polityka, 18
                      December 1982.
                      'Próba marksistowskiej analizy kryzysu',
                      Życie Warszawy, 21-22.3.81.
Markowski, D.   'Rzecz najważniejsza', Kultura, 14 June
                      1981.
Markowski, S.   'Nieubłagane prawą', Życie Warszawy,
                      26.9.80.
Mątkowski, S.   'Kościół a totalitaryzm', Spotkania, No. 3
                      (April 1978), pp. 53-85.

Bibliography

Maziarski, J.   'Czy chcemy silnej wŀadzy?', Kultura, 25
                         January 1981.
                         'Po roku', Kultura, 30 August 1981.
Mieszczankowski, M.   'Warunki powodzenia', Polityka, 13
                         December 1980.
                         'Kryzys w gospodarce-przyczyny i drogi
                         wyjścia', Nowe Drogi (December 1980).
Michnik, A.   'Polska wojna', Aneks, No. 27 (1982),
                         pp. 9-21.
Misiuna, B.   'Kultura polityczna', Kultura, 12 July 1981.
Moczar, M.   'Historyczne tradycje PPR a wspóŀczesność',
                         TL, 27.1.81.
Moszyński, P.   'Ruch w partii', Polityka, 24 January 1981.
Pajestka, J.   Polski kryzys lat 1980-1981 (Warsaw, KiW,
                         1981).
Pomian, G.   'Reżym-Dziennikarze-Solidarność', Zeszyty
                         Historyczne, No. 61 (1982), pp. 32-50.
Rakowski, M.F.   'Skutki centralizacji', Polityka, 22
                         November 1980.
                         Partnerstwo (Warsaw, KiW, 1982).
                         Interviews in Kultura, 4 October 1980, and
                         The Times, 22 & 23.2.82.   Major articles
                         cited in text.
Ranko, S.   'Socjalizm jednomianowany', Literatura,
                         30 October 1980.
Redelbach, A.   'Centralizacja decyzji politycznych-jej
                         mechanizmy', Studia Nauk Politycznych, No. 4
                         52 (1981), pp. 101-119.
Rolicki, J.   'Zjazd Historyczny', Kultura, 19 July 1981.
Rybicki, M.   'Partia-państwo a organizacje spoŀeczne',
                         Kultura, 15 February 1981.
                         'Pozycja ustrojowa rządu w systemie
                         politycznym PRL w latach 1970-1980',
                         Państwo i Prawo, XXXVII, No. 10 (October
                         1982), pp. 39-51.
Sokolewicz, W.   'Rząd w remoncie', Prawo i Życie, 26 July
                         1981.
                         'Konstytucja spoŀeczeństwa a spoŀeczna
                         rzeczywistość',Państwo i Prawo, XXXVII,
                         No. 7 (July 1982), pp. 3-15.
Strońska, A.   'Bierny aktyw', Polityka, 13 December 1980.
Sufin, Z.   'Nadzieje i Obawy Spoŀeczeństwaˊˊˊˊˊ', Polityka,
                         17 January 1981.
Szubert, W.   'Spoŀecznoˊˊˊˊˊ-prawne problemy związków
                         zawodowych', Państwo i Prawo, XXXV, No. 9
                         (September 1980), pp. 3-14.
Tejchma, J.   'Spoŀeczeństwo i kultura', Życie Warszawy,
                         12.11.80.
                         'Kultura reformowana i reformująca',
                         TL, 3.12.81.
Tomaszewski, J.   'Klęska pod Grunwaldem', Kultura,19 July '81.

Bibliography

Turowicz, J.	'Dialog, pluralizm i jedność', <u>Spotkania</u>, No. 3 (October 1978), pp. 38-46.
Tymowski, A.	'Polityka społeczna po sierpniu 1980', <u>Kultura</u>, 15 November 1981.
Werblan, A.	'W tyglu polskich przemian', <u>Życie Warszawy</u>, 10.10.80.
	'Dawne kryzysy i dzisiejsze problemy', <u>Życie Warszawy</u>, 13.1.81.
	'Spór o granice władzy', <u>Polityka</u>, 21 March 1981.
Wiatr, J.	'Odpowiedzialność za oceny', <u>Życie Warszawy</u>, 10.12.80.
	'Rok próby, rok nadziei ', <u>Życie Warszawy</u>, 30.12.80.
	'Lekcje minionych kryzysów', <u>Kultura</u>, 21 June 1981.
Wójcik, J.	'Oczekiwania i obawy', <u>Życie Warszawy</u>, 31.12.80.
Wójcik, P.	'Marksowsko-engelsowska teoria alienacji i dezalienacji', <u>Nowe Drogi</u> (May-June 1981), pp. 276-282.
Żabiński, A.	Interview in <u>Polityka</u>, 31 January 1981.
Zabrowski, J.	'Sprawa Żydów czy antysemityzmu', <u>Spotkania</u>, No. 1 (October 1977).
Zawadzki, S.	'Społeczne przesłanki wychodzenia z kryzysu', <u>Życie Warszawy</u>, 1.3.81.
Zieliński, T.	'Strajk (Aspekty polityczno-prawne)', <u>Państwo i Prawo</u>, XXXVI, No. 4 (April 1981), pp. 3-16.

INDEX

(Individuals mentioned in main text only. Functions referred
to concern post occupied in 1980-1981 unless otherwise stated.)

KEY:
CC   = Member of Central Committee   K7FS = Factory First Secretary
CCS = Central Committee Secretary   M   = Minister
Chm = Chairman   P   = Full Politburo member
FS   = First Secretary   P*   = Candidate Politburo
KWFS= Provincial First Secretary   member

Index

Index